The

The Fifth Special Forces in the Valleys of Vietnam, 1967

An Insider's Account

DOUGLAS COULTER

Foreword by General Henry Shelton

McFarland & Company, Inc., Publishers
Jefferson, North Carolina

*Douglas Coulter died in June 2022 after completing
and delivering the manuscript for this book. The publishers
are grateful to his friend Paul Magnusson for his subsequent help,
particularly in proofreading and preparing the index.*

LIBRARY OF CONGRESS CATALOGUING-IN-PUBLICATION DATA

Names: Coulter, Douglas, 1941–2022, author.
Title: The Fifth Special Forces in the valleys of Vietnam, 1967 : an insider's account / Douglas Coulter.
Description: Jefferson, North Carolina: McFarland & Company, Inc., Publishers, 2023 | Includes index.
Identifiers: LCCN 2022059074 | ISBN 9781476690209 (paperback : acid free paper) ∞
 ISBN 9781476648071 (ebook)
Subjects: LCSH: Vietnam War, 1961-1975—Campaigns—Vietnam—A Shau Valley. | United States. Army. Special Forces Group, 5th. Detachment B-52. | Vietnam War, 1961-1975—Reconnaissance operations, American. | Vietnam War, 1961–1975—Commando operations—United States. | Vietnam War, 1961–1975—Personal narratives, American. | Coulter, Douglas, 1941–2022. | BISAC: HISTORY / Wars & Conflicts / Vietnam War
Classification: LCC DS557.8.A2 C68 2023 | DDC 959.7043373092 [B]—dc23/eng/20221220
LC record available at https://lccn.loc.gov/2022059074

BRITISH LIBRARY CATALOGUING DATA ARE AVAILABLE

ISBN (print) 978-1-4766-9020-9
ISBN (ebook) 978-1-4766-4807-1

Front cover jungle image: *inset* author photograph; *background* © bere69/Pixabay

Printed in the United States of America

*McFarland & Company, Inc., Publishers
 Box 611, Jefferson, North Carolina 28640
 www.mcfarlandpub.com*

To the 2½ million Vietnamese
and the 59,000 Americans
who lost their lives in the Vietnam War

In vain have I looked for a single man capable of seeing his own faults and bringing the charge home against himself.

—Confucius

Contents

Acknowledgments

Thomas Patterson, Bradlee Professor
of Government and the Press,
Harvard Kennedy School,
for his subtle and wise editing of the text.

Gerry Krieg, for his invaluable help with the maps.

Jerry Estenson, Bruce Shirk, and Thomas Moore,
for their solid advice on the text.

Foreword

by General Henry Hugh Shelton

The Vietnam War remains one of America's most unpopular and divisive wars. More than 100,000 Americans fled the country or took other actions to avoid serving in the U.S. armed forces. By 1967, protests, demonstrations, and other forms of altercations with police were rampant. Against this backdrop, Doug Coulter, a true patriot, decided to leave Harvard, join the military, and serve in Vietnam.

During operation Delta 28 at Bong Son on 16 March 1967, 1st Lt. Douglas E. Coulter, side-by-side with Vietnamese Special Forces, infiltrated an enemy secret zone and found out Viet Cong unit at BS 758248. He himself guided artillery for precise shelling, thus causing almost 30 of the enemy to be killed on the spot.

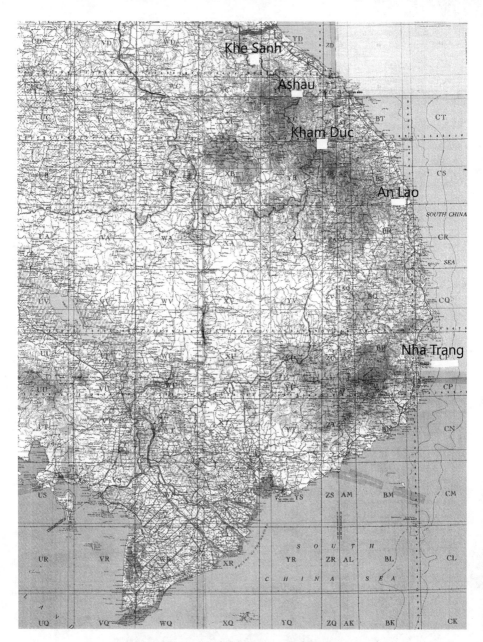

The map fighter pilots used during the war.

Electing to serve in America's most prestigious unit, Army Special Forces (or "Green Berets"), Coulter completed the arduous qualification and selection process and earned the coveted beret. But his desire to serve with the best didn't stop there. Arriving in Vietnam in September 1966, he became a member of the army's oldest and most respected reconnaissance unit: Project Delta, or Detachment B-52.

"Delta" (as the unit was commonly called) was a combined unit of American and Vietnamese Special Forces operating in areas of Vietnam that the Viet Cong and North Vietnamese considered sanctuaries, far from American or Vietnamese artillery or other indirect fire weapons.

Relying on special tactics and techniques that had been developed over years of operating "behind enemy lines" and equipped with a variety of special weapons, the Delta teams' operational areas were often designated by General William C. Westmoreland, then commander of all forces in Vietnam. Delta had its own helicopters, the 281st Assault Helicopter Company, for insertion and extraction of the reconnaissance teams, as well as its own assigned Air Force forward air controllers and an army radio relay capability to allow the team's radio transmissions to reach the base station in U.S.–controlled territory. It was a highly stressful operational environment and only the best survived a tour in Delta. Doug Coulter was one of those.

Coulter provides a riveting and insightful description of life in Delta as he examines the personalities of Delta leaders, fellow Delta officers, and the small cadre of highly qualified and courageous noncommissioned officers (NCOs) who made up the unit. In doing so, he provides the reader with insights into the caliber of individuals who served in Vietnam, the battlefield stress that most encountered, and the activities that many experienced with the Vietnamese civilians who worked the streets and businesses of Nha Trang and other populated areas.

After completing a highly successful tour of duty, Coulter returned to the United States to resume a life of politics and academia. Years later, he has provided a look back at Vietnam that should be required reading for all Americans who really want an inside look at America's involvement in a war whose legitimacy is still being debated today. Perhaps most important, Coulter's account shows that Vietnam veterans are as noble as the veterans of any previous wars America has fought, past or present.

The man to my right was Doug Coulter, a Harvard graduate who'd earned a commission and then gone through Special Forces training, determined to be the best recon-platoon leader in the Army. He studied hard, worked hard, and he was very, very good. We all looked up to him and aspired to be like him.—General Henry Hugh Shelton, Chairman of the Joint Chiefs of Staff (1997–2001), in his autobiography, Without Hesitation.

Preface

I didn't write this book simply to put a lid on what we know of the Vietnam War, but also to correct our failure to learn its lesson and to show that narcissism was the underlying issue that led to the war. According to the clinical definition, narcissism is not love of oneself but love of one's image of oneself and, therefore, is divorced from reality; if you look closely, beneath the other issues, I think you will see that we also pursued the war in Vietnam, as well as our later wars, out of admiration for our own image of ourselves. Narcissism to this day propels our foreign interventions, leading us to think that free elections in Afghanistan and Iraq would resolve these areas' age-old animosities. I believe it would be foolish to say that we weren't divorced from reality in Vietnam, Afghanistan, and Iraq and didn't believe something that wasn't true.

Vietnam began a series of wars of choice, including Afghanistan and Iraq. We lost in Afghanistan for the same reason we lost in Vietnam (our retreat from Afghanistan after twenty years being proof), and Iraq is now in worse shape than when we arrived, splintered into warring factions. The effects of these wars have been devastating to the people of the countries we have fought in, as well as to ourselves. The costs in blood and money are well-known from the statistics published by the government and in the media. The political and social costs, the decline of cohesiveness in our society, and the coarsening of our souls cannot be calculated and reduced to numbers on a sheet of paper, but they are all too real, nonetheless.

We considered ourselves the best; we knew best even when it came to cultures and peoples that we actually knew nothing about, and so we tried to impose our solution, the "right" one, on anybody we chose. Our self-regard was so great at the time of the Vietnamese conflict that we thought just showing up would bring victory (as we did later in Afghanistan and Iraq), and I shared this attitude of self-regard and self-glorification when I served in Vietnam. What have we learned since then? While chastened in Iraq and Afghanistan, do we not still exhibit the same attitude today?

The Vietnam War caused the greatest social crisis afflicting my generation, and the smoke from the war has continued, in one way or another, to float over the United States. I would ask whether the current profound divisions in our society—including the highly (and even violently) politicized media on both sides of the political aisle, with everything reduced to competing, intransigent ideologies, allowing no room for dialogue—didn't in some sense have their roots in the Vietnam War.

Prologue:
In the A Shau Valley

What I am about to describe changed my understanding of myself, the U.S. Army, the Vietnam War, and the United States.

In April 1968, after returning to Harvard to complete my undergraduate history degree, I came across the following *New York Times* headline: "U.S. Forces Begin Massive Assault of Ashau Valley" (see Appendix). A year earlier, I had led patrols in the A Shau, performing long-range reconnaissance with five-man teams up to twenty-five miles behind enemy lines. Our mission was to discover whether the enemy—the North Vietnamese army and its South Vietnamese allies, the Viet Cong—was marshaling forces in the A Shau preparatory to attacking Hue, the ancient capital of Vietnam. Now, a year later, the First Cavalry Division had launched the largest helicopter-borne assault of the war so far into the valley. The *Times* article stated that "five to six thousand North Vietnamese troops have held the valley for two years." Although the First Cav intended to wipe out these forces, I doubted that they knew what they faced.

Many of our A Shau patrols had barely gotten out of the valley alive. Two of our recon teams tried to land in the southern part of the valley, only to have machine guns open up on them. We had to call in night airstrikes by jet fighters based in Da Nang to save them. A Vietnamese Ranger company sent into the valley to help rescue a downed crew got so bogged down in the twelve-foot-high elephant grass that they had to withdraw or face annihilation. One crew member was left behind.

The A Shau's deadly reputation was such that, in the spring of 1967, we were given hero-like status just for entering the valley. We were the first to make the attempt after the A Shau Special Forces camp was overrun by North Vietnamese forces in March 1966. The fall of the camp had left a bad taste in everyone's mouth. The command had done nothing to help the camp's defense, even though it knew of the enemy's buildup in advance and the approximate date on which they would strike—in March, at the height of the monsoon, when clouds would blanket the valley and make reinforcement difficult and air support almost impossible.

The fall of the camp punctured the American forces' sense of invincibility. We refused to set foot in the valley, even though the enemy was transporting huge quantities of equipment and supplies down it every night. The unit that I belonged to, Project Delta, was the first to reenter.

Approached from the air, the A Shau Valley appeared deserted. The valley, two or three miles wide and thirty miles long, along the border with Laos, stood between sharp slopes to the east and deep-blue mountains to the west. Tall elephant grass carpeted the valley floor. The slopes on each side stretched up to the sky and seemed to pull it downward into the valley—a serene image that masked its deadliness.

The illusion was dispelled by a bright yellow line that ran straight down the middle of the valley. This line marked the road that the North Vietnamese used to transport arms, ammunition, and other equipment south to the battle zone. Empty during the day, it revealed its purpose every morning when our forward air controller (FAC) in his single-engine Bird Dog flew over and saw the fresh tracks. He would call in airstrikes, and yet overnight, the craters from the bomb blasts would be filled in or a new branch road would be built to keep the supply line open.

Flying south along the valley, one would observe an ash-colored triangle, which became more distinct up close. This was the old Special Forces camp, filled with debris. Empty mortar canisters and pieces of corrugated roofing littered the ground. Bomb craters pocked the airstrip. A twisted, blackened airplane fuselage lay at an angle across the strip, and white parachute silk from flares dropped during the battle for the camp dotted the surrounding elephant grass. South of the camp, the road twisted through terrain marred by huge B-52 bomb craters before vanishing into the jungle.

The *Times* article I picked up in April 1968 confirmed my expectations. The valley remained a place of danger, even terror—at least in the minds of the Americans who served there. "The importance of the valley to the North Vietnamese was underscored by the intensity of their 22-mm, 37-mm, and 57-mm antiaircraft fire—which was called the heaviest antiaircraft fire of the war in the South," the *Times* breathlessly told its readers. An unnamed executive officer was quoted as saying: "I'll tell you this. If you fly over that valley you have a good chance of getting killed. It's bad down there, very bad."

Over the next three days, I searched the newspaper for news of the fighting at A Shau. There was nothing. Then, on the fourth day, it was reported that "the assault had cut off a major infiltration route for the North Vietnamese." The article went on to discuss American helicopter losses: "The number of allied helicopters destroyed or damaged is unusually high. On the first day of the operation 10 helicopters were shot down by antiaircraft fire. Since then a total of 50 are believed to have been destroyed or damaged by North Vietnamese gunners hidden in the valley's ridges." But then there was this statement: "The helicopter units, except for antiaircraft fire, had only sporadic ground contact."

A week went by without further word, and then the *Times* reported, "Allied forces have taken control of the Ashau Valley." I thought this must mean that the road rather than the entire valley had been taken. General Robert Cushman, who commanded the Marines in Vietnam at the time, told the press otherwise: "Enemy resistance in the valley was sporadic in some areas and nonexistent in others."

A week later, the American command announced that the operation had ended. It didn't seem possible that the valley could have been taken by U.S. forces in less than a month, but the command put out the following statement: "Heavy fighting was reported during the first few days of Operation Delaware, but only light to moderate action has been disclosed since then." In addition, there were reports that "the initial allied landing in the Ashau was opposed only by enemy engineer and security forces."

Reading these accounts in the *New York Times* from the comfort of Harvard affected me as much as anything in my Vietnam experience, as they demonstrated how blinded we had been by our preconceptions. The U.S. Army was unable to conceive that the North Vietnamese—or anybody else, for that matter—could control such a large valley with anything less than five or six thousand combat troops. As a result, the guesswork became "fact." The enemy simply had to have a force of that size in the valley.

The truth was that the North Vietnamese had kept us in the dark for two years by lining the mountains surrounding the valley with antiaircraft gun emplacements manned by minimal crews. Their deadly fire led us to believe that an even worse fate awaited those who tried to land in the valley. The valley did not contain full-strength combat units, but rather engineers and maintenance crews charged with keeping the supply road open. For two years we bought into the idea of the valley teeming with well-armed enemy soldiers—bought it hook, line, and sinker.

A few days after Operation Delaware ended, the *Times* was at it again: "Highly informed sources said today that there was 'quite a bit of evidence' that the North Vietnamese had moved back into the Ashau Valley with large forces." We had just been through this. Did anybody—not just the *Times* but also the people on the ground, in Saigon, in Washington, D.C.—know what they were talking about? Was it willful ignorance? Self-deception?

I had already come to see that the issue went far beyond five or six thousand nonexistent enemy troops in the A Shau Valley. The root problem was our inability to function without believing that Americans had the answers. After all, we were living in the "American Century." We had never lost a war and never would, as Hollywood's version of General George S. Patton told his troops in *Patton*, which was filmed shortly after the time of the First Cav's assault on the A Shau.

If A Shau was too dangerous for ground troops, then the enemy had to be lurking behind every blade of elephant grass. How else could we account for the fact that, despite being the mightiest nation in history, we were not masters of the valley?

PART I

My Road to A Shau

One

My life has bridged the unfolding of the so-called American Century. In February 1941, Henry Luce, the powerful owner and publisher of the magazines *Time*, *Life*, and *Forbes*, wrote an editorial titled "The American Century." In an overly long and rather turgid paean to American exceptionalism, Luce sought to awaken the American people to their historic responsibilities. The son of missionaries, Henry Luce was well versed in zealotry. Whether he was wise to do it in this instance is another matter.

At the time of his writing, Adolf Hitler had conquered Western Europe. Britain stood alone, fighting for its survival. It had no real hope of defeating Hitler on its own. To the extent that Luce was arguing for American intervention in Europe, he was right in the sense that Britain needed our help. But Luce was seeking more than Hitler's defeat. He wanted to remake the world in America's image.

The Russian army laid the foundation for an Allied victory by crushing the Nazis in the east. Had the Normandy landing been attempted before Stalin's armies had crippled the Wehrmacht, it would almost certainly have failed, a fact played down in American news accounts of the time, accounts that fed a belief in American exceptionalism. That belief intensified with victory in 1945 over Germany and Japan, which provided an opportunity to realize Luce's vision. And we seized it. As a people schooled on Manifest Destiny, Americans were primed to remake the world.

I was in Vietnam as a soldier when Henry Luce died in 1967. The American Century was then barely twenty-five years old, and it was not yet clear whether the United States of America would succeed at remaking the world in its own image. Today the answer is clearer. But I'm getting ahead of myself. I first need to go back in time, to the month before Henry Luce published "The American Century." It was the time of my birth.

* * *

I enjoyed a privileged upbringing. My parents were white, college-educated Protestants and embodied the American upper middle class. My paternal grandparents were highly educated, my grandfather a graduate of Princeton, as was my father.

My grandfather, Eugene Calvin Coulter, heading a new preparatory school for boys in Chicago, formed a friendship with Marshall Field (the founder of the famous department store), who guided his investments and substantially improved my grandfather's finances. My grandmother was Anna Eleanor Brewster, an eighth-generation *Mayflower* descendant. They had eight children, the youngest of whom was my father, Eliot Brewster Coulter, who spent his working life in the Foreign Service until his retirement in 1957 as assistant chief of the Visa Division in Washington, D.C. Here, shortly before World War II, he met my mother.

In contrast, my mother, Elizabeth Clarke, grew up in hardship, which may partly explain her later fate. Born in Chicago, her father died in a railway accident before she reached school age, and her mother moved constantly in order to find work. Therefore, my mother studied at many different schools before graduating from Lowell High School in San Francisco.

Being in San Francisco likely was the reason she applied to Stanford, which limited to 500 the number of female students admitted. My mother was the first woman in her family to go to college and ultimately received an MA from the University of Chicago. She later served as secretary to Mary Yost, dean of women at Stanford, and saved enough money for a trip to Europe with a female friend, Gerry Kinne (later my godmother), visiting Austria shortly after the *Anschluss* and attending a youth festival at which Hitler spoke.

After returning from Europe, my mother worked for the Works Progress Administration in San Francisco and then with the Intergovernmental Committee on Refugees in Washington, D.C. Seeking to help a Jewish acquaintance she had met during her European travels, my mother went to the Visa Division at the State Department to make the plea. My father was the official with whom she met. He secured the visa and likely saved the person's life. It was the start of their courtship.

Almost a twenty-year age gap separated them, but both were educated and well traveled, and they shared many of the same values. My father had a subtle, dry sense of humor, in keeping with his background and upbringing. My mother's humor was more boisterous. My father was not conventionally handsome and was shorter than average, with a full head of prematurely white hair. His new wife was a pretty woman in the prime of life.

The early years of the marriage were happy ones. They settled down in a house in Arlington, Virginia, twenty minutes from Washington. I was their first child, born in January 1941. Three more children followed—my sisters Holley and Jean, and then my brother Malcolm.

Two

I was not yet five years old when World War II ended, and I have few memories of it. My early childhood was happy and carefree. My father was kind and gentle. My mother ran the household and likely did a good job at it, though she approached parenting as if it were a formal obligation.

During the postwar period, the Washington suburbs expanded, and a new house built below us was bought by General Edward Rowny, an advisor to presidents who became a good friend of my parents. Rowny had served in Italy during World War II and then was sent to the Pacific after V-E Day to join General Douglas MacArthur's staff. Five years later, he helped plan the amphibious landing at Inchon, the first large-scale landing of U.S. troops in the Korean War. He had a master's degree in international relations from Yale, had attended both the Command and General Staff College at Leavenworth and the War College at Carlisle Barracks, and was serving as a deputy to the army chief of staff at the time my parents met him. Rowny died in 2017 at the age of 100, and I will have more to say about him later.

In the late 1940s, a neighbor in the next block over sold his house to a Jewish family, and a large group of neighbors tried to make him go back on the sale. He came to the front door with a shotgun and told them he would sell his house to anybody he pleased. The only person who spoke up for the homeowner was my mother.

I had a privileged education, attending Alexandria's very progressive Burgundy Farm Country Day School, founded in 1946 and the first desegregated school in the United States south of the

Mason-Dixon Line. Then I went on to St. Albans, a prestigious private boys' school in Washington, whose graduates include Henry Cabot Lodge, Jr., Al Gore, and John Kerry.

The school intimidated me. The other boys were sons of senators, congressmen, or high-powered lawyers, while my father was simply a bureaucrat. Worse, I was not a jock and thus not the kind of well-rounded young man preferred by Canon Charles Martin, the headmaster. Although I was never really happy at St. Albans, I liked many of my teachers. I was a shy intellectual, not "one of the boys," and never felt accepted. I devoted myself to my studies, became class valedictorian, won several prizes, and got early acceptance to Harvard. I made a friend in Bill Bechhoefer, another shy intellectual. We roomed together our first year at Harvard.

My academic success did not soften my mother. She loved us, but tenderness was not in her nature. As she grew older, trapped in the role of housewife and mother, she became increasingly critical of us all, including my father. The warmth of their early years together had faded, and their relationship became distant. Although all of her children were targets of her criticism, I, as the oldest, bore the brunt of it. It didn't help that at that age I was rebellious.

With the passing of time, I've come to believe that my mother may not have been able to control all of her thoughts and actions. For a time, she saw a psychiatrist, and after her death the psychiatrist told my sister Jean that our mother was what we now call bipolar. It helped explain why her life had come to its tragic end.

Three

In my second year at Harvard, I won the Jacob Wendell Scholarship Prize, an annual award given to a sophomore student identified by the selection committee "as the most promising and broad-ranging scholar in his or her class, without reference to financial need." The Wendell committee gives a dinner for the recipient, to which I invited my father. There is also a cash prize, which back then, if I remember correctly, was $800. That was a lot of money in 1960, and in high school I had done summer work as a construction laborer. I had by then accumulated a bit of a nest egg. I was tired of school, having pushed myself academically since my first day at St. Albans. I was twenty years old and itching to see the larger world. At the end of my sophomore year, I decided to make a break for France.

Jet travel was very expensive, so I booked passage on the Holland America line and sailed from New York in early September 1961, the cost of my round-trip ticket $200. I can still feel the exhilaration of arriving at the wharf in Le Havre. I was free in a way I hadn't experienced before. I planned to hitchhike across France to Aix-en-Provence, and during my journey I discovered a world different from the one that I knew. The narrow roads, the French habit of shuttering windows (born, I think, of their long history of violence), and the smell of farmland, less odoriferous than back home, let me know that I was in a foreign land. I slept in the fields and lived on twenty-five cents a day.

One evening, sitting on a hill overlooking the village of Saint-Flour in the Auvergne while listening to the tinkle of sheep bells and smelling the dry forest, I seemed to have traveled back in time to the Middle Ages. You've likely seen Vincent van Gogh's pictures of Provence, and that's just how it looked when I was there— square white houses, yellow fields, and rows of green trees planted to block the strong winds (known as "Le Mistral") that blow down the Rhone Valley.

While I was in Aix, I became friends with a free-spirited Dutchman, Albert Koetsier, who had left his high school teaching job in Utrecht to study law in southern France, following van Gogh's route across France to get there. Albert was in his late twenties. He was tall, over six feet, blond and pale like many Northern Europeans. Charismatic and deeply irreverent, "Ab" (as I called him) spoke good English, but I refused to speak English while in France, so we conversed in French. We usually had supper together in his room, and he talked about his time as a commando in the Dutch army, in which he had served before becoming a teacher. It was the first stirring of my interest in becoming a soldier.

After getting his law degree, Albert went on to work for the French oil company Elf Aquitaine in Dutch-speaking Suriname. He went on to become a vice president for Elf Aquitaine, first in Norway and then in Malaysia. He and his wife retired in New Zealand. We stayed in touch until his death a few years ago, and I remain in contact with his widow, Brigitte, a Norwegian.

Four

In Aix I was doing nothing productive and had found that I couldn't write the novel I had planned. I wanted a full French experience, so I decided to go to Burgundy, hitchhiking north through the French countryside. I wanted to try to find work on a farm, having always enjoyed farm work back home. At the first couple of farms where I stopped, I was turned down. One cold night I sneaked into a barn and slept on the hay—the first good night's sleep I'd had since leaving Aix. In the morning, I asked the farmer whether he needed help, and he told me that a farmer down the road had just let his Spanish helper go. I walked there and entered the courtyard of Bernard and Monique Dubois.

A young couple in their mid-twenties, they had just started out in farming and had a small daughter, Elizabeth. Bernard had been a paratrooper in the French army, having served in the Algerian War. He had a broad face with strong features and light brown hair, which he kept covered with a cap. He was about my height, a little under six feet, but more heavily built and far stronger. With massive forearms and strong hands, he could lift up the tongue of a trailer and put it on the tractor as if it were toy, a task that took all of my strength. He could cut barbed wire as if it were butter.

Monique was tall and pretty, with black hair and graceful movements. She was a quintessential rural Gallic woman. She cooked on a wood stove, washed clothes in a basin outdoors during summer and winter alike, and could carry two full milk cans.

Every Sunday, without fail, Bernard and Monique alternated lunch with their respective parents. The families had lived in the same villages for generations. Except for new machinery, life was lived much as it had been lived for centuries. It was a world utterly unlike the America I knew. For me, it was a revelation and challenged my sense of American superiority, as there was a rhythm and depth to how they lived that was somehow missing back home, a natural beauty to how they spent their days and a touching and deep sentiment in how they treated each other.

They had about thirty cows that had to be milked morning and night. My time on the Dubois farm was my first experience with truly hard work. I used to gauge the strength I would need to do a job. Bernard never gauged anything. He just applied whatever strength was needed to get the job done. He taught me the art of carrying a 240-pound sack of wheat on my back. I was never stronger in my life than when I worked with him.

Bernard would sometimes talk about his time as a paratrooper in Algeria. Like most combat soldiers, he didn't dwell on the experience, but it had clearly helped shape his character and outlook. Like my friend Ab, it set him apart in my mind from ordinary men, bold men out of an earlier age compared to those I had known.

I had always wanted to sail around the world. I made about forty dollars a month working for Bernard and Monique, and I was able to save all of my earnings. Madagascar was another place I had romanticized, probably because of the name. After harvest, despite guilt over leaving Bernard and Monique, I bought a third-class ticket on the Messageries Maritimes line, leaving from Marseilles. We sailed through the Mediterranean, the Suez Canal, and the Red Sea before landing at Majunga (now called Mahajanga) on the west coast of Madagascar.

An American in first class, a Jesuit missionary, would stand by the railing in a short-sleeve shirt, which revealed that most of his left biceps had been torn away. He invited me to his cabin for a glass of whiskey and told me he had been a paratrooper in the 82nd Airborne during World War II and had landed with the first wave on D-Day. During the advance into Belgium, he was shot in the arm. He said that when the division reached Paris, the men got drunk and tossed those who were still virgins onto naked prostitutes. I felt privileged to be in the presence of someone who had risked his life in battle.

On the way to Madagascar, our ship stopped at Djibouti on the Horn of Africa, where I caught a glimpse of the French Foreign Legion—impressive-looking men who spoke bad French. Their uniforms were immaculate. The enlisted men had three neat creases down the back of their shirts, the officers five, and they strengthened my desire to become a soldier.

Our ship landed at Majunga after a voyage of twenty-two days. The feeling of being in this out-of-the-way place, of looking across the Mozambique Strait at sunset, was exhilarating. The next morning, I took a harrowing sixteen-hour bus ride to the capital, Tananarive (now Antananarivo). A first shock was the price of the cheapest room in Tananarive—two or three times what I had paid in France. Another shock was true poverty. In the market a girl, her face covered with dirt and flies, tried to sell a single mango displayed on a leaf in front of her.

Madagascar, which had been colonized by the French in the 1890s, had become an independent nation in 1960, but it was still under French influence. I had arrived with sixty or seventy dollars in my pocket, and, given the price of my room, that money went fast. I went to the offices of the French companies in Tananarive, Crédit Lyonnais and others, and asked them whether they knew of anyone who needed workers.

I was nearly broke when I got word that Jacques Galland, a rice farmer located outside Ambatosoratra (a village on the western shore of Lake Alaotra in the center of Madagascar), wanted me to work for him. Galland had a government contract to build a rice storage hangar and wanted a white man to supervise the construction. I used my last dollar to take the single-track train out there, riding in a boxcar. I was met by a driver who took me to Galland's plantation on the western side of the lake.

Lake Alaotra is about thirty-seven miles long and twenty-five miles wide. It is surrounded by reeds that extend a mile or so beyond the shores. In the early 1940s, Galland had asked the local Malgache whether there was a current running through the reeds to the lake. They told him there was, and he dug dikes from the shore through the reeds to form a large square, after which he drained the water and burned the reeds to provide fertilizer for his first crop of rice. It became collateral for a loan that allowed him to expand his operation. When I arrived in 1962, he had about 6,000 acres of terraced rice fields that were now the rice basket of Madagascar. He was shipping something like 50,000 tons of rice per year to Tananarive and exporting high-quality rice to Germany.

Polished rice is rice with the husks removed. Galland used the husks as fuel to power his steam engine, which provided the farm's electricity. He had built a machine shop, could repair virtually any combine or tractor himself, and had personally trained the mechanics who kept the place running.

When I met Jacques Galland, he was about sixty and had just learned to fly a plane. He was about my height but heavyset and with a bald head that was deeply tanned, the result of working in the sun without a hat. He had great *joie de vivre*, despite his unhappy marriage; his wife was a member of Mauritius island's French aristocracy and very severe of manner. She rarely came to the lake, preferring to stay in their house in Tananarive. They had no children. As time went on, I began to think that Galland saw me almost as a son.

In the 1940s, a national independence movement sprang up in Madagascar, which the French called the *Insurrection Malgache.* One night in early 1947, Malgache militants, armed with primitive weapons, staged a series of attacks on French plantations and military bases. They massacred a small French garrison near the town of Ambatondrazaka, on the eastern shore of Lake Alaotra. The French prefect called all the French in the surrounding area to shelter in the town. Soon after Galland arrived, he learned of the reprisals being carried out against the Malgache. He told the prefect, "You know what your people are doing? I'm not being a party to this." He went back to his plantation. The militants threatened to kill him, but his workers protected him, and while the war was going on and famine threatened, he gave rice to his workers and their families.

After having me repair dikes for about a month, Galland came to me and handed me a three-by-five card with a diagram of a rice hangar on it. He pointed to an empty plot of ground and said, "I want you to build this here." He switched his gaze to iron beams piled on the ground. "The metal you need is over there." Then he gestured toward three workers who had suddenly appeared at my side. "These three speak French, and they can weld. If you have any questions, ask." We built the hangar in seven months.

At this time, the government of Madagascar was in the process of nationalizing privately owned land, including Galland's rice plantation, and Galland later retired to Mauritius. In the 1970s, Didier Ratsiraka, a naval officer known as the "Red Admiral," seized power in Madagascar. He had attended the École navale (the French naval academy) and hated the French. Diplomatic relations were broken off, but in the 1980s, after François Mitterrand became the president of France, relations were restored. The French insisted that Frenchmen whose property had been nationalized be compensated. In recognition for Galland's actions in 1947, Ratsiraka decreed that he be the first to receive compensation.

I had abandoned my plan to sail around the world in order to finish Harvard and to get it over with. In July 1963, I took a boat back to France, where I worked the harvest on Bernard and Monique's farm. Then I went to Holland to catch a boat back to the States, visiting Ab on the way.

On the boat trip across the Atlantic, I met Huib Muller, a

Dutchman. We immediately hit it off. Huib had just finished his military service and was on his way to Michigan State to pursue graduate work in economics. He had been a Russian interpreter while in the army and would have been assigned to interrogate Soviet prisoners if war had broken out. Years later he became executive director of the Dutch Central Bank and was the Dutch member of the Committee of Five that created the euro. When I was in Russia in the early 1990s, we met again while he was on a trip to Moscow to consult with Russian central bankers. Huib died soon thereafter, but I have stayed in touch with his family.

Our ship docked in New York, and I took a bus down to Arlington. I had been away from home for two years, with almost no contact with my family. As I approached the house, a feeling of dread came over me. But I couldn't know just how fateful my homecoming would be.

Five

Stopping at our door, I took a deep breath and knocked. The door opened, and there stood my mother. "Oh, it's you," was all she said. Nothing had changed. I returned to Harvard. There were several phone calls with my mother, and she would go on about how we (all of us, not just me) had hurt her and didn't appreciate her. I tried to make peace, but whatever I said was misinterpreted or twisted to fit her persecution narrative.

I was walking across Harvard Yard one crisp fall afternoon when I heard the bells of Memorial Church starting to toll. I soon learned that President John F. Kennedy had been assassinated.

I felt a deep sense of loss at Kennedy's death, as did everyone I knew. I revered him. He seemed a breath of fresh air after the presidencies of Harry Truman and Dwight Eisenhower. His confidence and idealism captured how Americans thought of themselves and their country.

With time, however, I have changed my mind about Kennedy. Like his father and his brothers, he was cocksure and arrogant. His hubris led to the Cuban Missile Crisis. FDR, Truman, and

Eisenhower were prudent men. Kennedy was not. Although a student of history, he had forgotten Talleyrand's foreign policy maxim: *Surtout, pas de zele* (Above all, no zeal). Kennedy inherited America's entanglement in Vietnam. The Eisenhower administration had aided the French. But it was Kennedy who started the real buildup of U.S. forces in Vietnam.

* * *

I arrived home just before Christmas. All of us were under the same roof for the first time in years. The morning after my arrival, my father came to me and said my mother had disappeared during the night. He had a premonition that she had walked to Fort Scott Park—a large, wooded area up the street—and asked me to look for her. I had no idea where to start looking and, after searching for a while, went home.

We waited that day and night for her return. The next morning, I went with my father to the police station to report her missing. I can still see this sad, shrunken old man talking to the officers. She was found in Fort Scott Park, as my father had thought. Her body was lightly covered with snow. If I had searched longer that first day, I might have found her. She had taken sleeping pills and gone out to lie in the woods. I believe that she did this deliberately, hoping that we would find her and feel sorry for her. I felt responsible and yet relieved. My sisters and I had worried about how we would manage her if our father died first.

On returning to Harvard for the spring semester, I had lost my focus and lacked any interest in studying. It didn't help that other students seemed so self-assured. I had always envied such people. Bruce Shirk, a friend, introduced me to Pat Gallivan, a Harvard jock, very cocksure, and someone to avoid. I began trailing in his wake, drinking beer and shooting pool. Pat had already been thrown out of Harvard once but somehow managed to get himself reinstated.

After our midterm exams, Pat and I tied one on. We barhopped all over Cambridge and then raised some hell at Wellesley College, stealing several traffic signs. We somehow got back to Cambridge without a problem. We were very drunk. Pat hated Harvard's clubs and saw someone coming out of the Fly Club. We followed him down a dark side street, and Pat jumped on his back. He didn't hurt the boy or threaten him, but the kid was petrified. His glasses fell off, and he threw his money—about seven dollars—on the ground. Pat picked up the money, and I took the glasses. We ran down an alley and hid them. Then we got back on Massachusetts Avenue and stopped at a coffee shop to celebrate.

We were having coffee when a policeman came through the door, followed by our victim. The cop handcuffed us and put us in the back of the police car. After a night in jail, we were arraigned on charges of assault and battery and unarmed robbery, and then released on our own recognizance, likely because we were Harvard students.

In our next court appearance, the charges against us were dropped "pending action by Harvard." Since the boy had suffered no bodily harm and the amount of money stolen was tiny, and with all three of us Harvard students, the court had decided to let Harvard handle it.

Harvard expelled both of us. Pat's expulsion was permanent; I was told privately that I could reapply for admission. The worst blow for me was a Harvard letter to my father filled with righteous indignation about my behavior. That letter killed whatever loyalty I might have had to Harvard.

Since I was going to be drafted anyway, I decided to enlist in the army and first consulted with General Rowny, our family friend. I mentioned that I was interested in Special Forces, and he apparently made a mental note of it.

I enlisted as "airborne unassigned"—emulating my paratrooper friends, Albert and Bernard—and was assigned to Fort Knox for basic training. My fellow recruits came from all over the country. I remember Borrodino D'Alessandro from New York City, whose name was so long it couldn't fit around the inside of his boot, where we printed our names. After a fifteen-mile route march, I was standing near him as he took off his boots. The bottoms of his feet were so blistered that the skin had peeled away. During the march, he hadn't made a sound or complained.

After basic training and a week's leave, I reported to Fort Gordon in Georgia for nine weeks of advanced infantry training and, after AIT, having made it up to private first class, became part of the cadre responsible for a basic training platoon. The 1964 presidential election happened while I was at Fort Gordon. I had to have my vote notarized by my commanding officer, a lieutenant. He was a right-wing Republican who backed the GOP nominee, Senator Barry Goldwater. When I told him that I was voting for Lyndon Johnson, he subjected me to a lecture aimed at changing my vote. With no choice but to hear him out, I then asked for the notarization. When he gave it, I said, "Well, sir, I guess that takes care of your vote." The first sergeant, who had been listening, doubled over laughing.

Just over a year after my mother's death, I got news that my father had died. He passed away on New Year's Day in 1965. None of his children were there. I was in the army, Jean was in France, Holley was serving with the Peace Corps in Niger, and Malcolm, who was attending boarding school in Connecticut, was staying with friends.

After attending my father's funeral, I returned to Fort Benning and went to Airborne School. The three weeks of jump school were an unforgettable experience, not least because I was in the minority. About 60 percent of my fellow trainees were black. Back then, airborne status was a point of pride for a lot of African American soldiers. The black master sergeant issuing our equipment said, "Yo is going to roll up yo poncho and put it on yo pistol belt, and yo is not going to unroll it, 'cause in de airborne it do not rain."

You have to make five jumps to graduate. We jumped out of C-130 transport planes from 1,200 feet. What's striking is the dead silence that surrounds you after you jump and the noise from the aircraft has abated. The biggest challenge is the descent and keeping your eyes on the tops of the trees. You are instructed to look ahead as you approach the ground. If you look down, you tend naturally to draw your legs toward your body, which can result in serious injury. When your feet touch the ground, you are taught to roll to the side. Night jumps (which I did later when stationed in West Germany) are tough because it's hard to see the treetops, which themselves are a risk.

Being jump qualified is a big thing in the army. You get extra pay, and there's the pride that comes with wearing the Parachutist Badge on your uniform. I felt pretty good about myself. I likely had the most privileged background in my group of trainees, but nobody gave a damn about that or whether I'd attended Harvard. I had stood on my own two feet, one soldier among many.

After jump school, I was accepted for Officer Candidate School. My OCS training was also at Fort Benning, and it was brutal: physical training, field exercises, classroom instruction. Nobody went to bed before 1:00 or 2:00 a.m. We couldn't retire until we'd cleaned our equipment and spit shined the floors. Every now and then, one of the

TAC (Teach, Advise, and Counsel) officers would come in and grind the heels of his boots into the floor, and you'd shine it again.

I finished OCS at the head of my class and, as such, led the closing parades and received a large silver bowl. By tradition, the company sergeant major gives you your first salute, and you give him a dollar. As a newly minted second lieutenant, you need to adjust to the terrifying fact that you suddenly have authority.

Shortly before training ended, I learned that I'd been assigned to 10th Special Forces in West Germany. Later I heard that General Rowny had inquired about me while I was in OCS and was told that I was first in my class. He was by then a major general in command of the 24th Mechanized Infantry Division in Augsburg, West Germany. I don't know for sure but believe he pulled a few strings to get me sent to the 10th Special Forces. It was as plum an assignment as a young officer could get. President Kennedy had made Special Forces a priority and had spoken about it so fervently and often that the Green Berets were cemented in the public mind as our finest soldiers.

Six

The 10th Special Forces headquarters was at Bad Tölz, a medieval town on the edge of the Alps. During the Nazi period, it was the site of an officers' training school for the SS. I arrived there at the same time as another second lieutenant, Andy Irzyk. Andy was a naturalized U.S. citizen who'd been saved from death in his native Poland by a Soviet general when the Russians liberated Poland from the Nazis. Andy was as tough as they come. He joined the U.S. Army as a private and rose through the ranks, ultimately retiring as a full colonel. Except for a tour in Vietnam commanding a company of the 101st Airborne in the A Shau Valley, Andy spent his military career in special operations. Andy was in the A Shau two or three years after I was there and at a time when the valley was crawling with enemies. Of the company commanders there, Andy had the highest kill rate and the lowest death rate. The army rewarded him by sending him to college. He likes to say that Ho Chi Minh put him through college.

I've stayed in touch with Andy and mention him because his roots were like those of other members of Special Forces. When people today think of the Green Berets' history, they think of counterinsurgency operations in Vietnam. But the Green Berets originated as specialists in unconventional warfare in Europe. They were to carry out sabotage and guerrilla operations behind enemy lines in the event of a Soviet invasion of Western Europe. Many of the first Green Berets were émigrés who had been part of the Nazi resistance in Poland, Czechoslovakia, Hungary and other parts of Eastern Europe. Some of them had continued their resistance after the Soviet takeover of that region but then left for the West.

While Vietnam was heating up, our training at Bad Tölz was still focused on the possibility of a European land war with the Soviet Union. We practiced setting up ambushes, sabotaging infrastructure sites, and finding ways to get across rivers and other obstacles.

The headquarters of the army command in our part of Germany was in Garmisch-Partenkirchen, which sits on the Austrian border near the Zugspitze (the tallest mountain in Germany). On Saturdays, a weekly dance was held at the headquarters facility. I went there looking for girls and met Karin Maybach, a Hungarian American, whose American father had been a teacher at a school for the children of U.S. forces in Germany. Karin might have come to the dance to find a husband who would take her back to the States. Her German husband had died, leaving her with a small son.

I was immediately attracted to Karin. She was around my age and quite beautiful, with straight brown hair that she wore at shoulder length. We danced, and I was taken by her friendly but modest demeanor. As the night was ending, I asked her to meet me at next Saturday's dance. I was filled with anticipation all week, and when I got there my heart was in my mouth. I was ecstatic when she accepted my invitation to dinner.

I had bought a secondhand Austin-Healey from an American sergeant who was returning to the States. That Austin-Healey was the best car I have ever driven—we were inches above the road. I squired Karin in that car to Munich and places like St. Moritz and Vienna. At the time, U.S. soldiers stationed in West Germany were not allowed to leave the country, so my trips with Karin to Austria or Switzerland broke the rules. But the risk seemed worth it.

On one of our early dates, instead of going home afterward, Karin came with me to my room at the BOQ (Bachelor Officer

Quarters). We were inseparable after that. She was a superb skier. She raced downhill, slalom, and grand slalom. I was an average skier and kept up with her as best I could.

By this time, the war in Vietnam was on everyone's minds. The "Big Push" of 1966–1967 was beginning; back home, the antiwar movement was still in its infancy. Men from our unit were being sent to Vietnam all the time, and our morning formations became skeletons. But I had a year left on my tour in West Germany and stood little chance of getting reassigned.

My desire to get to Vietnam doubled when the Special Forces camp in the A Shau Valley came under attack by the North Vietnamese in early 1966. One of the officers I knew in Germany, Captain Blair, had been transferred to Vietnam and had arrived at the A Shau camp just as it was coming under attack. We followed the unfolding battle in *Stars and Stripes*, the U.S. military's daily paper. We read about how the Americans and their South Vietnamese troops in the camp held out for two days as it became increasingly clear that the area would be overrun.

Yet Special Forces command hesitated to evacuate the camp, perhaps out of fear of handing the enemy a propaganda victory, perhaps out of a belief that the defenders could hold on. By the afternoon of the second day, however, it was clear the force would be annihilated if it wasn't withdrawn, and the withdrawal order was given. When our helicopters reached the camp, the South Vietnamese troops panicked, storming and overloading the helicopters, making it impossible for them to take off. Our men were abandoned on the ground and forced to flee on foot. They scattered over the valley and were picked up individually over the next few days. Blair was one of the last ones to get out.

Reading about Blair in the *Stars and Stripes* deepened my desire to see combat. I had spent hours talking with men who had returned from Vietnam, listening to their stories of being under fire with the sound of bullets cracking past their heads. One of our sergeants suggested that I send a copy of my request for Vietnam duty directly to the Pentagon while withholding the original from my commanding officer. Soon thereafter, I got my orders for Vietnam. My commander was livid and tried to shame me by showing me the laudatory Officer Efficiency Report he had given me.

Facing Karin was more difficult. We had not discussed marriage, but I'm sure she had expectations. And I was very much in love with her, probably more so than she was with me. I can still picture her expression when I told her that I had volunteered to go to Vietnam. Her face just froze. She was shocked, but whether it was more about my going or having placed her trust in a man who would leave her for the chance to go to war, I do not know.

PART II

Vietnam

Seven

Like many American soldiers before us, and an even larger number later on, we landed at Tan Son Nhut Airport outside of Saigon, where our papers were checked and our destinations confirmed. I would be joining the 5th Special Forces Group, which had been activated early in the Kennedy administration to spearhead counterinsurgency operations in Southeast Asia.

I went first to the Special Forces transit station in Saigon, which was a two-story stuccoed building constructed during the French colonial period. Inside the matching surrounding wall, the grounds were immaculately kept and it was eerily silent. Just a couple of blocks away, there was the hustle and bustle of downtown Saigon, with Vietnamese on bicycles everywhere. When they took off at a green light, it resembled a charge in a Kurosawa film. After being given a room on the second floor, I walked down to the small bar on the first floor. Over a beer, I could faintly hear detonations from bombing and artillery fire, which I later discovered was taking place in what was called the Iron Triangle and War Zone C. It seemed surreal, a feeling that came over me many times during my year in Vietnam.

At the Special Forces transit station, I met a lieutenant who was on his way out of the country. He had a bullet wound in his forearm and was quite proud of it. "Now I know what it's like to be shot," he said. Secretly, I felt a sense of envy.

The headquarters of 5th Special Forces was in Nha Trang, which is located on the south-central coast of Vietnam, half an hour from the American airfield at Cam Ranh Bay, where, shortly after I arrived, President Lyndon Johnson landed for a firsthand look at the country that was seeing the effects of his military buildup. Nha Trang today is a tourist destination, known for its beaches and scuba diving. In the latter part of 1966, it was a boom town, courtesy of RMK-BRJ, the American construction consortium that had the contract to build the infrastructure for the war effort. New barracks were going up everywhere I looked.

The headquarters building for the 5th Special Forces looked like those in the States. The entrance walkway was lined with spotlessly painted white stones, with a captured Chinese antiaircraft gun placed near the door. The main hallway was decorated with brass plaques engraved with the names of the Special Forces soldiers who had been killed in Vietnam.

I had imagined that my stay at headquarters would be short, that I'd quickly be sent to a field unit. Full of anticipation, I was called, along with other new arrivals, to the office of Colonel Francis Kelley, the commander of 5th Special Forces. As it happened, I was the only lieutenant there; the other men were captains. Kelley wasn't the hardened warrior soldier I was expecting to see. He had an aquiline nose and a slight paunch, with jowls starting to sag. Rather than speaking in the clipped tones of a gnarled combat veteran, he was affable and gracious. I later discovered that, as a captain in World War II, he had been in the first wave to land at Normandy on D-Day.

Colonel Kelley had done his homework. He spoke to each officer individually, listing his background and describing the details of the camp to which he had been assigned. He seemed to know all ninety Special Forces camps by heart and appeared to have taken the time to carefully match each officer with his assigned camp. When he came to me, I was anxious to hear the location of my combat assignment. As a lieutenant, I would have been in line to become an A-team executive officer.

When Kelley announced my post, he might as well have slapped me across the face: I was being assigned as the Headquarters Secret Document Control Officer, a desk job. I felt a sense of betrayal. I had volunteered for war only to find myself assigned (or, rather, confined) to "the cage," a concrete vault a couple of yards square where we received, recorded, and distributed classified messages. There were thousands of these messages each month, and for each message six or eight separate receipts. If one got lost, I, as the control officer, would be held responsible.

I didn't challenge Colonel Kelley on the spot about my assignment, but, as soon as I could, I went to Major Assionte, the 5th Group's personnel officer, and appealed to him, saying, "I don't even have a top-secret clearance." Assionte, who looked a lot like the comedian Danny Thomas, stared at me with a blank expression. "We'll give you one," he said flatly, and that was that. I then made a pitch to Assionte's assistant, Tom Patterson, who later became a good friend. He was sympathetic, having recently come up to headquarters after having been in the field. But he couldn't override

Assionte's decision. I then went to each of the captains I knew and begged them to ask for me as their executive officer, but none of them wanted to stick his neck out.

The control officer's job was even worse than had I expected. Compounding my anguish were the war stories of friends I had made in Germany as they came back from the field and passed through headquarters. I began to worry that by the time I got out of the cage, it would be too late to go to the field. *Stars and Stripes* had begun running articles about the possibility of a diplomatic settlement to the conflict.

The rumors of peace quickly faded, and I heard that slots had opened up for Project Delta long-range reconnaissance. Most officers steered clear of Delta. It accepted only volunteers, and its missions were the most dangerous of those carried out by Special Forces. The missions involved patrols of two or three Americans and three South Vietnamese deep into enemy territory. The missions were out of direct reach of radio communication, and messages had to be relayed by plane. It might not have been my first choice, but I was willing to do anything to get out of the cage and into the field.

On January 8, 1967, I began my Project Delta training. Five other Delta lieutenants had arrived together around the same time. Each of us would be assigned to head a recon team. Given that we were all the same rank and would work closely together for the next few months, I anticipated that a tight bond would form between us.

To my surprise, they all gave me the cold shoulder. All five seemed to regard me as an outsider. When I approached Richardson while he was cleaning his rifle, he looked up briefly from the patch he was running through its barrel but showed no interest in talking. I tried the next cubicle, where Heddern, a rather delicate-looking kid with blond hair, was admiring his new Special Forces shoulder patches. He mumbled a hello and then looked back at his patches. The others—Larrabee, Best, and Estenson—were talking in the cubicle across the hall. In truth, Larrabee was doing the talking. He did not have what you would call a warrior's physique, and I wondered how he had gotten through the rigors of training. But he was glib and spoke with an air of confidence. His features were malleable, enabling him to take any position a situation required. Best, who had a nervous air, and Estenson, who looked physically strong, acknowledged my entrance with slight nods, but Larrabee just gave me a quick glance and kept on talking. I wondered whether they resented me because I had been on staff. Or did they somehow sense that I was a privileged kid who hadn't come up the hard way as they had done?

As I was dealing with my rude reception in Delta, Karin sent me a Dear John letter saying that she had married an old friend in State College, Pennsylvania. I had sent her a letter a short time before, asking her to marry me after I got back from Vietnam. Had I asked her to marry me *before* I went to Vietnam, she might have said yes—or at least waited until I came back to see whether I was the right person for her. I loved her and believe that she loved me. But I had inadvertently misplayed our relationship. I'm sure she felt betrayed by how I had volunteered for duty in Vietnam. It was a bitter life lesson.

Eight

We started Delta classes the next day in a small wooden barracks at the end of the compound. The white sand outside, visible through the screens, shimmered in the sun. The wooden benches creaked uneasily whenever we shifted our weight, and when an instructor paused in his presentation, we could hear hornets buzzing in the rafters or a child crying out on the road to town.

Three sergeants were instructing us. Sergeant Reddick was an imposing figure, the very image of a Special Forces NCO. High cheek-boned with a hard, rough face, he moved with a panther-like grace. It wasn't hard to imagine that he had spent so much time sneaking around in the jungle that he couldn't break the habit back at base.

Reddick was aware of his image, and so he behaved in as undramatic a way as possible. When lecturing, he leaned over the lectern self-effacingly, speaking in a dry, barely audible twang. But he contrived his modesty a bit and made it clear that he knew a lot more than we did and wouldn't be able to teach us everything we'd need to know.

Regarding the enemy, he said the following: "They'll very likely get a tail on you at one time or another. And they're pretty good at it, too. They'll move only when you move and stop when you stop.

So, you have to keep your ears perked. If you hear something that doesn't sound like other jungle sounds, like a stone rolling or a stick breaking, or if it suddenly gets quiet—because the birds and insects usually screech at the top of their lungs—keep on going for a while, and then stop all of a sudden and listen hard. Do this a couple of times. You want to catch them when they're still in the middle of a step, so that they'll keep on moving after you've stopped. Then part of your team can keep on going, so that Charlie hears you moving, while part stays behind to ambush them."

He went on to say, "At other times, if they know you're in the area, they'll split up. One group will chase you, and another will loop around in front to ambush you. Or they'll try to head you in the direction they want you to go. They'll beat sticks or fire off rounds to force you across a stream or into a valley. And then they'll move right up on you."

The calculations we were being asked to make seemed impossible. How could we know when the enemy was trying to drive us into unknown territory? How could we determine when to stop and start shooting, and when to keep going and lead them on? How long should we wait for them to get close enough before we fired?

For Reddick, these weren't problems but trivialities. He got a kick out of reading the enemy's mind and doing the opposite of what they expected. To him, it was all a matter of instinct, but you had to have those instincts in the first place, and we didn't know whether we had them. The aura of recon had lured us without our having any idea what it really meant or whether we could do it. Reddick's class gave us our first glimpse of what we had gotten ourselves into. My desire for philosophical truths and physical challenges gave me no help now. But I had gotten myself into this situation, and as a matter of honor, I had to see it through.

Our next instructor, Sergeant Simpson, presented himself without embellishment and taught the same way, laying out the facts and reducing everything to simple logic. He offered us a set of principles and practical actions we could take and left it to us to decide which ones we would use. He felt that once we had absorbed his teaching, we would know exactly what to do. Reddick had employed a similar method, though not nearly as heartlessly.

Simpson had a thin, almost delicate physique, but he conveyed a sense of being indestructible. With hard, piercing, almost hawk-like gray eyes, he had eliminated all fear in himself and made it abundantly clear that anyone who couldn't do the same had no business being in Delta. His voice was much deeper than his slight build suggested, and he discussed bone-chilling topics in a flat tone. You never knew what he was thinking. Simpson's immaculately pressed fatigues and stern formality added to his presence. He illustrated his points on the blackboard with precise diagrams that resembled architectural drawings. He answered questions as if we weren't there.

I remember him telling us, "After you get off the chopper, you go about a hundred meters straight into the jungle. When you think you've gone far enough, you turn sharp right or left, and go fifty meters in that direction. Then turn at a right angle and go back toward the landing zone you came in on. The enemy may track down where you came in, but it will be hard for them to find where you've turned, especially when it's getting dark." He illustrated the movements by drawing thin lines on the blackboard.

He continued: "Now make a right angle back toward your first trail and go about twenty-five meters. Then take one more measure. Turn back toward your first cutoff and go twenty-five meters." Simpson had drawn a series of precise, concentric circles. "You go until you can't see and sit down where you are. Then you wait to see if the enemy has come after you." What he had just told us, he said, was the method of night defense, the first night being the most vulnerable period for the patrol.

He went on: "If they've heard you come in, they may not find your trail or know exactly where you are, but they can get a pretty good idea, and a lot of times they'll set up a line of small kids with flashlights, say, ten or fifteen meters apart. Then they'll hang back, so if you fire, you'll wipe out the kids in front and your muzzle flashes will give you away. Don't fire at the flashlights.

"You want to wait and see if they're coming right on top of you. If they are going to the side, your tiger suits give pretty good camouflage, and they may not spot you. Just make sure you cover any bare skin. A flashlight will pick up bare skin in a second. Even if they're coming right at you and you figure they're going to walk on top of you, keep quiet. If you keep quiet enough, they can walk almost right over you without knowing you're there."

He then told us about an earlier mission: "On the first night a team was sitting there in the dark, and one of the guys saw a firefly coming nearer and nearer. He reached up to brush it away, and, all of a sudden, he had hold of someone's wrist. That firefly was Charlie's watch dial, and he was holding Charlie's wrist. He grabbed Charlie and lay on top of him all night." They didn't kill him because prisoners are an invaluable source of information. And the team managed to bring him out.

Simpson told us what to do if evasion was impossible: "If they are coming right at you, let the flashlights get up close to you and then throw a grenade to blow a hole in the line. Then run through the hole. If you stay quiet, you can usually surprise them. Just remember when you throw the grenade to make sure you shut your eyes. If you don't, that flash will do a real number on your night vision. Also, before it gets too dark, memorize where the trees are, so the grenade won't bounce back at you."

I didn't see how I could survive. I envisioned lights among the trees and not being able to tell whether the enemy was going to walk over me. I could feel a foot sliding around on top of me, and it seemed awfully hypothetical to suppose that the man wouldn't notice me. And how could I possibly memorize every tree in a strange jungle to keep a grenade from bouncing back on top of me? With the enemy a few yards away, how could I let my team know that I was about to throw a grenade, so they could shut their eyes too?

Each class produced the same inevitable conclusion: we were going to get killed. We would go into the enemy-controlled jungle with branches and vines everywhere, avoiding trails, surrounded by an enemy who could hear us but whom we couldn't hear. We had to move through the dense jungle without making noise. How could one do this on a patrol without once scraping a vine, breaking a twig, or stepping on a branch?

Our third instructor, Sergeant Markham, addressed these concerns in our next class. Unlike Reddick and Simpson, Markham tried to make things easier for us. He treated us with respect, putting himself in our shoes and trying earnestly to help us learn how to survive.

Markham embodied vitality. To this day I haven't met anyone possessing as much energy as him. Hailing from Tennessee, with a lightly freckled face, he looked like a country boy. Strong as an ox, he had hunted all his life and felt as much at home in the jungles of Vietnam as he did in the Tennessee woods. We were drawn to him, admired him, and paid extra close attention to what he was saying.

Markham's manner and physical presence gave him great authority, but he respected us as officers, saluting flawlessly when he encountered any of us in the compound. It was a different experience—a man so worthy of respect showing us respect—and his behavior seemed especially striking after the condescension we got from Reddick and Simpson.

Much like Simpson, Markham reduced everything to specific principles, and I credit him with keeping me alive. One principle governed all others: Don't use force on the jungle. Abide by the jungle, don't try to get the jungle to abide by you, and never try to do something the jungle won't allow. While this seemed a simple principle, it had many components.

First, we had to stop before every vine or branch in our path, take it delicately between our thumb and forefinger, and move it over our head or around to our side, without disturbing anything. Then we had to place it behind us, not releasing it until we were sure it wouldn't spring back, and we would step forward only after we had a clear space. There were no exceptions. We had to do this with every single branch or vine.

Second, we had to plan exactly each step we were going to take, never taking our eyes off where we were stepping, avoiding leaves that looked brittle enough to rustle or ground soft enough to leave a print. We had to put our heel down first and roll slowly onto the ball of the foot to crush the leaves so that they made no noise, never lifting the next foot until we had put the first one down. Between steps, we had to keep both feet planted firmly on the ground.

If a large vine or fallen tree blocked your way, you had to step over it, assuming that it was low enough to let you get over without scraping. If not, you had to squat down and duck walk underneath it. No getting down on your knees and crawling, because this action left tracks. If you couldn't get over or under the obstacle, you had to look for another way around.

We were not to move or come into contact with anything that we didn't deliberately plan to move or come into contact with, and we had to keep track of the relationship between the jungle and every single part of our body at all times, ducking up and down or twisting from side to side all day long. The jungle was so dense that we wouldn't be able to see past our outstretched arms, and we had to rely on hearing the enemy before they heard us, which required us to stop every couple of steps to listen and move so slowly that we might make only a mile or so a day. We were to halt for the night wherever we were and lie down on the jungle floor close enough to touch each other.

We were never to speak—only to signal by hand, hissing, or whispering in someone's ear. We would have only three radio contacts a day (at dawn, noon, and sunset) and were to stay on the air as briefly as possible, cupping the mike and speaking so softly that we couldn't be heard from a foot away. Radio contact was the most dangerous part of the day, as the enemy had receivers in the jungle and would try to locate us by triangulation. Nor did we want the radio relay plane to fly too close and give our position away.

I had no idea whether I could do all these things, but I could sure as hell try. Sergeant Markham had given me my first ray of hope.

Nine

Something happened during these early DAYS that I found quite revealing. During a break in classes, as we were heading to noon chow, two Vietnamese platoons came tearing out of their barracks. As they rushed to put on their equipment, I could see our commander, Lieutenant Colonel Hoyez, standing in the middle of the compound. He was watching them and obviously relishing the moment. His appearance still sticks in my mind. He was wearing a new, unused field harness with as many ammunition pouches and grenades as it could hold. He looked positively delighted.

A Vietnamese security patrol had radioed that they had been ambushed part of the way up the mountains about three miles to our west. We took this news with a grain of salt, because the Vietnamese tended to exaggerate when there were no Americans with them. But Hoyez was getting ready to lead a charge to rescue the patrol.

It was startling to see a lieutenant colonel preparing to lead two platoons into combat, an assignment normally given to a lieutenant. Hoyez was bringing everyone available, including the lieutenant assigned to the Vietnamese platoons, plus two senior American sergeants and, oddly, Major Tat, the Vietnamese Delta commander. Tat commanded our South Vietnamese Ranger battalion as well as the Vietnamese recon and Roadrunner platoons. He had no more business getting involved in this small action than Hoyez did, and he looked embarrassed to be out there.

Senior officers rarely see combat. General George Patton once ordered a general whose troops had failed to take a hill in North Africa to lead the second assault in person, but it's rare. Hoyez was deliberately exposing himself to combat to further his career. It would allow him to get a leg up on his peers and gain a bit of fame. And he'd be doing so right under the nose of his commanding officer, Colonel Kelley, who'd be writing his Officer Efficiency Report.

The relief force under Hoyez headed out right away, but, surprisingly, they stayed at the base of the mountains for the rest of the day. It was not until the following afternoon that they made contact with the Vietnamese patrol. Then, as the combined force worked its way down the mountain, the enemy attacked them. In response, Hoyez ordered in artillery. Word quickly spread that he was landing artillery practically on his own position, and we all left what we were doing to watch from the perimeter wire, standing on oil drums to get a better view.

This was my first sight of combat. Anybody who called in artillery on his own position had to be in a tough fight, and I pictured men beneath the trees shooting at each other from point-blank range and engaging in hand-to-hand combat. The fact that we would be facing the same thing soon gave their struggle a special meaning for us.

Yet something odd was going on. A howitzer would fire, and eventually a puff of gray smoke would appear on the mountainside. The smoke would turn white and then drift off in the wind. Then there would be a distinct pause before another round went out. Hoyez was calling in rounds one at a time, waiting to see what each strike did before he called in another. The mountainside gave no appearance or sense of anything happening beneath the trees.

Beyond the barbed wire, the rice paddies rippled and glistened peacefully in the sun, and small figures in white conical hats bending over their work took no notice of the rounds flying over them. The mountains looked beautiful in the approaching twilight. The battle seemed to have died down. As we were leaving for chow, a sergeant beside me muttered, "Who ever heard of a lieutenant colonel leading a platoon?"

Hoyez and his group got back the next morning, and we couldn't wait to hear about the men's combat experience. Instead, we heard, "The goddamn motherfucker!"

It turned out that Hoyez had called in the artillery for show. He had transformed a nondescript patrol into a firefight in order to attract attention to himself and further his career prospects, putting his men in danger to satisfy his ego. His troops were forced to hug the ground as the howitzer rounds came in. There were many big boulders on the mountainside, and whenever one of them was hit, shrapnel flew in every direction.

Hoyez had probably planned the show from the moment the distress call came in from the Vietnamese. Back at base, when he spoke of the mission, he would say, "Did you hear how close I called in the artillery?" to anyone who would listen. Word got back to headquarters as well. I can only guess what Hoyez put into the after-action report to dramatize the venture, given that there were no casualties on either side.

Hoyez might have been inspired by Captain Bill Carpenter (known as "Lonesome End Carpenter" from his days on West Point's football team), who had gained fame by calling in airstrikes on top of his own position when his men were on the brink of being overrun by the North Vietnamese. But Carpenter had acted to save his men. Hoyez, by contrast, had needlessly risked his men's lives. Carpenter went on to have a distinguished career, commanding the 10th Mountain Division and retiring as a lieutenant general. Hoyez deserved a court-martial.

Recon classes had been scary enough, with the thought of enemy troops lurking behind every tree. Now, on top of that, we knew we had a commander who was perfectly happy to get us killed for his own benefit.

* * *

I remained excluded from the circle of young lieutenants in Delta, which Larrabee continued to dominate. Larrabee did not impress me as an officer or a man. In the mess hall, he would tell infantile jokes about his time as president of his college fraternity. He spoke loudly, so that the sergeants sitting nearby could hear him. He was under the illusion that his conversation and ideas were sophisticated. He was too self-absorbed to notice the wry smiles of the sergeants overhearing him. However, I was worried. On recon patrols we would need all the help we could get from the sergeants, who had been on recon many times and knew their business. We needed their respect and goodwill more than we had needed anything in our lives. Larrabee, however, was doing everything possible to confirm the low opinion senior sergeants often have of junior lieutenants.

In the early days of the war, sergeants had commanded recon

patrols. This was one of the few areas in which they called the shots and determined their own fate. Their prestige within Special Forces and in the outside world was enormous. But in late 1966, the command began to question some of their reports and, believing that lieutenants were more reliable, had brought us in to lead the patrols. Putting a lieutenant in charge of a five-man patrol was a great extravagance.

The sergeants took this development as you might expect. First of all, they didn't like being called liars, but in recon the issue went deeper. Men will undertake recon voluntarily only if nobody back at base camp, or up in a helicopter, has the right to second-guess the man on the ground. Nobody at base camp or up in a helicopter can possibly know what is going on down in the jungle better than someone who is actually there, and anyone who has had the courage to jump out of a helicopter and go on a recon patrol has, by definition, already proven himself in many ways.

Even worse than this injustice, I think, was the loss of the sergeants' independence, which hurt their self-esteem. They now had to take orders from boys with a fraction of their experience, who had never set foot in the jungle, much less gone on a reconnaissance patrol. The sergeants thought that the command must have lost its grip, putting hardened soldiers under a bunch of rookies. Later on, sergeants began to lead patrols again, but their resentment lingered.

This situation helped to explain the blood-curdling teaching methods used by some of the sergeants. The more terror they could inspire in us, the further they could put thoughts of actually running a recon patrol out of our minds. This strengthened their authority. Conducting a recon patrol would become so out of reach for us that we wouldn't dream of trying to do it by ourselves and would therefore do whatever they told us, giving them back the power they had previously wielded, in fact if not in name.

My first week in Delta was discouraging in another respect as well. Major Assionte, the personnel officer at headquarters, appeared outside the orderly room as the new deputy commander. Assionte departed so dramatically from what one would have expected in Delta that we suspected his assignment as deputy had a nonprofessional explanation, which does happen in the military. He had no combat experience and, as best I could tell, no leadership ability. Why make a personnel guy the deputy? I suspect, though without proof, that Assionte, as personnel officer, simply assigned himself to the position. Nothing would look better on his record than a Special Forces long-range reconnaissance posting, even if he didn't have the qualifications or aptitude for the job. Nor did it take much effort to figure out why Colonel Kelley went along and rewarded Assionte's incompetence. Assionte would have done any number of favors for Kelley and making him deputy at Delta was payback. Kelley probably believed that, as deputy commander, Assionte couldn't do much damage, and if he did something foolish, those around him would fix it.

Offsetting the incongruity of Assionte's promotion was the arrival of Major Allen as our new operations officer, or S-3. Allen had already served a previous tour in Vietnam. He had been the executive officer at Khe Sanh, one of the most dangerous camps in Vietnam. The story was that Allen's commanding officer stayed back in camp drinking, never going on patrols. Allen grew so frustrated with this behavior that he wound up getting into a fist fight with his commander, during which he struck his superior—a court-martial offense. Because of the circumstances, Allen was able to avoid a court-martial, but he was passed over for promotion to major the first time he became eligible. He only received promotion on the second try.

Our first sight of Allen confirmed our expectations. His broad shoulders and barrel chest seemed to fill any space he occupied. He looked like he could pick up any man and toss him like a stick. Yet it was his extraordinary intensity that impressed us the most. He seemed always to be engrossed in his duties and the mission.

Allen's arrival had a dramatic effect. We now had a leader of whom we could be proud, and we trusted him instinctively. We all felt his presence would improve our chances of succeeding and surviving.

Ten

Once classes were over, we began to go out on practice patrols. These patrols raised our spirits because they made recon seem like something we could actually do. The patrols went into the same mountains where Hoyez had called in his artillery strikes two weeks earlier. Although these practice patrols didn't approach the real thing—the city of Nha Trang was six miles away—you couldn't have known this from the importance we attached to them. We all crowded around as Estenson and Richardson prepared to go out, watching them adjust their shoulder harnesses and load their magazines, as if we might never see them again.

Their absence that first night created a void in the barracks, a feeling to which we would become accustomed. Their first radio messages the next morning caused jubilation.

When they returned, we treated them as oracles and gleaned every scrap of information we could from them: how they had moved the vines, handled thorns, and stepped on leaves and what it felt like hauling sixty pounds of equipment and getting no sleep.

At the end of his patrol, Estenson came out on a small basalt cliff overlooking the ocean about six miles to the south. He said he had never seen anything so beautiful, with the surf pounding between the rocks and emerald-blue water stretching to the horizon. This news gave me comfort. If Estenson could forget himself and find beauty in his surroundings, the patrol couldn't have been too awful.

Our lives seemed to end, though, when Hoyez called us into the briefing room and issued the order for the Kham Duc operation. He waited next to the wall map as we assembled, as if he dreaded what he had to say. When everyone was there, he pointed to a mountainous area on the map next to Laos and said, "Agents report a North Vietnamese–Viet Cong headquarters here. We're supposed to locate it and take prisoners."

For the first time, the significance of maps in Vietnam sank in for me. The jungle here showed not a single clearing in which we could get in or out. Once we did get in, if we got into trouble, we would never come out again. On the ground beneath the triple-canopy jungle, our enemies could do anything they wanted. They'd have large camps cleared under the trees and could move troops along trails they knew by heart. Somehow, we were supposed to sneak up on them and capture prisoners, even though the slightest noise would almost certainly spell disaster. Up until now, we had left the enemy in this area alone, and for very good reason. I doubt any of us anticipated making it past the first night.

Hoyez gave us all the supplementary information, which none of us registered (much less retained), and ended with "They'll be guarding it pretty strongly. Some of us may not come back." I remember walking out into the blinding sun afterward, the hot sand squeaking under our boots. No one said a word.

But then the operation was postponed for some unknown reason. This reprieve took the pressure off temporarily, but Hoyez didn't want us hanging around doing nothing, so he sent us to the Recondo School, which stood at the far end of our compound and taught reconnaissance to the regular army. We would be taking the same classes we had just completed.

From Larrabee's reaction, you would have thought Hoyez had just turned us into kitchen help. Not only were the other students at the Recondo School from straight-leg, non-airborne units, but they were also enlisted men. This meant that we, Airborne Special Forces officers, had to sit in the same classroom with non-airborne enlisted men, most of whom were privates. Nobody felt stronger about this situation than Larrabee, who paced up and down the barracks muttering, "I refuse!" and trying to persuade the rest of us to go to the orderly room on Monday morning and refuse with him.

I wondered what kind of asylum I had fallen into. Although we were preparing to undertake the most dangerous task that we had done in our lives, which none of us really knew the first thing about,

Group picture of Delta recon members before our operations.

Larrabee was latching onto this kind of thing, standing on his dignity as an officer. He had apparently given no thought to how Hoyez would react, though he had been in Delta long enough to know what the lieutenant colonel was capable of doing.

But when Monday morning arrived, Larrabee seemed to have suffered amnesia. I couldn't tell whether somebody had gotten to him or he had just chickened out. In any case, he walked meekly over to Recondo School with the rest of us.

We arrived ahead of the other soldiers and watched them march up in formation. They had been specially selected and looked like good, solid men, although none wore airborne wings. As they stood at attention and then peeled off to run into the classroom, Larrabee pointed at them and said in a tone of disgust, "Legs!"

We sat on a raised dais at the back of the classroom, as befitted our status. Larrabee sulked the whole time, making it plain that he was there under duress and had been drilled to the hilt in this material already. Heddern took this situation as his cue. If an instructor departed one bit from what we had been taught two weeks earlier—things Heddern really didn't know anything about—Heddern's arm shot up like a rocket. When the sergeant said that after getting off the helicopter we should go seventy-five meters before turning to the right or the left, whereas two weeks earlier Simpson had said a hundred meters, Heddern raised his hand and asked, "Sergeant, isn't it better to go a hundred meters?" Not wanting to have a dispute with an officer, especially a Special Forces officer, the sergeant would answer with exemplary military courtesy, "Yes, sir, if you can."

When a sergeant forgot to mention shutting your eyes when you throw a grenade at night, Heddern said, "Sergeant, shouldn't you shut your eyes to keep from losing your night vision?" The sergeant replied, "Absolutely, sir, but you want to throw the grenade and then shut your eyes, so you know where you're throwing it."

For two days, Heddern didn't miss a beat, and each time I couldn't help but cringe. Finally, Captain Jaegels, who had just arrived to be our platoon leader, pulled us together and said, "What's this bullshit about undercutting the sergeants? Don't you guys know any better than that?"

As improbable as it may sound, I saw Recondo School as my first chance to prove myself to the other lieutenants. However, it actually precipitated a chain of events that culminated in one of the bitterest moments of my life.

The end of the Recondo School program required us to run eight miles in an hour while wearing a forty-pound pack, climb a rope ladder and then rappel back down. I had always done well running long distance and had rappelled a lot in mountaineering, so I felt confident that I could beat everyone else.

Defending our collective honor, though, was another issue. Airborne Special Forces officers should be able to beat non-airborne enlisted men with their hands tied behind their backs, but the other soldiers looked strong, while most of us did not. Furthermore, Larrabee had raised the stakes by ridiculing the "legs" all week.

I felt we could count on Estenson and the two newest members of our group, Shelton and Ford, who looked strong and fit as well. But Best and Richardson were not in really good shape, Heddern was weaker still, and Larrabee was the weakest of all. The night before, while the rest of us weighed our packs and fixed our harnesses, Larrabee, a cigarette dangling from his fingertips, held forth about everything except the eight-mile run.

The run started at 4:00 a.m. The enlisted men started faster than I had expected, staying together and not stringing out. I did my best to keep up with them, assuming they couldn't maintain this pace.

As soon as we got past the glow of the camp, I lost sight of my fellow lieutenants. I couldn't really see the road and was guided by the shadows of the bordering barbed wire. The darkness swallowed the forms of the men ahead of me. I focused on maintaining a half-walk, half-run pace. I ran along this road every day and was worried that after I passed the point where I usually turned around, I would lose a sense of how much strength I needed for the run back.

I was startled by a man running straight at me out of the darkness ahead. He had already reached the turnaround point and was heading back. I couldn't believe that someone had gotten so far ahead. A moment later, two more men came out of the darkness. This spelled disaster. I had no hope of catching them.

I made the turnaround before I met anyone else, which gave me hope. I had a good lead on everyone but the three men I had seen. I then ran into some men who were still on the first leg, but no lieutenants. Finally, I encountered Estenson and Shelton, followed by Ford and bunches of enlisted men, and after them Best and Richardson. I encouraged them to keep up the pace in defense of airborne honor.

I overtook one of the three enlisted men who had beaten me

to the turnaround, then another and then a third, as they tired and couldn't maintain their pace. I worried that I had lost count of those in front of me.

The green glow of the lights over the compound gate came into view. I crossed the finish line, confident I had done well, since nobody at the gate looked like a runner who had just finished. But I still had to get past the rope ladder before I could stop to find out.

I assumed that they would time the run, climbing the rope ladder, and rappelling down all together, so that if I hadn't won the run, I could at least make up time here. But I hadn't practiced climbing a rope ladder with a pack on, and when I stepped on the ladder with my forty-pound pack, it bucked out in front of me. Unable to get any leverage with my feet, I had to pull myself up entirely by my arms. When I reached the rappel, I was exhausted and fumbled with the carabiners, wasting more time.

I couldn't tell how well I had done but thought I might have finished in the top three. Overall, Delta didn't fare too badly. Shelton and Estenson came in near the front, Ford not far behind, Best and Richardson around the middle, and Heddern, though well back in the pack, at least finished.

After the race had ended and the sergeants had coiled the rappel ropes, Larrabee appeared. As he approached the finish line, he clutched the air in front of him, as if trying to pull himself forward while he struggled to stay on his feet. After crossing the finish line, he collapsed against the nearest barracks wall.

Here I failed to follow Larrabee's thinking. You would think that an airborne Special Forces long-range reconnaissance officer who had spent all week ridiculing non-airborne regular army enlisted men would want to keep a failure of this magnitude to himself. However, Larrabee apparently believed anything that happened to him was infinitely more important than anything that could possibly happen to anyone else.

As it turned out, I hadn't come in first, but I had beaten the other lieutenants and won their respect as a result. Larrabee's reaction gratified me the most. He fell mysteriously silent, as if trying to figure out how to handle me.

Colonel Kelley had organized a "prop blast" for that evening. A prop blast is an airborne tradition to initiate newly jump-qualified men into their new unit after they have completed their first parachute jump with the unit, much the way you get dunked for "crossing the line" when you cross the equator on a ship for the first time. Special Forces, however, had not upheld this ritual as rigorously as other airborne units, and many of us hadn't been prop blasted. To correct this discrepancy, Kelley got the names of all the uninitiated Special Forces officers in Vietnam and closed down headquarters for the evening. This was during the Tet truce at the end of January. Larrabee was really looking forward to this event. He had barely been able to contain himself all week.

Without actually knowing how other units do it, I suspect all prop blasts are pretty similar. Ours took the form of a watered-down version of jump school harassment. We started out by running around the motor pool, sentry towers, and most of the barracks, shouting that we were idiots, while a sergeant passed a bottle of whiskey up and down the line to warm us up. When we were sufficiently warmed, they lined us up in front of the mess hall and had us enter it one by one to slide down a plank into a child's plastic swimming pool. Then, while dripping wet, we stood at attention and read an oath that was written in Gothic script on a large scroll. The room burst into applause.

After sliding into the swimming pool and reading the oath, Heddern and I stood off to the side. With puddles forming around our boots, we cheered as each new man was dunked. Heddern had consumed a lot of whiskey, was bright red, and looked as if he was having a great time. Then he suddenly turned to me and pounded on my chest, saying, "You goddamn sonofabitch!"

I thought at first that Heddern had finally opened up and become a friend, and I slapped him on the shoulder in return.

But I was mistaken. A fierce look was on Heddern's face. "You worthless bastard!" he shouted. "You're a goddamn spy for Assionte!" (Major Assionte, you'll recall, was the personnel chief at headquarters who had assigned me to "the cage.") Heddern started pounding on me again.

I still thought Heddern was joking, so I laughed and said, "What do you mean? He was the one who put me in the cage."

But Heddern persisted. "You goddamn sonofabitch! You're a fucking spy!" He was hard to hear because of all the noise, but his blows were getting harder, and he was turning a brighter shade of red. Eventually, a sergeant, detailed to monitor the prop blast, came over and stepped between us, saying, "All right, sirs, break it up!" But Heddern didn't stop, and the sergeant had to restrain him.

Markham and Simpson during our Tet celebrations in January 1967.

Larrabee during our Tet celebrations in January 1967.

Heddern wasn't joking. He really thought I was a spy for Assionte. All of the other lieutenants must have thought that, which explained why I had been treated like an outcast. Heddern's outburst was probably precipitated by the run (plus the whiskey), because if he believed I was a spy, he would expect that I'd inform Assionte of how poorly he'd done.

Imagine the effect of a sergeant having to stop me and another officer from fighting, in full view of a crowd of witnesses. I felt like I had been dropped into a wasteland and left to make my way among ruins. To endure the stares of everyone else boring into me, I remained standing at attention until the prop blast was over.

Eleven

The suspicion the other lieutenants harbored about me being a spy hurt more than being expelled from Harvard. I got some perverse satisfaction, though, from wallowing in the injustice of the accusation, which saved me from succumbing totally to despair. Despite all I'd had to drink at the prop blast, I lay awake that night wondering what I should do.

As much as I hated to abandon my dream of leading a long-range reconnaissance team, I couldn't stay in Delta if the other lieutenants thought I was a traitor, a spy for the command. If the other men didn't trust me, life would be unbearable; I'd have to watch my back at all times, and not just for the enemy when I was out on patrol.

It seemed a fairly simple matter: recon was voluntary, so I'd just cease to volunteer. It meant swallowing my pride and telling them that I'd had no idea what was involved, and after training, I realized I wasn't cut out for the work. I felt that I was actually upholding the principle of solidarity by bowing out rather than accusing the other lieutenants of suspecting me of spying and ostracizing me.

The question remained: Who should I go to? I felt I had no chance with our commander, Lieutenant Colonel Hoyez. But Major Assionte, the personnel officer for whom I was supposedly spying, had just been promoted to become Hoyez's deputy, and I had no choice but to try him. In retrospect, it seems odd to have gone to

Assionte, given that I had spent all my time in "the cage" trying to persuade him to allow me to transfer to a combat unit. But at the time I saw no alternative.

I showed up at the orderly room and asked to see Assionte for "personal reasons." The sergeant major hesitated, because sergeant majors rarely do anything in a hurry, but he reluctantly complied, honoring a soldier's right to see his commander.

Assionte's eyes narrowed when I entered the office. He growled, "What do you want, Coulter?"

"Sir, I apologize for all the trouble I've caused you, but I've let you down. After trying my best at this, I realize it's too much for me, and I ask to be transferred to an A-team."

Assionte leaned back in his chair and scrutinized me. The pause seemed endless. Then he spoke: "Is that all, Coulter?"

"Yes, sir," I said. He dismissed me without another word.

I expected another assignment, but nothing happened, and life continued. Apparently, I had overplayed my cards with Assionte; I was stuck in recon whether I liked it or not, for which I was very grateful later.

To my relief, we got orders to move up to Kham Duc, about two hundred miles northwest of Nha Trang. This news meant we were finally going into the field, which to me represented the chance to pursue higher goals and truths, a purer experience in which you succeeded based on objective accomplishments, and a sharp contrast to our time in Nha Trang, with its infighting and petty jealousies.

Everything in Vietnam took longer than it should have, and the move to Kham Duc was no exception. We waited on the scorching tarmac for three days for the clouds to clear over our destination. We officers stood beside our packs all day, braving the sun to set an example—except for Larrabee, who found his way into the air-conditioned conning tower nearby. Sergeant Brown, who was irrepressibly irreverent, played poker on the tarmac with another sergeant and called out at large, "Don't anybody wander off and get lost."

Three days later, we took off.

No one observed flight security in Vietnam or used seat belts; for takeoff, the Vietnamese steadied themselves against a truck chained to the transport plane's floor. Once we were aloft, they wandered around joking with each other.

The clouds over Kham Duc swirled around a tiny patch of red

dirt that the pilots lost sight of more than once as we descended. We landed so hard that I thought we had crashed. Kham Duc was a netherworld of rusted barbed wire, sickly green claymore mines sticking out of red clay, and a placard written in Vietnamese over the gate that seemed to say, "Abandon all hope, ye who enter here." Wooden walkways twisted between dilapidated shacks half submerged in mud. Our guide said, "You'll be living in luxury. Just watch out for the rats."

The surrounding mountains began to turn dark. It was very wet. To heat C-rations, the sergeants lit a fire on the one piece of dry ground available, using scrap lumber and an old tire for fuel. They began to reminisce about past operations and the men they had known. I felt happier than I had been since arriving in Vietnam.

The next morning, we had to move to an adjacent field, because the camp couldn't hold us; as a result, we had to dig our own fortifications. The recon platoon was responsible for the mortar, and we had to dig the mortar pit. Hoyez ordered that both sergeants

Sergeant Robinette, relaxing while we wait for our patrols to start at Kham Duc, the location of some of the hardest battles of the year in October 1967.

Lieutenant-Colonel Hoyez in Kham Duc.

and lieutenants would dig it, which led to another one of Larrabee's tantrums.

Hoyez couldn't order the sergeants to dig the pit while we stood around doing nothing, but Larrabee didn't see it that way. Exemption from manual labor was a key distinction between officers and enlisted men. Hoyez had made Larrabee sit through Recondo School with enlisted men, and now, in Larrabee's mind, he had turned him into one.

This affront to his dignity made Larrabee forget where he was. He tore around our hovel shouting, "He's making us dig mortar pits! Who ever heard of an officer digging a mortar pit? Wait 'til I get back to Nha Trang!" Larrabee evidently thought he could bring the wrath of Headquarters down on Hoyez's head. Bemused, Captain Jaegels watched Larrabee's antics for a while before telling him, "Shut up and get the shovels."

We didn't know Jaegels that well yet, since he had arrived at Nha Trang three weeks after we did. But we all suspected that the army had made a mistake in assigning him to Delta. Jaegels came from the straight-line army, where there was a sharp division separating officers from enlisted men, bearing no resemblance to the dynamic in Special Forces. In Jaegels' world, an officer simply compelled his subordinates to do anything he positively hated to do, and he knew that for senior sergeants digging a mortar pit was more degrading than it was for young lieutenants.

We started looking for a place to dig the pit. Larrabee straggled behind the rest of us, grumbling to himself. As some of us dug with picks and others shoveled dirt into sandbags, Sergeant Brown said, "Leave some for the rest of us." Ford didn't seem to be putting in a lot of effort, prompting Brown to say, "Those look like lieutenant shovelfuls to me." For a while, Larrabee held a sandbag for others to fill. Then, somehow, he managed to disappear.

* * *

The mountains enclosed Kham Duc so tightly that a gap had been cut out of one of them to allow planes to get in, and the pilots had to reverse propellers as soon as the plane touched down in order to keep it from rolling off the end of the runway. One plane came in at such a steep angle that it careened down the entire length of the runway on only two wheels, barely righting itself at the last moment. The men who staggered out said they hadn't expected to make it.

The tops of the mountains came into view only when the clouds lifted, and the shifting mists hung over us at night. We waited for the weather to clear so that we could start our patrols. We spoke little, unable to voice our thoughts, but our behavior spoke for us. Best would stand up and sit down again for no apparent reason. Estenson stared off into space, and I lay on my cot thinking about making too much noise on patrol.

On the fourth morning, I heard somebody shout, "The operation's been cancelled! We're going back to Nha Trang!" But before we could leave, the weather closed in again. We spent several days waiting around and playing poker.

Larrabee wanted to involve Hoyez in our poker games. He

managed to persuade Hoyez that this bit of fraternization with junior officers would be good for morale and not undermine Hoyez's authority. When Hoyez joined us, Larrabee made a point of sitting to his right, so he would receive his cards first and could react to the hand Hoyez had. When Hoyez won a hand, Larrabee would be sure to say, "You really got us that time, sir." More daring was his reaction if he won and Hoyez lost: "We can't just let you take all the money, sir." This was Larrabee's way of getting close to Hoyez, and, surprisingly, it worked.

Finally, the weather cleared. Our destination, after a short stop in Nha Trang, was An Lao, eighty miles southeast of Kham Duc. In Vietnam, you could travel from one geographical extreme to another in a shorter distance than anywhere else in the world, and at An Lao we landed in a plain of flattened rice stubble. If at Kham Duc we

Ford (left) and Graves (right) swimming at a waterfall while we relaxed at Kham Duc, harmless now but deadly eight months later.

Estenson, my closest friend in recon at Kham Duc.

couldn't see the enemy, at An Lao we could see them all around us—almost. It was impossible to tell who was an enemy and who a friend in the welter of people that surrounded us—old women carrying baskets, boys atop water buffalo, and men (mostly old) carry bundles of firewood on their shoulders.

The slender barrel of a 175-millimeter gun protruded from a hill half a mile away. It fired at fixed targets in the jungle, and the noise it made was so loud that at first we thought we were being attacked. Smaller 155-millimeter howitzers, firing barrages of twenty or thirty rounds at a time, startled us less, and the rounds continued to explode out in the jungle long after the firing had stopped. They had a better chance of hitting something because they were firing at targets somebody had called in.

Six miles to the north, a gap between two mountains marked the entrance to the An Lao Valley and the beginning of enemy territory, with nothing between us and them except rice stubble and a few water buffalo. The valley looked empty, but the enemy controlled it by night, and the nearby First Cavalry Division never entered it. The enemy had once run up a Viet Cong flag in a deserted village in the valley, taunting the First Cav, and it took days for the First Cav to build up courage to send down a helicopter to pull it off.

Larrabee hitched a helicopter ride over to the First Cav and returned with a new lease on life. "You should have seen the guys over there when I told them I was from Delta," he began. "They think we eat nails for breakfast. They said nobody could get them to go where we go. They don't go beyond 105-millimeter range, and you can call in a 105 round on a dime. I told them we didn't know what that was." A 105-millimeter howitzer has a six-mile range, and within six miles you have constant radio contact and can call in artillery anytime, even at night. Delta patrols always went well beyond six miles (and usually beyond the fifteen- to eighteen-mile range of a 155-millimeter). On top of that, we never had radio contact at night.

It rained constantly. We dug trenches and filled sandbags and got very wet. The rain fell in sheets. The trench floor became as slippery as glass, and we struggled to stay upright. Jaegels occasionally came out of the command tent, squatted next to the trench, and said, "How do you like it out here? I hate this as much as you do." Brown would respond with a yawn, throw down his shovel, and stuff clay into a sandbag. The senior sergeants' distaste for Jaegels was palpable, and the feud really began to fester. Eventually, the sergeant major flew up from Nha Trang to complain to Hoyez about Jaegels' treatment of the sergeants.

As usual, Larrabee was the first to find out what had happened. He burst into our tent with a schoolboy's air of excitement: "Hoyez just gave Jaegels an hour to get out of here!"

Hoyez was responsible for bringing Jaegels into the unit and by rights should have supported him. But Jaegels was an outsider, and in any case Hoyez's first concern was retaining the sergeants' goodwill.

The other men dispersed, while I remained in the tent to work on my equipment. A few minutes later, Jaegels came in, unrepentant as ever. "The sonsofbitches! Worthless bastards!" He was almost crying with rage. "This will ruin my chances of making major!"

Power and promotion were what mattered most to Jaegels. Duty and honor were secondary. Unfortunately, his attitude was all too prevalent among many members of the U.S. military forces in Vietnam.

Twelve

The first patrol in a new area always involves the greatest risk, and so Delta assigned the best man to lead it. Hoyez, of course, wanted someone who would make him look good, so he wasn't about to give our first patrol at An Lao to a green lieutenant. Instead, he selected Sergeant Reddick. While this decision hurt the pride of the lieutenants, we felt sure that Reddick could run circles around the enemy, while we couldn't—at least not yet.

We watched Reddick in fascination as he prepared for the patrol, marveling at his attention to the smallest details. He was scheduled to go in a little more than twenty-two miles to the north of us, but that night it rained, and the helicopters couldn't take off. A couple of nights later, Reddick tried again but had to return. The next night, his patrol was cancelled just as he was about to board the helicopter. He then spent several hours in the mess tent commiserating with the other sergeants. He could keep up his own edge, but he didn't know about the rest of his team.

After five days the clouds finally broke, and the helicopters began to thump beyond the palm trees, the cadence embedded in the soul of any soldier who has gone on recon, as it conjures up the memory of his own patrols. Reddick and his two sergeants emerged from their tent, the three Vietnamese emerged from theirs, and then they made their way to the helicopters.

Everybody in the camp emerged and followed them. As the team climbed in, sergeants squeezed the men's elbows or touched their shoulders, whispering, "Good luck" and "We're counting on you."

Reddick sat in the helicopter door, the last rays of the sun turning his face yellow. His hand grenades were taped to his ammunition pouches to allow him to retrieve them quickly, his rifle's upper hand guard was taped to break its outline in the jungle, his radio antenna was woven into his pack flap to keep it from getting caught in the vines, and his sheath knife was taped upside down on his shoulder harness so that he could get at it faster. This last choice was perhaps a bit of bravado, but in a tight fight it might make all the difference.

The play of sunlight and shadows sharpened Reddick's features and gave him a heroic appearance. I don't know what he was thinking, but, looking back on my own experience, I imagine he was concentrating on memorizing his route in and rehearsing the actions he would take when he hit the ground. Flying in constituted as much a part of the patrols as the patrol itself, and if the flight in embeds itself in the soul of every man going on recon, so does the sight of the departing helicopters embed itself in those back at camp. The helicopters rocked back and forth as they lifted into the air. We stepped back, holding our hats to avoid the backdraft and watching solemnly as they flew toward the mountains at the entrance to the An Lao Valley.

Men departing on recon represent a courage and even grandeur seldom seen elsewhere. Nothing else has ever given me a greater sense of my own insignificance. Reddick represented the few of this world who willingly devote their lives to what they believe a man should live for—in this case, gambling his life on his ability to keep himself alive. Nobody had forced him to do it. His was an act of free will.

No one broke the silence after the sound of the helicopters faded away, and silently we threaded our way through the palm trees back to camp. Shortly afterward, the commo tent passed the word that Reddick had gotten in, and a little later we heard the helicopters return.

A man's first night on patrol always affects his fellow soldiers deeply. The thought of Reddick out in the jungle created a great hole in the darkness. Although we never believed anything would happen to him, we tried not to think about the possibilities.

The next morning, we gathered in fairly good spirits in front of the command tent for Reddick's first radio message. Larrabee burst out from the door flaps with a frightened look on his face. "Reddick's in trouble!" he said. "He saw flashlights last night and heard mortar rounds!"

"Jesus Christ!" someone whispered as Larrabee reentered the tent.

We had recognized this possibility but had not taken it seriously. Reddick wouldn't get into trouble; he had more experience than anybody except possibly Simpson and Markham. We remained in place outside the tent, each man struggling with his own thoughts as we awaited more news.

After a while, Larrabee came out again and said, "Reddick's hearing movement all around him! He's surrounded!" Our gloom deepened.

Twenty minutes later Larrabee burst out once more, now

sounding indignant. "Reddick asked to come out, and Hoyez refused. He ordered him to stay in!"

"You're kidding!" said Estenson.

Heddern was blunter: "Second-guessing the team on the ground? He's never been on a fucking recon patrol in his life!"

Hoyez had never given us any reason to believe that he cared whether we lived or died, but this incident laid it out in the open. He couldn't possibly know how many enemies Reddick and his men were surrounded by, or how tightly, and Reddick could radio only the bare minimum of information. The last thing Reddick needed was to have someone who didn't have the faintest idea of what was going on tell him what to do.

Hoyez had broken recon's Rule Number One: never second-guess the men on the ground. I pictured myself out in the jungle, the enemy drawing closer as I radioed to come out, with Hoyez showing no more mercy for me than he had for Reddick.

We milled around in front of the command tent, staring at the ground and kicking at the tufts of rice stubble. Vietnamese laborers arrived and began stacking sandbags. The palm shadows flickered on the canvas, and the growing heat marked the passage of time.

Larrabee emerged again, pale and shaken. "Two men have been hit!" he said. Reddick had reported that a squad had attacked them with grenades and small arms.

Shortly afterward, Hoyez pushed the tent flaps aside and literally mowed through us, glaring straight ahead with a look of grim determination on his face. He had his pilot's helmet in one hand and his rifle in the other. Larrabee emerged from the tent and watched Hoyez as he headed for the helicopters, their blades already turning in preparation for takeoff.

"Wait until Nha Trang finds out," Larrabee said. Hoyez's decision to wait until a man was hit before taking him out would, we thought, finish him as a leader.

I didn't see how Hoyez could reach Reddick in time. By now, the enemy had probably closed in on Reddick too tightly for us to get him out. I agonized over the time it took the helicopters to reach the entrance of the An Lao Valley, become specks, and then disappear.

To my disbelief, the helicopters got to Reddick and recovered everybody without even taking fire. In spite of our joy, we felt the world had witnessed one more injustice, what with Hoyez emerging unscathed.

We all went down to help the wounded, pushing close to Reddick's helicopter even before it completed its landing. Any casualties on the helicopter could be in bad shape, and I expected to see men bleeding and in agony. The crowd and the dust raised by the downdraft prevented me from seeing anything at first. When the view was clear, I was shocked to see no blood—no casualties whatsoever. They all looked exactly as they had the night before, except for a growth of beard stubble and some mud on their fatigues. Someone had a broken pack strap.

Hoyez hustled the men into the command tent for the debriefing even before they dropped their gear, and the debriefing lasted for an eternity. Then the news spread through the camp without an identifiable source. I would have guessed Larrabee was the culprit, but not even he wanted to get this news out.

According to Reddick, he had heard the enemy during the night. As daylight came on, he heard twigs snap and leaves rustle—clear indications that the enemy was close. Reddick crawled ahead of his team. He saw two men moving in on him, one in khaki and the other in black pajamas and carrying an American carbine. To get them before they got him, Reddick prepared to throw a grenade, but the man in black pajamas had gotten too close, and so Reddick had to shoot.

This is how we preserved the incident in the records. However, Reddick had reported two of his men hit, but in fact only one—Reddick himself—had been wounded. And he had not suffered a gunshot wound, only a slight laceration from grenade shrapnel—so slight that it barely needed attention. This omission was significant, because when Reddick radioed that two men were wounded, he knew perfectly well that we would assume the injuries were gunshots, not insignificant scratches.

Worse still, the only grenade thrown appeared to be the one Reddick had thrown. The other men were unable to provide any details, which weighed against him even more. None of them could verify that they had seen the enemy or even heard gunfire, and a lot of us now questioned the enemy's actual whereabouts. We suspected that Reddick had been wounded by his own grenade. It began to appear that Reddick had become so terrified during his first night that he had collapsed by morning and fabricated a story to get his team pulled out. That would explain how they got back to the clearing and onto the helicopters without any apparent difficulty.

I passed the mess tent later and could hear Reddick explaining the events of his patrol to other sergeants as they sat at one of the tables. I stopped for a moment to listen. Reddick spoke earnestly, searching their faces. I couldn't hear everything but caught some of what he was saying. He spoke rapidly, without excitement. He was letting the "facts" speak for themselves and tied everything together so neatly that it almost seemed he was telling the truth, far-fetched or no. But Reddick had lost his audience. Some of the men looked pained, others averted their eyes, and still others picked at the edge of the mess table with their fingernails.

The next day, Hoyez kicked Reddick out of Delta, and I never heard anybody discuss his patrol or mention him again. We didn't want to know more, since this couldn't help but raise questions about ourselves and whether we had any more integrity than Reddick did. If word ever got out, Delta would be disgraced, finished. We hoped the whole mess would just disappear. We had nourished ourselves on the courage we believed we possessed, but Reddick had shown how difficult putting that courage into practice could be.

Thirteen

You had to be crazy not to be scared on recon. A man's first patrol is the most terrifying experience of his life, with each step possibly being his last.

My first patrol remains indelibly impressed in my mind. First came the briefing. With an air of regret, the intelligence officer pointed to a small valley on the map. Here, twenty miles to the north (and three miles southeast of where Reddick's patrol had gone in), we suspected there was a North Vietnamese headquarters. The intelligence officer then listed the enemy units known to be operating in the area, which all briefings include and nobody remembers.

After receiving the patrol order, I faced perhaps my most agonizing decision: choosing a landing zone. This choice would make or break the patrol, and anyone who doesn't understand its importance doesn't understand recon. Choosing the right site meant getting the team into enemy territory and safely out of the helicopter.

Choosing the wrong site could get the team killed before the patrol even started. There was no way to know in advance whether you'd picked the right site.

Eventually there was a break in the continual rain, and we were able to fly up to pick our landing zone. We took off and flew over deserted rice paddies and the burned ruins of the village where the Viet Cong had flown their flag, followed by mile after mile of cold mountain jungle with dreary gray columns of mist floating above the drenched foliage. For the first time, recon became something more than an abstraction for me; it was a life-or-death reality. I had grown up in suburban Arlington, Virginia. Now I had to decipher Vietnam's inscrutable jungle and bet my life on what I'd learned in our classes.

Vietnam never spoiled us in terms of landing zones, and I had to choose between a deserted-looking valley that was a mile outside of my patrol area and a ridge saddle that was right in the middle of it. The ridge saddle looked like it might have been recently cleared, and during two quick preliminary passes at a few hundred feet, I had to search for signs of cultivation in the red, muddy ground. I had figured out early on that you never wanted to land in an area where you might run into someone, even a noncombatant.

The sound of the helicopters revving up signaled that it was time to go. I met Sergeants Brown and Bartlett, plus the three Vietnamese who would accompany us, in the center of camp, and we crossed through the palm trees to the helicopters.

The helicopter lifted off, the air becoming colder as we rose into the sky. My concern over choosing the right landing zone transformed into fear of not recognizing the landmarks to get there; somehow everything looked different than it had when I had flown over before. Pilots didn't care nearly as much about where they dropped us as we did, so the pressure to get it right was on me. Landing the least bit off in a jungle that limited visibility to about six feet could leave us with no idea of where we were.

I had opted for the ridge saddle, and the pilot dropped into a diversionary flight pattern. Unfamiliar ridges and strange new clearings popped up as we descended. Warm, nauseating jungle air hit us, a shock after the colder air of our previous altitude. Rough brush, thrashing in the downdraft, rose to meet us, and before I knew it the black jungle hemmed us in on all sides.

The clearing looked right, more or less, and I signaled for the others to stand up as I balanced at the door's edge, looking for a place to jump among the tree stumps. Once I hit the ground, I paused to make sure the others were following, and then I sprinted for the jungle.

Anybody who says he didn't expect to get killed during his first night on recon is lying. After the almost dreamlike nature of the flight in, everything becomes extraordinarily concrete. Dusk fell on us with all its uncertainty, and the jungle's gloomy darkness and the overpowering smell of rot filled our senses. Once the helicopter left, the silence was overwhelming, all encompassing, and oppressive. Breaking the silence would likely give us away, while not breaking it was a challenge in itself.

We faced a wall of vines and brambles, and the Vietnamese point man stopped frequently to figure out a way forward. Rotted logs were everywhere on the ground; their loose bark fell away at the slightest touch, causing us to slip whenever we stepped on them. I was at a loss as to how we could mask a six-man trail in this terrain.

I kept the point man moving until it was completely dark. We sat down close enough to touch each other, propping ourselves against bushes and saplings to keep from slipping down the slope we were on. We waited in silence to see whether the enemy would come after us. The men tried to shift quietly, but even the subtlest movement made noise. Sergeant Brown knocked his rifle butt against the ground a couple of times, potentially a big problem because the sound could be easily distinguished from normal jungle noises.

The jungle creaked, and rotten branches fell to the ground frequently. Each sound made me think the enemy was approaching. Fireflies blinked everywhere, and each one was a flashlight searching for me. Phosphorescent mold glowed at the base of trees and produced purple forms that glided from place to place and stood right over me. I felt I lacked the courage for this work. I couldn't remain silent while someone walked over me. I couldn't remember where the trees were, so any grenade I threw would likely bounce back at me. I might shut my eyes to keep from being blinded by the blast, but how in the world could I silently alert Brown and the Vietnamese team leader right beside me, to say nothing of Bartlett and the other two Vietnamese farther off? Even if I somehow managed to warn the others, throw the grenade correctly, and blow a hole in the enemy line, I had no idea of how to get us all through it.

The first night brings personal weaknesses to the surface, making them impossible to ignore. Thoughts were almost uncontrollable. I didn't care about success or even about the other members of my team. I just wanted to live, and Reddick's disgrace was the only thing that kept me from radioing for help and running back to the landing zone.

After what seemed an eternity, bird calls started coming from far down in the valley, leading me to hope that dawn would soon break, but the darkness continued for hours. Eventually a faint gray mist replaced the darkness, revealing the outlines of trees and of the other men on my team. We nodded silently to each other and continued to stare at the jungle. Our eyes were hollow from lack of sleep, our pants were out of our boots, and our boots were caked with red mud.

The trees had protected us all night, and when it got light, we looked on them with affection. After a night like that, you stare at everything with wonder. The smooth gray bark of the tree in front of me resembled the leg of some huge animal, and I half expected it to shiver when an insect crawled across it. A leech started to inch toward me over the dead leaves. I marveled at its instinct to back away when it encountered the scent of my insect repellent.

Finally, we heard the forward air controller (FAC), a one-engine Bird Dog, coming from the south—the sound of life and deliverance. I cupped the radio handset and whispered our map coordinates in code so softly that Brown at my shoulder couldn't hear. We had made it through the first night.

Nobody forgets his first night on recon, and nobody forgets his first day either. The joy of making it through the night evaporated very quickly. The sergeants had told us that the enemy liked to hit teams just after they got off the helicopter the first night or first thing the next morning. Since the jungle made it hard to attack at night, they often waited until morning when they could hear the team moving. Making it through the night didn't mean we were in the clear, and we wouldn't actually know whether we had gotten in undetected until about noon. We waited another hour to see whether the enemy had picked up our radio call.

Nothing characterized these patrols more than your inability to see beyond six feet and the belief that someone was waiting beyond the next leaf, someone who could hear you, though you couldn't hear him. We started from zero with every move, each new step as perilous as the last, aggravated by the fact that we couldn't hear above the birds and cicadas. We stopped to listen as best we could after each step.

The jungle, in all its aspects, conspired to kill. Vines and brambles crisscrossed the air in front of you like barbed wire. The vines had three-inch thorns that were as hard as steel. At each step we fought to squeeze through the diabolical latticework. No sooner had we made it through one than it closed behind us and we faced another, making us feel as if we hadn't moved at all.

Heavy knotted vines, two or three inches thick, rose from the ground at our feet or hung down from the trees above. In places, a wall of leaves encased an entire tree, revealing a sinister green-copper glimmer inside. A huge vine might wrap itself entirely around a tree, engulfing it, while the tree seemed to undulate in folds cascading one on top of another. Knee-high buttress roots fanned out so close together that they caught our feet, and to get around a single tree, we often had to step over each root, taking care not to trip.

The jungle seemed to breathe on us. Specks of dust danced in the hot air, giving the only hint that light made it down this far. To get a sense of the canopy's height, I tried looking up one of the enormous, smooth, gray tree trunks. But the thickness of the canopy made it impossible to see beyond a few levels.

I clung to the rules Markham had taught us as if they meant our salvation, which they probably did. I'm sure I applied them more conscientiously than even he did. I caught each vine between my thumb and forefinger, paused to figure out how to move through each thicket, and then repositioned the whole thing behind me before advancing.

I can't remember whether I concentrated more on my hands or my feet, but moving my feet took more work. Humans have a natural inclination to pay more attention to what is in front of us than what is below. I constantly reminded myself to look down, causing me to work harder watching my feet than I did when picking apart the vines. I looked for pliable (not damp) leaves, free of twigs, and put my heel down first to test the ground before rolling onto my sole. I made sure I stood firmly on one foot before moving the other, and each step required the same amount of effort.

I checked behind me to see whether I had disturbed anything, but jungle leaves hold a lot of moisture, give way under pressure, and restore their shape easily, so I seemed to be doing all right.

Occasionally, I rustled some leaves accidentally, but the sound didn't carry beyond me, and I just told myself that I couldn't get everything right the first time.

With me on patrol were three Vietnamese and two American sergeants, Bartlett and Brown. Nobody put more heart into his work than Bartlett. Unfortunately, he was tall and somewhat uncoordinated—not the best combination for silently slipping through the jungle without leaving traces. As much as he tried not to, Bartlett made noise. I would scowl at him and he would look mortified, but sooner or later he'd make noise again.

I liked Bartlett, and I couldn't come down hard on him anyway because I needed the goodwill of the sergeants as a group. I was impressed by the fact that Bartlett spent most of his spare time devouring books on Vietnam. He was seeking knowledge, including self-knowledge, just as I was.

Brown was short and stocky, which also made him a less-than-ideal physical type for recon. He gave the impression of general bitterness and a strong dislike for authority. He seemed to feel he had gotten the short stick in life and was suspicious of even those people who exhibited the best of intentions, letting you know with brutal humor. When I had reviewed tactics before our patrol, Brown said, "That's not the way we did it in fifty-five, sir." He was highly intelligent and went about everything he did with precision. His intelligence seemed wasted on a buck sergeant.

Brown seemed to place little value on life, including his own. I feared that he would bristle at anything I told him to do. Yet he looked to me for guidance and did his best not to make any noise. He focused on what he was doing at all times. As the patrol proceeded, I felt I had won his grudging respect.

We made it past the half-morning mark and expected to reach the top of the next slope at noon. The rule of thumb was that if you made it to noon, you were probably in good shape. I couldn't have felt more elated than when we topped a rise and my watch pointed to twelve.

As the FAC approached, I unhitched the handset from my shirt and whispered our map coordinates and no change in status, letting the facts speak for themselves, knowing the effect they would have on those back at base camp. Hoyez would be delighted.

We took the obligatory two-hour "pock time" (the Vietnamese term for a siesta), because all Vietnamese sleep at noon and any movement at that time would arouse suspicion. By the time we stopped, we hadn't eaten for eighteen hours and wouldn't have traded our rehydrated indigenous rice rations for the world. We mixed them with dried fish or sausage and ate with twigs for chopsticks, rehydrating our rice for the noon meal by pouring a canteen of water into it in the morning.

We continued to move through the jungle during the afternoon. We could hear distant shots in the valley to our west, and I began to fear that base camp might think I was strolling along and purposely being idle. I had gained greater confidence in my feeling for the jungle and thought I should try to do something more, so I decided to head down into the valley.

We immediately ran into a world-class briar patch. I would no sooner pull one bramble off my sleeve than have another catch on my shoulder. After an hour, we'd barely made a few yards—very slow even for the jungles of Vietnam. We were making too much noise and stayed so long in one place that we were leaving tracks.

"To hell with this," I whispered to the others. "Let's go back up on the ridge and call in artillery." The shots we had heard earlier had to be the enemy. The shooting was target practice, perhaps, or they could have been hunting.

I called the radio relay and, since I didn't recognize the voice, assumed it was one of the relays the First Cav had provided for us. I gave the coordinates of the rifle fire and my compass line to him, the "observer-target azimuth," as taught in training. I expected the radio relay to understand, but he didn't adjust according to my compass line from the target, but rather according to the "gun target line," directly south of us. As a result, the round crashed through the trees over our heads and exploded less than fifty-five yards down the slope. The relay's stupidity had nearly killed us. I told the relay, "We don't need any more help." This incident led to my realization that war is just a crap shoot or a traffic accident waiting to happen.

We made it to 6:00 p.m., and the FAC came for our last radio message. I threw it down almost like a gauntlet; for a moment, the whole jungle seemed to scintillate. I had made it through the entire day—a rarity. I imagined Hoyez walking around the command tent saying, "God damn, Coulter!"

I had succeeded from a tactical perspective, and I had also succeeded with my men, especially Sergeant Brown. For a young lieutenant on his first patrol, nothing counted more than that. As the shadows lengthened and darkness began to settle in, I felt a sense of exhilaration.

I picked a level spot, and we ate our rice as we listened to the last bird calls. I arranged my canteens in order to lie between them with my shoulder harness on, and Brown said, "If I snore, just poke me in the ribs, sir." The jungle grew black and silent. We had survived day one.

We stayed on the ridge the second day and came across a ridge trail, and on the third day I decided to try the valley to the east, a small basin among mountain ridges and one of the patrol's objectives. On the first day, the jungle seemed to personify death, with the enemy ruling everywhere and us at their mercy. But after remaining undetected for two days, some of the terror had worn off. We had turned the tables on the enemy and placed the jungle between us and them; we, not they, were the hunters. Now the jungle almost seemed to welcome us, and I moved through it with more confidence.

Despite its cruelty, the jungle bursts with rare richness and unique beauty. Drops of water sparkle gaily off leaves that seem to be on the verge of putting your eyes out, and sharp palm fronds lunge down threateningly and then fan out gracefully over your head.

As we descended into the valley, light began to appear among the treetops. I ruled more strictly over the team now that we had a greater chance of running into somebody. Suddenly, we were on a valley floor, and the underbrush vanished as a large clearing opened under the trees, branches arching twenty yards over our heads, tree trunks standing in columns, and the ground packed absolutely smooth. After growing accustomed to the heavy jungle, this shift caught me off guard, and I felt curiously weightless. The clearing came into view so suddenly that I thought it was a natural phenomenon. My point man, though, knew better and had ducked behind some trees.

We had stumbled on a camp, one where the enemy had been present not long ago; their presence still hung in the air. We tiptoed from tree to tree, peering into foxholes and bomb shelters, which were impressively deep. A lashed bamboo hut stood in the middle, probably the headquarters.

This was a pretty large encampment. I estimated that it would hold a battalion, four or five hundred men. They must have been here a long time and had probably felt so well hidden under the trees that they could have stayed on forever. But, for whatever reason, they had left quickly at some point, probably within the past two or three weeks. That was fortunate for us, for if they'd still been there, we all would have been killed or captured.

"These must be the guys we were sent to look for," I said to Brown. We sat down against the trees to eat and celebrate.

Suddenly the three Vietnamese members of the patrol grabbed their rifles and leaped to their feet. The point man put a finger to his lips, stared at the nearby stream, and then motioned for silence. The water tinkled over rocks in the stream bed, and we braced ourselves against the trees with rifles pointed toward where we expected the enemy to appear. The leaves obstructed our view, and we could shoot only the men in front; the rest would be out of our line of sight. They would almost certainly know the area and be able to flank us.

But instead of enemy soldiers, two old Montagnard women came into view, on the rocks. They were about four feet tall, with deeply wrinkled, rubbery faces and oddly distorted features. They wore rough shawls made out of gray bark. They were throwbacks to an ancient time who had never entered the modern world; they were unlike any person I had ever seen before. We had them in our rifle sights but couldn't fire. When they caught sight of us, the women's eyes widened, and they spun around and darted back downstream, their heads bobbing above the rocks until they disappeared from sight.

I had stupidly violated the rules of patrolling and deserved to be sighted. Now I had no idea what to do. Being seen and caught unaware was humiliating enough; realizing that I had no clue what to do next was paralyzing. Enemy units were undoubtedly nearby, and the old women would tell them where we were.

I had to decide between two bad options. We could take the time to find a good position from which to defend ourselves, or we could try to get away before the enemy found us. Making a stand against superior numbers would probably get us killed, but if we pulled out, where would we go? Going forward meant entering a new area, and the old women had seen us taking that direction. Going back the way we came meant possibly running into someone who had picked up our trail. Heading back like that was a mistake one of my friends from Germany had made, and it had cost him his life. However, there was a third possibility: I could ask Hoyez to let the team come out. But making that request because I had allowed us to be sighted by two old women would be humiliating.

I decided to move sideways into the valley. We came to some

brush that looked big enough to hide behind, and I ordered every-body down. But as soon as we got down, I realized that the brush wouldn't protect us and cursed myself for not seeing this problem before ordering the men to get down. Ordering everyone up again to search for a better place would make me look like a fool. Faced with the choice of getting killed or looking foolish, I actually hesitated and almost chose to save face. Only after a brief internal debate did I opt to seek a more defensible position.

"Dammit, this isn't any good," I said. "We've got to find some-place better." I ordered everyone to move closer to the ridge. The brush there should be thicker, I thought, but whether we would get there before the enemy was on us was unknown.

We ran around in the valley looking for a better position, break-ing all the rules and leaving footprints for the enemy to find. Sweat was pouring down my face, and I was desperately thirsty.

We had gotten back to where the ridge began to rise. With the enemy having to work through the underbrush to get to us, I felt more secure and began to act more in control. Since the enemy hadn't attacked yet, maybe they weren't at the entrance to the valley and the old women had been forced to go some distance to reach them. When they came after us, the enemy would probably take the same stream bed along which the old women had fled. Maybe they hadn't even entered that area yet. If I brought an artillery barrage down there, I could inflict casualties on anybody who was there or scare anybody who hadn't got there yet into thinking twice about pursuing us.

I got on the radio and called for artillery. I requested the first round long, and the shell whistled over our heads and exploded far to the north. I tried to bring the second round back into the valley where we were, in order to bracket the stream gorge the women had fled along, and believed I succeeded because the explosion seemed almost on top of us. I moved the third round back a little to the north, and the muffled explosion showed it had landed somewhere in the stream gorge.

"I'm going to blow the hell out of the place," I told the team and called for a barrage of thirty rounds. The old women had probably left the area, but if not, it was either them or us. The howitzers thud-ded away, and as each round hit the stream gorge, the sound trav-eled along the top of the ridge and reverberated all around the valley, like rolling thunderclaps. The barrage must have pulverized the stream gorge beyond recognition. Thirty rounds landed right where

I thought the enemy would be as I pictured them cowering under the rain of shells.

We pressed our bodies against the side of the ridge. The ground shook, and loose branches and other refuse fell down on us. At each round, the faces of the Vietnamese team members lit up, and I could tell Brown and Bartlett found the barrage comforting as well. I had restored my authority and hoped the memory of my panic would quickly fade.

We circled on the ridge to hide our tracks and could sense no one following us. I felt rejuvenated and congratulated myself on having limited the damage I had caused. I felt a sense of exhilaration and invincibility.

The next day, we went back into the valley. We found large bomb craters, explaining how the enemy realized they had been discovered. Suddenly the brush shook. I cursed myself and couldn't believe I was dumb enough to be caught in the open again. I pointed my rifle at the foliage and was about to pull the trigger when a water buffalo thrust its head through the leaves. I shook my rifle at it, and it pulled its head back. Then another appeared.

"Watch out he doesn't take a bite out of you, sir," said Brown.

Suddenly, buffalo were everywhere, and we had to make our way through a herd without stampeding it and alerting the entire valley. Brown stamped his feet and shook his rifle at them, while Bartlett studied each animal intensely, trying to discern its next move.

For our patrol's final night, I hid the team in brambles close to our exfiltration point. Mine would be the first team to actually finish a patrol. I couldn't believe I had done so well.

The following morning, we heard pots clattering barely ten yards away. It was peasants tending the herd of water buffalo. The buffalo grazed in our midst as if we weren't there. The helicopter approached, and, like a matador, the tail gunner waved his red signal panel at one buffalo just as a boy tending the herd came into view. The point man beckoned for the boy to come closer, but he disappeared into the brush instead. A moment later, the pots stopped, but I didn't care. We'd be long gone before they could bring the enemy after us.

Nothing beats the feeling of coming out from a recon patrol. The dense brush prevented the helicopter from landing, so instead it hovered overhead and lowered a hoist. After they pulled me into the helicopter, with the buffalo stampeding below, I caressed the cold aluminum floor, inhaled the fumes from the aviation fuel, and then gazed absently at the white clouds that dotted the deep blue sky above us. We headed back to camp. I had accomplished the hardest thing in my life. The events of that patrol are as vivid for me today as they were back then.

I have to add, however, that my first patrol also created an internal debate that haunted me for my entire tour. It had dawned on me that no one back at base camp could know what I might be doing in the jungle. I could do almost anything I wanted. The ridge we had been on seemed deserted, while shots and other noise could be heard coming from the valley to the west. I concluded that people (including the enemy) stayed in the valleys, where there was water, and not on the ridges, where there was none. Most of the jungle was, in fact, fairly empty, in contrast to our assumption that it was crawling with enemy troops.

This realization led me to the conclusion that I could spend the entire patrol on ridges, listening to the activity in the valleys without going down into them and getting shot at. I might not get the best intelligence, but I could finish my patrols and return with enough information to make it seem as if I had accomplished something.

I justified this approach to myself with the following reasoning: To obtain great intelligence, like troop sightings, I would have to go down into the valleys, which would inevitably lead to enemy contact and firefights. This in turn would mean being forced out early, assuming the patrol wasn't annihilated by the enemy's superior numbers. A firefight revealed nothing except what was going on at that particular spot. Anyway, our recon patrols weren't designed to get into firefights, and by staying on the ridges, I could gather *some* information of value—maybe not headline-grabbing stuff, but enough to satisfy my superiors. This was basically sound reasoning. But I never shook the suspicion that I had less-than-noble motives for adopting this strategy.

Fourteen

The other lieutenants were going out on patrols as well. When I returned, Larrabee was in the field with his team. In all his duties, Larrabee tended to "wing it" and assume everything would just fall into place. He had not prepared for his first patrol properly and wound up landing almost four miles outside his chosen landing area, and for a time it was feared that his patrol had been completely wiped out. The FAC finally located him by firing artillery rounds and having Larrabee identify where they landed. On extraction, he dishonored himself by getting into the chopper first, leaving his team members behind to follow. This behavior did not go over well, especially with the sergeants. Military principles carried more weight with them than they did with us. Foremost among these principles is that you work not for yourself but for the general good. This viewpoint creates cohesion between ranks, from privates to generals. Men recognize the right of another man to be placed over them only to the extent that he, on the deepest level, places himself under them and puts their welfare ahead his own. This idea expressed itself in clear, mandatory practices. In recon, when you went in on patrol, the patrol leader always jumped out of the chopper first, and when you came out, he always got on last. No one needed to be told this rule.

I was back in camp when Larrabee returned and watched as he literally threw himself out of the helicopter on top of Best, who had come to help, and then held on to Best as if the latter were a life preserver. Larrabee's pants were ripped to the thigh, his rifle smeared with mud. He clung to Best with one hand while gulping water from his canteen with the other. Not a pretty sight.

Larrabee had confirmed what the sergeants already knew: lieutenants are not real men, not as soldiers understand it. A real man has some kind of core. A lieutenant, shorn of his insignia, does not, or so the senior sergeants believed.

Larrabee was an embarrassment, but he wasn't all that different from a lot of the other men serving in Vietnam. He was self-centered and arrogant on the outside, but inside he was a zero, nothing. He allowed the fear we all felt to eat away at his sense of duty and honor. That made him a bad soldier. He represented a type that was all too prevalent in the Vietnam-era army, even in Special Forces.

* * *

As Sergeant Markham was coming back from his patrol, we got word that he and his team had captured six people. Prisoners were the Holy Grail in recon, live intelligence considerably more valuable than my empty enemy camp.

I can't deny that I felt jealous of Markham's success. Despite my jealousy, I went up to congratulate him when he returned. I barely recognized him. He looked tense and exhausted, his eyes darting nervously without fixing on anyone or anything. It was a far cry from the Markham I had known.

The six prisoners shocked me even more: three frail old men, an old woman, and two small children, a girl and a boy, all of them dressed in tattered peasant clothing. Blindfolded, their hands tied behind their backs, to be sent over to the First Cav for interrogation, they tried to keep their balance in the back of the truck, the children barely visible above the truck's sides.

Capturing innocent civilians had never occurred to me. I could have captured the buffalo herders and perhaps the old Montagnard women had I chosen to do so; it simply hadn't entered my mind. The fate of these unfortunate "prisoners" is unknown to me. The army's interrogation process could take weeks, and we heard nothing more about them after they left our camp.

Heddern went out on his first patrol and reported being attacked, with two of his men wounded. They got the team back safely, and when the chopper landed, we went down to see whether we could help with the wounded. But it was Reddick all over again. The wounds looked like scratches from thorns, and no one could confirm the enemy presence reported by Heddern.

Whenever I reflect on Vietnam, our indestructible belief in ourselves amazes me the most. Shortly after Heddern's patrol, one of our sergeants, Archer, was killed on patrol.

We didn't think his patrol would run into much trouble. They were going in two and a half miles southeast of where I had gone, and the isolated mortar rounds and machine gun fire they reported during the first night didn't seem to trouble them. But as dawn broke, they were attacked by thirty to forty men.

The other men on Archer's team kept close to the ground, knowing that fire usually comes in high. Archer, however, despite the others' gestures for him to stay down, raised his head to see what was happening. He was shot in the chest. When the other men on the team started moving and saw that Archer wasn't with them, they hesitated to go back to retrieve him. If Archer didn't have enough sense to save himself, they weren't going to get killed trying to do it for him.

When the other sergeants got back, they were beside themselves with anger. "That motherfucker! That dumb sonofabitch! What the fuck did he expect?" The feeling was that anybody that stupid deserved to get killed, and they were lucky he hadn't gotten them killed as well. The fact remained, though, that they had all been prepared to abandon him.

The sergeants' judgment took the weight of guilt off Archer's death. It suggested that Archer had gotten killed for a mistake that no normal, capable man would make. You only got killed on these patrols if you were as dumb as Archer, which none of us believed we were.

I now got to know the First Cav better. After the fiasco of Larrabee's first patrol, Hoyez had sent him up to the First Cav as liaison. The day Archer was killed, Hoyez ordered me to go over there to replace Larrabee, so that Larrabee could be sent to retrieve Archer's body and get some much-needed experience in the field. Larrabee had worked his peculiar form of magic on the First Cav, and as he introduced me, everyone looked sad to see somebody bland like me replace him.

Since the First Cav's patrols didn't go beyond the range of a 105-millimeter howitzer, they knew little about what was happening outside their own perimeter and had to base their estimates of enemy strength and intentions mainly on agents' reports. While the First Cav ran many patrols, these tended to be more reactive to whatever the division happened to encounter, as opposed to seeking out the enemy. They were essentially passive, not active. But in a just a few weeks, Hoyez had changed things and shed new light on the farthest reaches of the First Cav's territory. This development occurred despite the fact that most of our patrols accomplished very little. What we did produce seemed pure gold to the First Cav. The commanding general didn't know what he would have done without us. When Hoyez visited the Cav, the general came out and, after returning Hoyez's salute, went over to him and punched him on the arm like a buddy. Hoyez had accomplished more in a few weeks than the First Cav had thought possible.

I had never served as a liaison before, and Larrabee had barely introduced me, so I had no idea of what I was supposed to do when Ford went on patrol almost four miles west of where Heddern had been. We had put so many teams in by now, though, that it was hard to imagine what could go wrong. So, with nothing else to do, I went over to the commo tent to monitor the radio.

I heard footsteps outside, and Major Gillespie entered, sat down on a cot, and lit a cigarette. Gillespie was the First Cav's liaison with us. He had an intimidating reputation. He was one of the first Special Forces soldiers to be sent to Vietnam and had gotten on the cover of *National Geographic* in 1964 after helping to subdue a revolt among Montagnard soldiers in the Central Highlands. He had shown up to be with me while I monitored the patrol going in. His presence made me very uncomfortable.

Ford had taken off, and the helicopter pilots made their first radio checks. Suddenly, a loud screech broke the routine radio squelch. It was Hoyez. "They're firing artillery right under us!" he yelled. "Why haven't they kept this corridor clear? Get them to stop, now!"

I cranked the field telephone to contact the First Cav's operation center and explained to the duty officer what was happening. This should have resolved the issue. But within a few moments Hoyez was on the radio again, sounding even angrier. "They're still firing! Right under me! I told you to do something! Find out what's happening and get the bastards to stop, or I'll take my unit and go home!"

Gillespie had heard everything. He got up slowly, came over, and cranked the field telephone in a leisurely manner. He asked for someone by his first name. After speaking with him briefly, Gillespie turned to me. "The message took a while getting down to the battery." Then he added, dryly, "If he's at five or six thousand feet with rounds falling right below him, they can't hit him."

He resumed his seat on the cot. The darkness became complete, and I could see only his cigarette glowing as he puffed on it. Nothing more broke the squelch until word came over that Ford had gotten in. Gillespie stood up, said a curt "Good night," and disappeared into the night.

Administrative messages followed, one of which said, "Unaccounted rifle found on the infiltration aircraft." As it turned out, Ford had forgotten to take his rifle when he jumped off the helicopter—another embarrassment. Ford had done what the dumbest private wouldn't do on his first day of basic training. Nobody had ever heard of anyone forgetting his rifle. Your rifle was the one thing, besides water, that you absolutely needed to go on these patrols, and you would no more go out on a patrol without it than you would go out there stark naked.

* * *

I hate to recount the next episode because it resembles the original A Shau battle in early 1966, when the Special Forces camp was overrun and the men had to scatter into the jungle in order to save themselves.

After establishing his reputation with the First Cav, Hoyez probably feared that he would lose his new status if he failed to build on it. Our eighty-man Ranger companies could take on large enemy units but made noise and left trails. Recon patrols, by contrast, moved stealthily but couldn't stand and fight against units of any size. Hoyez came up with a way to solve this dilemma by using a platoon on recon. A platoon, he felt, would be big enough to fight but still small enough to maintain stealth.

Hoyez wanted the best man to try this experiment, and he chose Livingston, a second lieutenant with the least time in grade. He was also less pretentious than the rest of us. Livingston had gotten Hoyez's attention when he performed well on his first operation with the Vietnamese Rangers. As a further sign of respect, or perhaps as insurance, Hoyez assigned Sergeant Simpson to go with him. We thought the whole idea was ridiculous. No one could possibly control twenty-nine men to the extent of keeping the enemy from hearing them. But Livingston proved us wrong and moved like clockwork for two days, three miles north of where I had gone and twenty-three miles north of base camp, and by noon on the second day he had reached an observation point on a well-used trail.

Three men and two women came along, unarmed and without using any precautions. Shortly after, a group of two men and a woman appeared; one of the men was carrying an AK-47. Both groups had the air of a high-ranking Viet Cong or North Vietnamese cadre. Livingston's men fired on the second group and killed the woman, but they somehow missed the two men, who escaped. Papers on the woman verified that she was a highly placed Viet Cong official.

High-ranking officials moving about freely implied a large unit nearby. They wouldn't take the woman's death lightly and would soon know exactly where Livingston had killed her. Livingston, therefore, had to get away quickly. Later that afternoon, he felt he was safe, but then a man with a red bandana jumped from a tree and ran into the brush, obviously a lookout on his way to report. With dusk falling, and unable to move in the dark, Livingston had to hole up for the night as best he could.

Livingston's first radio message the next morning brought relief, as he reported that during the night he had heard nothing more than some machine gun fire about half a mile away. An hour later, however, Livingston reported groups of men—first five, then twenty, then forty—passing on both sides of his ridge, in standard web gear with loaded rucksacks, wearing black pajamas and armed with AK-47s, all moving in an orderly manner and clearly North Vietnamese troops, not Viet Cong. Forty troops took off their packs and sat down under the trees to rest for twenty minutes before moving on.

Reading Livingston's messages up at First Cav, I felt as if I could touch the enemy soldiers streaming by on each side of the platoon. I was very worried. With the enemy so close, Livingston couldn't call in an airstrike, as he could easily get his platoon wiped out by friendly fire, or, if the strike landed beyond the enemy, it could stampede them right into him.

Most of Livingston's twenty-nine men crammed together on a small ridge and would be out of his sight and beyond his control. All one of them had to do was knock his rifle butt against a tree or, worse, accidentally fire a round. Plus, the enemy could read the jungle better than we could and distinguish anything that didn't harmonize with it. Then Livingston reported that one of the men with the woman they had killed the day before had approached the ridge he was on and was probing the edge of the foliage, obviously looking for signs of the patrol. At this point, base camp ordered me to coordinate with the First Cav, and I had to leave the radio.

In the S-3 tent, the battalion commander—a lieutenant colonel—waited as his company commanders hurried in, all of them wearing pressed fatigues and immaculately shined boots, old-fashioned cavalry hats with one side turned up, gold braid, and crossed-saber cavalry insignia. A couple had saffron or camouflage silk neck scarves, and one had a .45 in a shoulder holster strapped under his arm. Each one stamped the ground, sprang to attention, and shouted which company he was from.

The lieutenant colonel asked how soon they could get their men ready. "Five minutes, sir," some said, sounding as if they didn't actually need that much time, while the others said ten minutes, because they were "still cleaning up from the last patrol." The Cav needed to keep five hundred men waiting in their tents with all their equipment on to react that fast.

The lieutenant colonel asked me what I had to say, and, not knowing exactly what to reply, I said, "I'm here to coordinate, sir," which caused the captains to exchange knowing smiles. By 1967, many in Special Forces were on their second or third tour in Vietnam; however, the regular army now did most of the fighting, and they considered us mavericks. They felt as though they did all the real work.

The lieutenant colonel told the captains to stand by. The captains hurried back to their companies, and I returned to our tent, expecting that the sky would fill with helicopters. The First Cav had been designed to land large quantities of helicopter-borne troops anywhere at the drop of a hat and thereby catch and kill an enemy who was otherwise able to move much faster in the jungle than we could. "Air mobility" had received a lot of publicity, and one would think the First Cav would welcome an opportunity to demonstrate their capabilities, since they rarely found large enemy units like this and we had, in effect, presented them with one on a platter.

But, as it turned out, Livingston didn't meet their criteria. The enemy could have moved on from where Livingston had first reported them, and the First Cav required absolute precision before committing themselves. Therefore, while deciding what to do, they wanted a recon team to keep track of the enemy for them. Besides, there were always plenty of enemies, and if the Cav didn't get these, there would be others.

Hoyez ordered me to return and head the team that would keep track of the enemy. Foolishly, I yielded to the military psychology of considering the most terrifying tasks a huge honor, and as I went over to tell the First Cav, I looked forward to the chance to place myself above the captains who had mocked me. But I came across only the S-3 sergeant, who couldn't have cared less where I was going or what I was going to do.

Just when the First Cav had left it up to us to get Livingston out on our own, we had to abandon him to take out two Vietnamese teams located almost twenty-two miles to the northwest. One team claimed that it had killed two Viet Cong and then been surrounded all night, while the other reported they had just been attacked. This could mean anything, but Hoyez wasn't going to jeopardize his career by questioning them.

I have to say very frankly that we considered the South Vietnamese lazy and cowardly, and while we maintained public harmony for the sake of the war effort and certainly liked some of the Vietnamese individually, our prejudice often broke through to the surface. The general feeling was that if we didn't have to carry the burden of the Vietnamese on our shoulders, the war would already have been won.

Our helicopter pilots detested going in for Vietnamese teams. "You can just kiss your ass goodbye" is how they would refer to these missions. The Vietnamese believed helicopters could get in anywhere, didn't require clearance for their rotors, and didn't need to worry about guns on any heights above them.

Just communicating with the Vietnamese was difficult. Their team would radio to the Vietnamese interpreter in the plane with the FAC, and the interpreter would explain what they said to the FAC; the FAC then radioed this information to the helicopter pilots, and the helicopter pilots replied by telling the FAC what they thought; the FAC explained this to the interpreter, and the interpreter would proceed to have a long conversation with the people on the ground. Needless to say, key details could often get lost in this process. You didn't know whether the interpreter had translated accurately from Vietnamese to English and vice versa, much less whether the team had given accurate details to begin with. They might report coordinates for one place and yet be somewhere else.

In this case, we didn't have men to rescue in just one location; rather, they were scattered all over the place. As a result, we spent hours picking them up one at a time, all the while hoping that nobody was an enemy decoy.

Livingston and his platoon got back safely, thanks to Sergeant Simpson. Late in the afternoon, I spoke with Livingston at the camp's back perimeter. His face was lined with exhaustion, his fatigues were caked with mud, and he seemed a little sheepish after all the attention he had received.

"I don't know what I would have done without Simpson," he said. "He laid down the law, and I did whatever he said." Livingston recounted how Simpson had picked their ridge for the night as if he had spent his entire life studying how to choose the best possible defensive positions. He organized the men's firing positions as well.

"The Vietnamese normally fool around and string up their hammocks to get comfortable for the night," Livingston continued. "Last night they just lay on the ground, and so we knew something was up. They didn't even take off their equipment. Then, this morning, man! There sure were a lot of them!"

He and Simpson had hung on to their little piece of high ground all morning long, with death moving around them just a short distance away. Livingston said the danger seemed to give Simpson new energy, as if he lived for outwitting the enemy. He went down to the edge of the jungle and peered through the leaves at the enemy soldiers, watching everything they did and calculating what to do next. "I wanted to stay as far back as I could, but Simpson dragged me down there with him."

The enemy officer who had been with the woman they killed climbed partway up the ridge toward their hiding place. At one point, he looked into the leaves not far from where Livingston and Simpson were hiding. "Boy, he got pretty close!" Livingston said with a shudder.

Livingston (right) at An Lao right after he miraculously returned after being surrounded by the North Vietnamese.

This was the tensest moment. Had the NVA officer come just a few feet closer, or had one of our men made any noise, it would have been all over. But Simpson never flinched. When the enemy officer turned away, Simpson whispered dryly, "Now we just have to make sure one of the men doesn't screw up." None of Livingston's men made a sound or moved a muscle, which said a lot for them.

Simpson's physical courage was not exceptional by itself. Courage has been displayed by men since the dawn of history (and probably before that as well). But Simpson's behavior went beyond courage. While the enemy officer was nearby searching for them, Simpson was thinking about how long it would take for the enemy to move on to a point where he could call in an airstrike on them. However, the enemy took a long time to move, and then other groups came along so that Simpson lost the sense of who was where and whether many of them were still too close to be bombed without panicking the enemy troops over our men. He held his hand, and then it was too late. "He didn't want to come out," Livingston told me. "He wanted to stay in and bomb the hell out of them."

Simpson did not want to depart one iota from the spirit of the order that had sent him on patrol or fail to justify the faith that others placed in him. He would sacrifice his life first.

When the situation finally allowed the platoon to be taken out, they moved down to the edge of the small valley through which the enemy had just passed. However, the helicopters overshot them and headed toward the opposite end of the valley. Seeing the helicopters going the wrong way caused Simpson to jump up and run down the middle of the valley after them, waving for them to turn around. After he had gone a few yards, automatic fire was heard, and bullets started hitting the ground at his heels. The shooting came from members of the enemy's rearguard, or possibly stragglers.

This action also required great physical courage. But Simpson probably didn't think twice about it. He saw what he had to do, and he did it. On another level, Simpson was aware that most of us were already in awe of him and may have wanted to reinforce that image by showing that he could do what few other men would even dare to try. Courage loves an audience, as someone once said.

Livingston radioed the helicopters to suppress the enemy fire, and every one of our men got out and back to base. For most of the day, Simpson and Livingston had hung on, surrounded by the enemy, and not knowing when or if help was coming. The first word they got from the command was that we would be taking out the Vietnamese patrols first. If it weren't for the coolness and bravery displayed by Simpson, together with simple luck, Livingston's platoon would have ended up just like the A Shau camp did, with our men scattering in the hopes of being picked up later. Or, worse, the platoon could have been annihilated.

Experiencing the character of other men is one of the things that make serving in the military one of life's great experiences. Some of the men I served with were so impressive that their strength of character has stayed with me and become etched in my mind. However, at the time I knew them I was not always able to avoid the human proclivity to turn such relationships into a positive reflection on myself.

Fifteen

Once I got back to camp after we extracted the two Vietnamese patrols, I went to report to Hoyez. I encountered Larrabee before I could reach the command tent. He gave me an odd look. "You won't believe this, but Hoyez just left."

"What?"

"Yeah. Kelley put him in charge of Two Corps, and he just flew out to take command. You missed him by about twenty minutes."

In the military, your commander dominates your consciousness in a way that rarely occurs in other parts of life. His judgment becomes your own, his approval is constantly sought, and his order becomes a personal responsibility that you have to him. As a result, you believe (or want to believe) that he is bound by a similar responsibility to you. Livingston had agreed to go on his patrol because, in the deepest sense, he believed that Hoyez was bound by a personal responsibility to him.

I would have thought that Hoyez couldn't help but feel responsible for a man he had placed in this perilous situation and would feel Livingston's peril almost as if it were his own. He would surely want to do everything he possibly could to save Livingston and his men, if for no other reason than to avoid feeling guilty if they died out there.

I would have expected him, even if he had been told to report to Two Corps immediately, to ask for a few hours so that he could remain on the spot to make sure Livingston and his men got out. But Hoyez had never given us any reason to think that he cared about us one way or another, and we couldn't expect him to care now.

Two Corps covered central South Vietnam, from the coast to the Cambodian and Laotian borders. It contained one-third of Special Forces camps in Vietnam and was Special Forces' largest command. A promotion like this put Hoyez well ahead of his peers and apparently drove any thoughts about Livingston and Simpson out of his mind.

I wondered why it had taken me so long to figure out how the army works. The army sees men as interlocking pieces that can be inserted in one spot or extracted from another without affecting the machine's operation in the slightest; one man's presence or absence makes no difference at all.

"Good riddance," said Larrabee. "Those poor bastards! Hoyez shouldn't command a squad."

"Is Assionte in command?" I asked.

"That's right," he replied. "Danny Thomas!"

* * *

Base camp had matured since I left, and the recon platoon had spent the previous morning blowing up the swimming hole behind camp to deepen it in order to swing out on a rope and drop into the water without hitting the bottom. They had exploded several charges of plastic when, to take care of any snakes that might still be hiding among the roots along the shore, Graves threw in a grenade for good measure. (On his last patrol, Graves had been bitten by a snake and fallen into violent convulsions, and the patrol had been forced to come out.)

Unfortunately, Graves' grenade failed to go off, and, as the water cleared, he glumly stared at it sitting innocently on the bottom. The other men shouted, "Good job, Graves! You sure took care of those snakes." Graves became uncharacteristically subdued for the rest of the day, and during the evening movie in the mess tent Brown said, "Guess who's got mandatory swimming tomorrow?"

The day I returned, Graves had taken his towel and gone dejectedly down to the stream while the other men hid behind the trees. Graves mechanically undressed on the bank and waded in until he got waist deep right over the grenade, gritted his teeth, took a deep breath, stared vacantly ahead for a moment, and then plunged in, picked up the grenade, and brought it carefully to the surface. The instant Graves lifted the grenade out of the water, the 175-millimeter gun nearby went off. Some of the men rolled on the ground from laughing so hard, while others held on to palm trees to stay upright. Graves turned white as a sheet and looked like he was going to fall apart, thinking he'd been killed.

*   *   *

Things didn't improve with the change in command. Assionte often seemed uncertain what to do. He had assumed command of a prestigious Special Forces long-range reconnaissance unit right in

Major Assionte and Major Allen relaxing at An Lao.

the middle of its greatest crisis so far, but with no qualifications or experience. Livingston and his team had gotten out of trouble thanks to luck and Sergeant Simpson's coolness under pressure; Assionte had played no part in their success. But as soon as the Livingston crisis had been resolved, a new challenge appeared on Assionte's horizon. My team had to infiltrate a plateau crawling with enemy troops, something we had never done before, and Assionte now appeared to be adrift and incapable of mastering the job. For the first time, he would be ordering men under his command into combat—orders that could send them to their deaths.

When I reported to Assionte, I saw a man who was clearly unsure of himself. His eyes seemed to plead for help. "You've got the whole unit at your disposal," he told me.

The broad plateau, almost twenty-five miles north of base camp, had few openings for a landing, and the passing shadows of clouds made what openings existed hard to evaluate. Furthermore, the flat, monotonous terrain made navigation difficult and clearings hard to recognize, meaning that I would have to memorize all the ridges leading up to my clearing and count them off as we went in. To make my clearing easier to identify, I chose one with high brush in one corner.

On the day we were going in, March 28, the command formed a line leading to the helicopter: Assionte, Major Allen, Shelton, and the platoon sergeant. Assionte looked more scared than I felt; he was probably envisioning disaster and a major setback to his career. They shook our hands and wished us luck. Probably everyone was convinced they would never see us again,

I had worked out my plan and memorized our escape route back to the First Cav. If we landed in the midst of the enemy, I planned to survive until dawn by keeping low and using the sound of the enemy's fire to cover any noise we might make. The enemy would give themselves away with their gun flashes, and, if we had to fire, we could aim at the flashes. We would fire from one side of the ridgeline and then run over to the other side and fire from there, always keeping the ridgeline between us and the enemy until we could get back to the First Cav.

The rotors started to whir. We got in, and the men on the ground shielded their eyes from the dust. As we ascended, the colder air made me think of the warm air we would hit just before we jumped off. The pilot dropped down, and we hit that nauseating layer of warm air. I stood behind the pilot and tried to count the ridges to our landing zone. I thought I had gotten the first ridge and then the next, but the tree crests zipped past too quickly for me to be sure, and at treetop level a ridge might not look the same as it did from higher up. I lost count, and clearings came and went before I could identify them.

A clearing with high brush in one corner suddenly appeared, though the brush looked taller than I remembered, almost the height of the surrounding jungle, and in the clearing was a tree I didn't recall seeing. I couldn't risk flying past, so I assumed the clearing had looked different from higher up. I yelled for the pilot to go in.

The chopper began to hover. The air became filled with the familiar smell of rot. I moved to the door and prepared to tell the other men to get up. Suddenly, the helicopter shuddered, reared back, and knocked me to the floor. I was certain we were going to crash. As the helicopter slipped to the left, I crawled to the right to avoid being crushed when we went down.

The pilot fought to keep us in the air. The chopper slipped sideways, the trees grew smaller, and it was clear that we were rising. I crawled up the floor and grabbed the pilot's seat to stand up. "What's the matter?" I shouted.

The pilot waited until we had leveled off and then yelled back, "Enemy fire!"

"Where?" I said. "I didn't see anything."

"The copilot saw it," he said and turned back to flying.

Maybe the copilot had seen a flash on his side, but I hadn't seen anything and didn't think the copilot had either. I was pretty sure the pilot had lost his nerve and made an excuse to abort.

Given the patrol's importance, an abort would kill me; we had to try the alternate landing zone, or else it would look like we had chickened out. On Best's last patrol, after three delays, he had tried to go in. His pilot had seen machine gun fire at his primary landing zone and taken them over to the alternate. The pilot saw nothing at the alternate site, but Best had refused to jump out, which had finished him with Delta.

"Try the alternate!" I shouted at the pilot.

The pilot initially ignored me, concentrating on flying. Then he spoke: "This is goddamn ridiculous." He sounded furious. "You're crazy! It's too dark!" He thought we had done enough already, but it wasn't his call, and he had no choice but to take us in to the alternate.

I couldn't picture the alternate landing zone nearly as well as the primary. I remembered its general direction and hoped I could recognize it once we got there.

Purple shadows obscured everything, and the clearings had become black spots. I had to pick one and hope. Something vaguely resembling what I remembered appeared, and I ordered the pilot to hover into it, standing at his back to make sure he did so.

The pilot craned to see the clearing, and the helicopter shuddered as we went down. We were approaching awfully high, and I couldn't tell whether we had actually gotten into the clearing. Suddenly the helicopter sprang back up, and the pilot ascended with full power. "VC were on it," he said. "I saw enemy fire. We're going home. It's too dark!"

I had been moving to the door and hadn't seen anything. I looked at the pilot to see whether he was lying, but I could see only the wires of his radio mouthpiece against his cheek. We always feared going into any clearing, but I didn't especially fear this one. I didn't argue with the pilot, though, and took refuge in the ambiguity of who has final authority in a helicopter. I outranked the pilot (a warrant officer), and as patrol commander I could order him into any clearing I wanted. But as aircraft commander he could decide whether to try to land, and disputing him on that point could land me in real trouble.

I had an air-tight defense and the best of all possible worlds, getting credit for going on one of the most dangerous patrols so far without actually doing so. I had simply refused to second-guess the pilot in the middle of a flight. I had probably done more than my duty by getting the pilot to try the alternate against his wishes.

We reached a safe altitude, and the pilot turned on the cabin lights. The air cooled again. I enjoyed the beauty of the jungle from this altitude at night. I would soon be back at camp, and somebody had to have a beer around someplace.

Suddenly, the Vietnamese team leader came over and began shouting at me. He was in a rage and looked like he was about to hit me. "We fly back? No can do! No! Go back! We try one more time!"

We had tried twice already. Nobody ever tried more than two landing zones, but he wanted us to go in on some random clearing we knew nothing about. All the black spots that represented clearings had blended in with the purple jungle by now, and we might have to turn on the landing lights to get in, possibly giving ourselves away.

I gestured at him helplessly and shouted, "The pilot says too dark! No! No can do!"

But the man refused to listen. "Major Tat get mad we no go in."

This moment affected me as much as anything in Vietnam, although I have never mentioned it until now because it contradicted what we wanted others to think about us and what we wanted to think about ourselves. The common belief was that the Vietnamese never wanted to keep going and the Americans never refused to go, no matter how great the danger. This man, though, felt more bound by Major Tat's trust in him than I felt bound by Assionte's trust in me. And he had put me in a difficult position, because if it ever got out that he had wanted to keep going and I had refused, this revelation would bring shame not only on me but also on everyone in recon. And word would get out, because he would have to explain the situation to Major Tat. Simply put, if he had wanted to continue while I had refused, it would look not as if I had aborted due to enemy fire but as if I had chickened out.

Asking the pilot to try again would be like moving heaven and earth, and I went over to him apprehensively, the Vietnamese team leader standing by my side. The pilot jerked around. "You're fucking crazy! It's pitch black out there now!"

"But he refuses to go back," I said. "What can I do? We have to go in."

"Jesus Christ!" he swore, but he swung the helicopter back around again, because he had the same problem I had.

The pilot gazed at the clearings just barely visible in the darkness. "Where? Where do we go?" His voice was filled with disgust.

"Anywhere," I said, looking at him knowingly. "Just try any clearing you can find." We both knew what this meant.

The pilot turned out the lights and began to descend into an indigo pit, going down for what could be passed off as a plausible effort and then immediately pulling back up. "It's too dark!" he said in a tone that left no room for argument. "That's it! We're going home!"

On the ride back, the Vietnamese team leader sat dejectedly with his head between his knees. He was almost in tears.

As I entered the command tent following our return, I feared Assionte would accuse me of cowardice, and I was prepared to argue that nobody else had gotten shot off two landing zones and tried a third. But I needn't have worried. Assionte couldn't have been happier. "You did a great job, Coulter," he said. Hoyez would have reacted differently. I didn't want to think about what Hoyez would have said and done.

We heard our call sign, and Larrabee picked up the mike. "Sir," he said. "It's the First Cav. What do you want me to tell them?"

"Tell them this is the last time we're going to do any of their dirty work," said Assionte. He seemed pleased with himself.

Major Tat, the commander of our Vietnamese compatriots, showing his dignity.

Assionte's reaction reassured me, but I still feared that some of the others might suspect I had chickened out. The helicopter pilots now took this worry off my mind, as they crowded into the command tent and regaled us with stories of their close calls. Tonight had just been one more very dangerous mission that had to be aborted due to circumstances on the ground.

But this episode illustrates how much of war is window dressing. The First Cav almost certainly expected us to do nothing. They simply wanted it on the record that they had tried to deal with the enemy-infested plateau. Had we gotten in, how in the world would a five-man team keep track of an enemy battalion in the jungle at night? If we had found the battalion, what were we actually supposed to do? It would have been a death trap. The whole business was really just for show.

Sixteen

My failure to capture the old women or the boy on my first patrol had weighed heavily on me, and I wanted to make up for it. I had deduced from the ridge trail that we found above our valley on my first patrol that the Vietnamese used ridges primarily for communication between valleys. Thus, I concluded that all I had to do to capture somebody was land on the back of a ridge and creep up to the trail on top.

My next patrol did not seem like much of a challenge, but I took no patrol for granted and devoted all my mental energy to choosing the optimal landing zone. My choice came down to a clearing on a ridge crest, near a likely trail, or a field of elephant grass farther to the west. I considered landing on my objective a gamble or worse, and so if I chose the ridge crest, I would be violating one of my cardinal principles. I finally chose the elephant grass, even though it faced slopes from which we might be observed. Chances were that at twilight no one would see us or would bother coming after us if they did.

Accompanied by Brown, Bartlett, and three Vietnamese, I landed on the elephant grass on the evening of March 30. I felt safe once we got under the jungle's cover. I planned to take three days to get up to the ridge crest. By then, anyone on the ridge who had heard our helicopter would have forgotten about it or been lulled into a sense of complacency.

The first three days went like clockwork. I could read the jungle now as if I had been doing it all my life, distinguishing animal trails from those cut in the brush by people. My biggest fear was not being heard but being *smelled* by the enemy. We reeked from sweat in the tropical heat.

In the thick jungle, it's hard to see beyond your immediate surroundings, and one depended to a great extent on one's hearing. The biggest challenge was the cicadas. Cicadas give off a high-pitched, almost hysterical scream that drowns out literally everything short of loud explosions. The noise permeates the air and surrounds you like a metal curtain. The volume of their calls increases with the heat of the day. The noise does drown out almost any noise you may make, but it serves the same purpose for the enemy. On balance, I'd rather be able to hear whether somebody else is creeping around the jungle.

On the third day, we approached the ridge top with the

anticipated trail. As the slope leveled off and the underbrush thinned out, I ordered the men to exercise even more caution. Suddenly, the point man signaled for us to stop. He had stepped over the trail before noticing it. It was only a foot wide, sunk in the ground but polished as hard as glass by constant foot traffic. And sure enough, shouts rose from the valley below.

I had nailed it! We had slipped past the Montagnards, who had lived in this jungle all their lives, to reach a point from which I felt confident we could take a prisoner. I wanted a soldier, in order to outdo Markham. The sparse underbrush made it impossible to wait close to the trail, so we had to hide behind rocks some distance away.

My hopes were dashed when the FAC made contact and told me the operation was ending a day early, and we had to come out in an hour's time. We were told to go to the nearest clearing for extraction. Rather than take prisoners, the command wanted a couple of extra hours to get back early for a new mission; in other words, instead of subordinating everything peripheral to what we were supposed to do, they were subordinating what we were supposed to do to everything peripheral.

When the helicopter arrived, it was unable to take us all because at this high altitude it didn't have a sufficient cushion of air to keep itself flying with all of us aboard. Markham, who was in the helicopter, jumped out and told me that the helicopter couldn't take me. We were picked up by a second helicopter a few minutes later. I stupidly almost got caught in the tail rotor as I was about to get onboard, but Markham warned me in time.

My disappointment at not taking a prisoner was compounded by the shame I felt at almost getting myself killed and needing Markham to save me.

* * *

Our time in An Lao came to an end. Everybody was pleased, and after their last flight in the An Lao Valley, the gunship pilots descended on the command tent and pounded each other on the back. The gunship pilots took great pride in their skill and daring, but they were even more proud of their function. The rest of us contributed to the war's goal more or less tangentially. But the gunships focused on the goal itself, killing the enemy, which made us all feel, more or less, that they were the only ones who really did anything.

Gunships carried nose-mounted 20-millimeter automatic

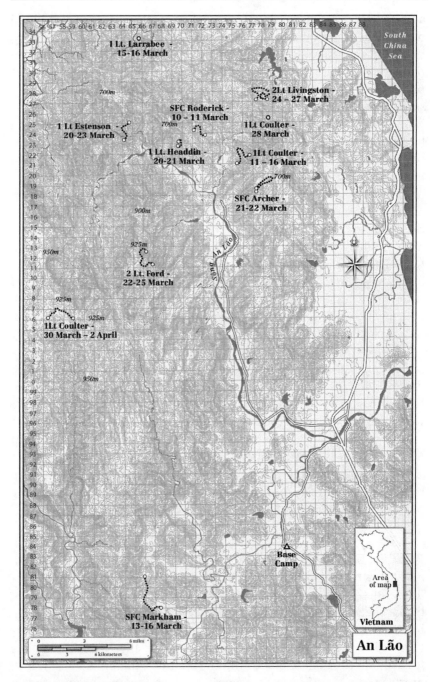

An Lao Map. All our major patrols in our first operation, which separated the sheep from the goats.

cannons or side-mounted rocket pods and were filled to the brim with ammunition, making them veritable flying powder kegs. If they caught the muzzle flash of an enemy position that dared fire on them, they locked onto it and poured everything they had into it. What they could do with just the touch of a trigger finger gave them an air of omnipotence.

Their commander, a major, told us of sighting two men in black pajamas and white coolie hats walking along a trail. When they heard the gunship, they started running, and he chased them with rockets into the tree line. "I fire at anybody who runs," he told us. "If they run, they have a guilty conscience. I don't know if I got them, but I sure scared the hell out of them!"

Seventeen

On April 5, we went back for a week to Nha Trang, where we would throw ourselves into the arms of the women. As soon as it got dark, we dressed in our civilian clothes and arranged for a jeep, agreeing beforehand who would drive it back. Nothing beats driving a jeep in Vietnam, with no constraints and total impunity. The rules for ordinary mortals didn't apply to us. Taking on the bare open road felt like taking on the world: the hot, humid, exotic night smelling of tropical flowers; the dark, lonely, shuttered houses bathed in unworldly silver moonlight; smoldering piles of palm fronds, coconut husks, crushed unrecognizable fruit, and rotting vegetables beside the road.

Reaching the city square signaled the end of the civilized world. A sickly green streetlamp disclosed the stumps of palm trees with their fronds torn off. Garbage moldered beside the road, cyclo drivers squatted in the dark, and indistinct forms darted in and out of bar entrances.

Nha Trang already had clear practices by the time I got to Vietnam, and while other cities probably had similar ones, Nha Trang had tailored its practices especially for Special Forces. Special Forces had arrived in 1964, before everybody else, and returned on repeat tours, so we had cemented deep relationships. Special

Picture of the Project Delta compound in Nha Trang, showing how immaculate we appeared on the surface in contrast to the chaos underneath.

Picture of the Project Delta compound in Nha Trang. It came under heavy attack and many men were killed during the Tet offensive the following January.

Forces had come to The Streamer, a local bar, since the beginning, and it had become our bar. The girls at The Streamer had little to do with men from other units, knowing that somebody from Special Forces would always pick them up, and they hustled us for "Saigon Tea" much less than women in other bars did; we didn't have to fend them off as much. Saigon Tea dictated life in Vietnam and ran through all transactions, lubricating the Vietnamese economy, and it is hard to understand why the term never entered the mainland American lexicon.

Saigon Tea was watered-down, worthless tea served in thimble-sized glasses, and the bar girls got half the price for every Saigon Tea they sold. They refused to talk to you unless you bought it for them, and to keep you buying it, they dragged out whether they would go to bed with you for as long as possible. The girls in The Streamer

Downtown Nha Trang, giving an idea of the civilized world we lived in when back in base.

took a more lenient approach toward us in this regard than other girls, but woe betide any non–Special Forces soldier who happened to walk in.

Our privileges at The Streamer had a drawback, in that you had to determine early on whether you were negotiating with a girl who was being kept by a man out on operations. A girl in any one of the regular bars could turn down someone she didn't like, but not in The Streamer. If you were from Special Forces, she had to give herself to you whether she liked you or not and could legitimately refuse only if she had a boyfriend out on operations, since no one could expect her to jeopardize the steady payments and presents from the PX. If you failed to sense the girl's situation early enough, you could spend a lot on Saigon Tea without getting anywhere.

The prettiest women were maintained by sergeant majors, senior sergeants, and senior officers. They received payments out of the man's salary every month, which had to approximate what they could earn by taking someone to bed every night, and this amount represented a lot of money, so we couldn't possibly compete. Girls in other bars probably had similar arrangements with men in other units, but they didn't do nearly as well as those at The Streamer, because, out of everybody in Nha Trang, only Special Forces got parachute jump pay. Thus, the girls at The Streamer considered themselves much better than their peers.

From the outside, The Streamer looked like any other bar, in that you had to step over a smoldering trash pile blocking the door to get in, but once inside there were better furnishings. For instance, The Streamer had a pink table lamp with a torn shade that provided enough light to see the peanut shells, cigarette butts, and broken glass littering the floor, and it also had a broken couch to sit on. On the wall, as a tribute to us, the girls had painted a red and green rendition of "a streamer" (a parachute that had failed to open).

I had learned the ropes right after joining Delta and had dropped into The Streamer before we left for An Lao. The conventions for negotiations in Vietnam were well established by now, and you couldn't deviate from them, although they did permit timing and brinksmanship. Bar girls instantly spotted anyone who hadn't yet bought a drink, and a pretty girl with a plump face, Western bangs, and an American dress rushed over and demanded that I buy her a Saigon Tea. I wasn't particularly attracted to her, and I didn't think she was especially attracted to me, but she looked decent, and a firm deal reached now outweighed waiting to find something better later.

These conversations took real fortitude. The girls alternated between expressions of great affection and complete indifference, asking you questions and paying no attention to your answers. This girl kept leaving and coming back to ask for more Saigon Tea, and I couldn't tell whether she went off to talk with the other girls or had several men buy her tea at the same time. Finally, when she came back for a moment, I asked, "You take me home?" This question did not help me. "You no have girlfriend?" she said contemptuously. "You butterfly. You number ten. Sau lam. Me have boyfriend." She was pretty enough to have a steady boyfriend but could just as easily have made this story up to extract more Saigon Tea or a higher price from me. They could string you along for half the evening before you figured them out, and they were good actors.

She left but came back again and asked quickly, "How much?"

"Two thousand 'p,'" I said. I used piasters instead of military scrip, because bar girls liked to count the exchange rate as 100 piasters for one dollar, though it was really 117.

"Number ten G.I. Cheap. Sau lam. Four thousand 'p.'"

"No way. Two thousand," I said. She pouted angrily, hesitated for a moment, and then nodded curtly. We all knew the going rates. Then she asked for another Saigon Tea.

Those of us who had been in Vietnam for a while always tried to get the girls to agree to go to bed with us before we bought too many Saigon Teas. This way we could go somewhere else to drink, without having to spend more on Saigon Tea, and could come back before curfew to pick the girl up. "I'll meet you back here at curfew."

"Me sure you come back?" she asked skeptically, although she and her friends knew other men in Special Forces and thus had a form of security. Plus a man couldn't break his word to a girl at The Streamer without completely discrediting himself.

"Me keep my word. You keep yours?"

"Me keep my word," she said haughtily. A girl at The Streamer wouldn't break her word to a man from Special Forces, even if someone else offered her more later on. The whole system operated on pitiless integrity. If a man couldn't count on a girl to keep her word, he wouldn't be bound to keep his word to her if he found someone cheaper.

Once back from An Lao, I went to The Streamer again to line up the same girl, who I now knew went by the name Gina. The instant Gina saw me, she went into raptures and bounced over as if she had wanted to see me more than anyone else in the world. We didn't even mention price. Brown suddenly appeared, in an unexpectedly freshly ironed civilian shirt, holding a can of beer. While I couldn't possibly hold my own in a conversation with him, nothing works your way into the hearts of your men better than showing you have all the same base instincts they do. Although nobody ever got what you would call open warmth from Brown, I detected that he felt real pride at finding me in the same bar with him, and he charitably overlooked my slower wit.

Out of nowhere, a girl appeared at Brown's side. I remembered her as the girl who had gone to sleep next to the fireplace the last time I was at Gina's house.

"So you've got her roommate," I said.

"Love at first sight," said Brown.

I didn't want to stay drinking here and buying more Saigon Tea, and I had already arranged with Gina to come back for her at curfew. Besides, managing a conversation with a bar girl was hard enough without also trying to keep up with Brown, so I went to another bar.

The Streamer insulated you from the real rough and tumble of Nha Trang, and you had to hit the regular bars to know the genuine article. There you entered a sphere like no other. If coming downtown offered a break from the old order, these bars liberated you from all trace of it. You had traversed the center of the earth and come out on the other side. You had no idea where you were, no control or boundaries, and had entered a world alien to everything you had known, requiring good nerves and a strong constitution. They kept those bars as black as a tomb, and you had to feel your way around, the sole aid being a single candle burning on a wooden plank that acted as the bar and illuminating the heavily lined face of the madam who ruled the place and subjected everyone to her icy stare.

You couldn't even see the beer can in your hand, and your experience consisted exclusively of smells and sounds, the intolerable thick incense mixed with women's perfume and the deafening music with women shrieking above it, trying to tell something to someone else on the other side of the room. Two inches from your face, the ugliest woman in the room would yell, "You buy me Saigon Tea!"

Once you adapted to the dark, you began to distinguish silhouettes of girls sitting on soldiers' laps, caressing the men one moment and jumping up and chatting with other girls the next. If you caught one of their expressions, you couldn't tell whether the girl actually acknowledged that the men were even there. They clearly didn't like having anything to do with us, and we couldn't tell which side they supported, us or the communists, or, if they sided with us, whether they hated us just as much as they hated the Viet Cong.

At curfew, I returned to The Streamer to pick up Gina. While the girls settled their shares for Saigon Tea, Brown and I went outside. Across the road, cyclo drivers in rags squatted around a small charcoal brazier, their calloused feet buried in the dust and their cyclos together nearby. As soon as we appeared, they scrambled to their feet and pulled their machines over, whispering, "Hey, G.I." They had been waiting all evening to give one American a ride, a trip that would earn them perhaps eighty piasters (seventy cents). One old man hung back, unable to keep up with the others. He looked as if he never got a fare, and I considered picking him, but his cyclo looked like it was about to fall apart, so I pointed to someone in the middle.

Women emerged from the bar and distributed themselves to the men, shouting to each other and running in different directions. One would come outside while another ran back in, and the others pushed among the mass of cyclos. Cyclos began to leave with a woman and a man, or two women without men, and things calmed down. Gina and her roommate finally appeared, and Gina and I left first in our cyclo. I called to Brown, "I'll take point."

These nocturnal cyclo rides satisfied every sensation. The dark house fronts hung over you ominously during the whole route; you couldn't see where you were going and always felt you were entering a mysterious, unknown world. The soft tropical nights were exciting by themselves for anyone who hadn't grown up experiencing them, and you spent the whole ride anticipating what would happen at the end.

We moved along, the driver grunting and the bicycle chain occasionally catching while Brown's cyclo squeaked in the distance behind us. Gina's house stood in a row of other single-story buildings made of stucco cement with metal shutters. Gina jumped out, saying, "You pay driver," and unlocked her metal shutter and lifted it up enough for us to crawl under.

Next, she opened the door in the back for her roommate and Brown, who had caught up with us. She lit a single candle and put it on the floor, exposing the fruits of her labor: a mattress covered with an olive-drab army poncho liner and a wooden army footlocker with a can of PX hairspray on it. "A real fancy place," said Brown. The girls went to work preparing the apartment; this clearly wasn't their first time. They laid a second mattress on the floor in the back room and hung a sheet in the doorway between the two rooms, shouting to each other in Vietnamese the whole time and hardly paying attention to us at all. Brown remarked, "We need a code card to understand them."

Brown and I made small talk, and he said, "A team that fights together fucks together," showing that he accepted me as his kind of man. Coming from a man who didn't care whether he lived or died, this was the highest compliment he could pay me. I could tell that he also appreciated that I, as an officer, was violating curfew with him, since we technically were supposed to be back in the barracks before bed check, although in fact nobody paid any attention to this rule.

As much as I prized Brown's respect, I can't say that I was delighted to embark on something like this at such close quarters and under more scrutiny than I was used to. Brown's absence of any qualm made the situation worse, but I had to show resolve and uphold my honor.

When the girls had finished their preparations, we each went to our side of the sheet; Gina sat on her bed, told me she loved me, and very nicely asked for her money. The next morning, all I had to do was get a cyclo early enough to make it back to base before reveille.

* * *

At Nha Trang, Assionte threw us a beach party, something Hoyez had never done. Parties took place on a special section of beach reserved for the American military and had a fixed format: mess hall steaks cooked on an oil drum that had been split in two to serve as a grill, with plenty of beer kept cold in trash cans filled with ice.

We started slowly, drinking in groups that were segregated by rank—the sergeants in one cluster, the lieutenants in another, and our commanders separate from both. Of course, Larrabee, despite his rank, had managed to find a spot in the magic circle with Assionte and Allen. As close as we had all grown in the field, we maintained distance socially. The one exception, besides Larrabee, was Estenson, who perceived no barriers and mixed easily with anyone. I always felt the sergeants looked on me as something of an egghead; I made them uncomfortable, although I was pretty sure I had gained their respect in the field.

After a while, the beer loosened us up, and the men began drifting between groups, eventually gravitating toward Assionte and Allen, who of course were the center of power in our small universe. Allen and Sergeant Robinette inevitably fell at one point to talking about weightlifting, since they both weighed 250–300 pounds, which led to them asking each other how much they could lift. We then learned how weightlifters prove this fact: you lift someone your own weight over your head and do deep knee bends with him on your shoulders. So Allen offered to lift Robinette over his head and do ten deep knee bends with him on his shoulders and challenged Robinette to do the same with him.

The beach party now took on a new character. We vaguely assumed—or at least I did—that sergeants had more manly qualities than we officers did, and since manliness and physical strength are inseparable, this meant that sergeants were physically stronger than we were and our superiority in rank was artificial. The contest now promised to put this assumption to a test.

With Robinette standing in front of him, Allen put his left fist between Robinette's legs at the groin and had Robinette lock his legs around his fist. Allen next grabbed Robinette's neck with his right arm and swung Robinette sideways off his feet and then over his own head and onto his shoulders. Then, holding Robinette across his back, Allen, sure enough, did ten deep knee bends. You had to see this to believe it, and we gave Allen an immense round of applause. Afterward, it was Robinette's turn, and he pressed Allen over his head, although he strained more visibly than Allen had. However, on his first deep knee bend, he squatted unsteadily, attempted to rise, hovered uncertainly, and then fell over on his side, ripping his pants down the middle and giving up. This was a great victory for the officers.

Allen's victory over Robinette, though, paled in comparison with its effect on Assionte. During the contest, Assionte had stood awkwardly to the side, his feet apart and his arms across his chest. As Allen lifted Robinette, I glanced at Assionte to see how he was taking it. His face had collapsed with jealousy and despair. He couldn't hope to do something like this, and Allen's strength made his own weakness that much clearer. This revelation had deep implications for Assionte's command. After a feat like this one, Allen would become the only force that mattered, and men would consider him their rightful commander. Assionte knew he had no business commanding Delta and that Allen rightfully belonged in his place. The men would see Assionte being in command as a huge injustice. Yet Assionte would still have to preserve the illusion of command to save his honor, knowing that everyone else thought it was a masquerade, and all of this appeared on Assionte's face.

Eventually, the relationship between these two men would split the unit in two. Allen had such a strong character that he could roll over Assionte without meaning to do so; he also possessed a temper that he sometimes found hard to control. We couldn't predict what would happen, and the uncertainty made us uncomfortable.

* * *

While Assionte had not shown himself to be a capable commander, he was smart enough to know that his performance depended a great deal on who he had beneath him. He had a knack

Shelton at Khe Sanh, after he made captain and showing just how vulnerable our site was.

for getting the right people in the right positions—not surprising, since he had spent his career up to now as a personnel officer. He shrewdly kicked Larrabee upstairs to become assistant S-3 (Operations). Larrabee had demonstrated neither character nor ability in recon, but it would be hard for him to do any damage as assistant S-3, while his talent for ingratiation and intrigue could prove useful. Major Allen, who had served as S-3 at Delta under Hoyez, now became deputy commander. We all saw Allen as the real force in Delta, the man who mattered and who should have been put in charge of us.

The other lieutenants who had joined Delta when I did or soon after were mostly gone. Richardson had gotten wounded by stepping on a punji stake, was sent to Qui Nhon for treatment, and never came back. Heddern and Ford were assigned to the Vietnamese Rangers as advisors. Best remained, but after the time when he refused to leave the helicopter, he never went out on patrol again. Shelton, however, made captain, a promotion he very much deserved. He and Allen were our rocks, the best officers in the unit.

* * *

The following day, we learned that our next assignment would be Khe Sanh. We had come to think of ourselves as exceptional, but we hadn't known we were this exceptional. You couldn't be assigned anywhere worse than Khe Sanh. There were many articles in the *Stars and Stripes* about Khe Sanh, and people spoke of the place as if it were haunted. Maybe it was.

Khe Sanh was a Marine base located at the northwest corner of South Vietnam, just below the so-called Demilitarized Zone (in truth, it was about as militarized an area as you could find). It sat right next to both North Vietnamese and Laotian territory, with the Ho Chi Minh Trail running right alongside. It was one of the most dangerous places in South Vietnam. The enemy mortared the area frequently. Planes landing at Khe Sanh often didn't stop their engines before taking off again.

Larrabee was sent there to head up the advance party, a move I would have thought Allen would prevent. But no, Larrabee would be the U.S. Marines' first exposure to Delta. We felt sure our reputation would be in tatters before we even arrived.

Eighteen

When we got to Khe Sanh, we found that Larrabee had picked an exposed spot for our camp, a bend in the road about half a mile from the Marine base, with level brush to the north and west. Fifty-five yards away to the south and east was a wall of jungle in which the enemy could creep up on us undetected and then start shooting.

The DMZ and North Vietnam were just over the horizon. The air was crystal clear on this high plateau, and the brilliant sunlight made objects stand out more vividly and appear closer than they actually were. The deep blue sky was a glorious sight, dotted with large white cumulus clouds that drifted slowly in the wind.

A ten-man Marine patrol moved silently past us. The men were all wearing flak jackets. Two men carried machine guns; their shoulders were draped with ammunition belts. Another carried a bazooka, with a vest full of rounds strapped on his back. The others carried extra bazooka rounds on their backs. The Marines were taking an awful lot of firepower out with them on patrol. We, by contrast, went twenty or twenty-five miles into enemy territory armed with nothing more than a rifle and a few grenades.

"Flak jackets!" said Heddern with a smirk.

We sat on crates of mortar ammunition or bales of empty sandbags and watched a FAC about four miles away arch and dip his plane as he called in airstrikes where a Marine patrol had been ambushed the day before, losing several men. The enemy, however, had probably left the area long before.

That evening, I got my first patrol order. My patrol area went right up to the DMZ, and with the enemy filtering through there constantly, it was hard to believe I wouldn't encounter some. But I considered being chosen to lead our first patrol at Khe Sanh a great honor. I had been singled out as the best recon man in Delta.

The next morning, the Marines radioed for Assionte and Allen to come over and discuss the possibility of sending us to A Shau, rather than keeping us at Khe Sanh. Apparently, they had gotten wind of enemy plans to attack Hue, the old Vietnamese capital, by emerging from the A Shau Valley.

Until the Marines made up their minds, we would have to stay where we were and fortify the camp. Then the Montagnard laborers who were doing the work went on strike because we were only paying them one canteen cup of rice per day, as we had at An Lao, rather than the two cups a day they got up here. I now saw an opportunity to strike a blow against Larrabee by getting the local French planter to persuade the Montagnards to return.

The day before, when I learned a French coffee planter lived nearby, I took the jeep up to see him in order to show off my French. He lived very simply in the beautiful stone house his father, a famous French botanist, had built. His deep attachment to the life in Vietnam had kept him here after the French left, and he had brought his wife to join him from France.

The planter's completely disarming, unassuming manner contrasted unflatteringly with us. We wouldn't think of going anywhere without our rifles, while carrying one never entered his mind. He paid so little attention to the war around him that you would never have guessed there was one going on. He lived in harmony with the Montagnards and knew they would never betray him. The Americans were the only ones who caused him trouble by jettisoning excess defoliant on his coffee trees before their planes landed.

Like a good Frenchman, the planter offered me a glass of Pernod, and I felt silly drinking it with my rifle leaning against my knee. I tried to impress him with my French and felt I had gotten him to open up more than he would have with the Marines, who probably considered him an enemy informant and had a low opinion of him in the first place because he was French.

As I drove back to see him the next day, I experienced one of those events that stay with you forever, especially since it occurred against the background of the Marines' fortified bunkers and the later fate of Khe Sanh. As I passed a small shack on stilts beside the road, I heard the voices of Montagnard children singing "Frère Jacques." The planter's wife was teaching them French.

The planter already knew the story about the Montagnards going on strike and, with the same simplicity and directness of the day before, explained that he didn't know our Montagnards well, because they came from a different village, but an American missionary at Lang Vei, six miles away, did know our Montagnards and might be willing to help. He had lived among them for many years and was translating the Bible into Montagnard, and if he thought it could help them, he might be willing to do something. But the planter warned me that the missionary hated the American military.

As I drove the six miles to Lang Vei, I drove very fast, so as not to give anybody in the jungle time to shoot. Before meeting the missionary, I dropped in on the Special Forces camp at Lang Vei, to impress them as somebody from Delta. I caught sight of their perimeter barbed wire only by accident, and, with North Vietnamese moving down the Ho Chi Minh Trail in Laos only a mile away, this situation struck me as awfully lax. The team room, in an old French fort, opened on the town's main street, and anybody could walk in.

I found the men sitting around a table with their feet on it, discussing hot rod transmissions, like a lazy afternoon in any country store back in the States. There was no sense of the North Vietnamese being present only a little more than a mile away. They later told me that for the past two months they hadn't run into anything within a roughly two-mile radius of the camp.

The executive officer, First Lieutenant Stallings, barely said hello before returning to his transmission. Given their location in one of the most dangerous parts of Vietnam, they would get visits from full colonels and generals all the time, and a visit by somebody from Delta meant nothing.

I expected a rough time with the missionary. His beliefs and ours had to be poles apart, and for him I represented evil incarnate. In his scheme of things, I wouldn't have any significance whatsoever. The last thing I wanted to do was take him on directly. I had to be the opposite of what he expected and put my Harvard background to use. I would be the most sincere, idealistic person he had ever met, with not an evil bone in my body—in other words, I'd be just like him.

When I reached his compound, I realized I had a more serious adversary than I had expected. He stood barefoot in calf-deep mud, with his young wife and two small children, also barefoot in the mud, their Montagnard shack on stilts behind them. A fragile ladder led to the door of the shack, with a rough fence of interlaced branches separating the courtyard from the surrounding jungle. Apparently, the missionary had decided to eliminate all differences between himself and the Montagnards in order to win their trust. If he and his wife and children had to walk around in the mud to accomplish this feat, they would. If he had to become a Montagnard, he would; he would do whatever it took. Not only had he become a Montagnard, but he had also mastered the language well enough to undertake the monumental work of translating the Bible into it. He looked completely unprepossessing but he had to have phenomenal will, conviction, and selflessness. To him, the North Vietnamese a mile away were irrelevant.

The planter's warning proved an understatement. The missionary couldn't control his distaste when he saw me, and my heart sank. I tried to make myself as ingratiating as possible and started by saying that I would be grateful to him for the rest of my life if he shared his knowledge of how to deal with the Montagnards. This statement made him at least willing to listen. I said that we knew we had offended them, wanted to apologize to them from the bottom of our hearts, and compensate them for every last ounce of rice. And I would do anything else he suggested. This caught him off guard. But as little as he had expected this attitude from an American soldier, I still hadn't won him over, so I went further, saying that I personally suffered from the injustice to the Montagnards, even more than they did, and, independent of anything else, wanted to right the problem for my own peace of mind. This declaration came so far out of left field that he agreed to help.

But even before I got back to camp, we got orders to move to A Shau.

Nineteen

The A Shau had got its evil reputation from the fall of the Special Forces camp there in March 1966. This battle perfectly captured the futile heroism and shameful incompetence that characterized the entire Vietnam War. The camp had known for two months that the enemy planned to attack, and that Special Forces command had decided to leave the men in place to fight it out with the enemy, even though our forces would be heavily outnumbered. The men in the camp knew they would have to die if necessary, in order to preserve their honor; the battle, when it came, was one for honor as much as survival.

When the camp was being overrun by the enemy, they still refused to ask to come out. The men in the camp hoped the command would see that they had held on from pride and a sense of duty and would spare them the indignity of asking to leave. However, honor, pride, and courage floated aimlessly over the camp like will-of-the-wisps and were not enough to move the command. Abandoned, the men rallied in the dark, under intense fire, with enemy troops in overwhelming numbers about to land on top of them. Only the extraordinary heroism of the men prevented the camp from falling on the first night.

The thirty-mile-long A Shau Valley lay in the far northwest corner of South Vietnam, along the Laotian border, fifty miles south of the Demilitarized Zone and forty miles west of Hue, the ancient Vietnamese capital. The A Shau camp stood at its southern end. We had established three camps in the valley originally but abandoned the two northern camps out of fear that they would be overrun. Ever since we built the A Shau camp, the enemy had let us know what they intended. There was no better highway south than the A Shau Valley, and so, for the first two months of 1966, the enemy prepared to first paralyze the camp and then strangle it to death.

I met a sergeant in Nha Trang who had helped recover the bodies of the Americans who died at the camp. This was two months after the battle. He had climbed up a ladder to get in over the wall; when he heard metal tinkling inside the camp, he said it had taken all his courage to look over. The tinkling turned out to be rats scurrying among empty mortar canisters. Skeletons lay bleached in the sun, eaten clean by the rats. The enemy had left the area immediately to avoid airstrikes.

The party found four dead Americans—Stahl, McKam, Allen, and Hall. They used grappling irons to move the skeletons before touching them, for fear of booby-traps. As a result, the recovery operation took considerably longer than planned, and the sergeant said that the whole time he felt the enemy breathing down his neck.

The position of the skeletons gave an idea of how the battle had progressed. The party identified forty South Vietnamese skeletons inside the camp. They estimated 110 South Vietnamese had died outside. The enemy's own dead gave a good idea of what they had thrown into the attack. The party estimated that several hundred North Vietnamese had been killed and wounded. In other words, the attackers had been several thousand strong.

After the camp's fall, we didn't venture near the valley. If the enemy had moved such a force into the valley and paid such a price to take it, it didn't take much effort to figure out what they would do to keep it, and so we left the valley to the North Vietnamese.

The worst aspect of this event is that long before it happened, almost anyone could have predicted what was going to occur. A reconnaissance flight in January 1966 reported the presence of trenches and tunnels a mile south of the camp, big enough to hold three companies, with dug-in mortar and antiaircraft gun positions. In the coming weeks, flights reported new works, plus extensions of the old ones. We called in airstrikes, but the ever-present clouds prevented us from knowing whether we had hit anything. Over the next two months, the monsoons thickened, visibility worsened, and the timetable for the attack was pretty obvious—March, when the monsoon clouds would be at their thickest.

The camp's fortifications actually made the situation worse. Twelve-foot-high elephant grass grew up to the camp's east and south walls and gave the enemy excellent cover for their approach. We couldn't cut the grass down because it grew over old minefields, and we couldn't burn it off because of the rain.

In some way, I am sure all wars provide examples of the same kind of command dereliction as at A Shau, but this event deserves special attention. Despite clear evidence of the enemy's buildup, and with the imminence of the attack plain for all to see, the command seemed to view it all as a nuisance that would ultimately go away. You would think the command would realize that the camp knew more about what was going on than they did, but for two months the command treated the camp's pleas for reinforcements as whining and most likely took comfort in the fact that the Marines were nearby. But the Marines would hardly take responsibility for an army unit and, moreover, would expect Special Forces to show just how tough they were. Headquarters at Nha Trang probably also counted on the Special Forces First Corps C-Team in case of trouble, although being this close to the DMZ meant that the C-Team would hardly have extra men to spare.

The command simply wanted the A Shau camp to shut up and do what it was told, because any Special Forces camp ought to be able to take on vastly superior numbers of North Vietnamese. By not taking the camp off the hook, the command could get the job done a lot more easily, backing the men into such corner that they would have no choice but to rise to the occasion.

Eventually, the command began having second thoughts and took the step of changing the camp commander, as if all they had to do was to bring in a new man to resolve the problem. I can imagine the shock that the new commander, Captain Blair—a short, athletic man I had known in West Germany—felt when he landed in A Shau with the camp already under siege.

In early February 1966, before Blair's arrival, the enemy began to tighten the noose. On February 18, one of our patrols killed a North Vietnamese soldier with a diary detailing the enemy's preparations. The man had watched the camp for two months from a tower less than eight hundred yards away, listened to our soldiers shouting inside and observing what they were doing. Three times at night he had crawled up to the second or third row of perimeter wire, looking for passageways. The sentiments that filled the diary, a mixture of excitement and conviction that the North Vietnamese would win, were telling.

Toward the end of February, the command thought they could get by with sending in four scout dogs to track down the enemy, but the dogs foundered in the elephant grass and proved to be useless. Around March 1, the command came up with another measure: a loudspeaker plane that would circle the enemy's area, drop leaflets, and broadcast that defectors would be well treated. This approach probably provoked the enemy's wrath, jeopardizing the camp even more.

Four days later, on March 5, 1966, two North Vietnamese soldiers appeared at the camp gate and gave themselves up. They had left a battalion equipped with heavy weapons, located three miles to the southeast. It appeared that an entire North Vietnamese regiment was preparing to assault the camp. The defectors finally provided the kind of information to which the command would listen. According to them, the attack would take place in five or six days.

Nha Trang finally gave in and sent in a company of Chinese Nung mercenaries, but it was too little, too late to change anything that was about to happen. For the next four days, with impending disaster hanging over their heads, those in the camp waited, merely sending out daily patrols that barely went beyond the barbed wire.

At midnight, March 9, the camp heard snaps in the wire to the south and sounds of digging. At 4:00 in the morning, the enemy started firing on the camp with mortars, and our men finally had to face what they had known was coming for weeks.

The mortar fire badly damaged the camp's superstructures and destroyed the radio antennas, cutting off the camp's communications. The battle had finally started, but the command back in Da

Nang didn't know about it. The first salvos killed two Americans and seriously wounded two others, one of whom later died. Four of the twelve Americans who were in the camp when the battle started were already out of the fight. Eight South Vietnamese were killed and forty-two were wounded, many of them seriously, reducing the number of Vietnamese defenders by a fifth.

After an hour's bombardment, the enemy troops began their assault. Two North Vietnamese companies attacked through the barbed wire and elephant grass along the south wall and almost took the camp by storm right away.

An American, Captain Carter, in command of the Nung mercenaries who had arrived four days earlier, showed the kind of courage that some men display in such circumstances and got his Nungs through the bullets and mortar fire to the south wall, where they pushed the enemy back. No sooner had the Nungs restored the south wall than the enemy's fire intensified and pinned them down. The camp had been saved temporarily, but ammunition was already running low and the camp was unable to communicate with the command.

At 9:00, five hours after the attack began, the South Vietnamese got their radio to work and contacted their command in Hue. An hour later, the Americans got their backup radio working and began to relay messages to Da Nang through other camps like Khe Sanh.

Those at A Shau knew what lay in store for them when darkness fell, and yet they still didn't ask to come out.

The messages from A Shau led Nha Trang to take a couple of steps. They ordered three ammunition drops onto the camp, one of which landed on target; the other two fell outside the perimeter. At noon, the camp asked for reinforcements, and Nha Trang decided to send in a second company of Nung mercenaries. The company, though, didn't arrive at Da Nang until 1:00 p.m., and the Marines couldn't provide armed helicopters to take them in until 4:00. By then the disappearing daylight and bad weather made it impossible to go in. The Nungs remained on the runway at Da Nang and never reached the camp.

At the camp, the fog and rain had cleared a bit and the defenders could see enough to do what they had wanted to do since the beginning of the battle: call in airstrikes. Calling in airstrikes through heavy clouds close to your position requires a lot of trust in your own and others' judgment, especially when communications are bad. The men had to relay requests for bombing through camps as far away as Khe Sanh and then hope the pilots would drop their bombs somewhere near the coordinates they had given. Unable to see where the bombs were hitting, the men had to make adjustments by ear and relay these instructions through distant camps, hoping the pilots could orient themselves well enough above the clouds to bomb more accurately. Then the weather closed in again and the air support ceased.

Army pilots made heroic efforts to help. Two small army planes came in for the wounded. The pilots had to have perfect timing to come down through the clouds and into the valley without crashing into a mountain. They then had to pick out the camp's landing strip in the fog and rain, all the while hoping they could avoid getting shot by enemy machine gun and rifle fire. Once they landed, they risked being shot at out of the elephant grass alongside the airstrip. Both pilots made it in, the first stopping long enough to pick up a seriously wounded American, while the second was unable to stop and took off again the second it touched down.

The Marines hadn't lifted a finger before, but they now made up for it, with Marine pilots going to the same lengths the two army pilots had. Two Marine C-47 transport helicopters flew in for the Vietnamese wounded, and one rescued twenty-six of them. But the second helicopter was shot down by the North Vietnamese.

Now, an Air Force "Puff the Magic Dragon" arrived. Whatever other units may have thought about Puff the Magic Dragon, it warmed the hearts of Special Forces soldiers. Puff was an old, World War II DC-3 with a Gatling gun in the cargo door and a huge amount of machine gun ammunition on board. In Vietnam, it was used to circle any area we wanted to hit and saturate it with machine gun fire. Puff had saved Special Forces camps many times, and our men were very fond of it.

Unfortunately, at A Shau Puff got shot down before it could wreak havoc on the NVA forces. Another helicopter flew in to rescue the crew and managed to get three of the six out before the enemy killed those left behind.

Darkness brought another bombardment. Then the enemy infantry charged. The camp repelled two assaults, but the third breached the south wall. The defenders still managed to hold on for another three hours. With astonishing bravery, two Americans took turns jumping across a hole in the wall to provoke the enemy to fire, so that they could see the gun flashes and know where to throw their grenades.

As it became light on the morning of March 10, the defenders called in airstrikes and napalm right on top of the camp, which succeeded in breaking up the enemy formations massing for yet another assault.

Even now, the men in the camp hoped that their courage would cause Nha Trang to do something substantial to help them. They asked for reinforcements and told the command that without them, "you can kiss us goodbye." Despite facing almost certain death, they still couldn't bring themselves to ask the command to take them out.

That morning, President Johnson telephoned the army high command in Saigon and asked how many Americans were at A Shau. He was afraid of the political fallout from the fall of camp and the annihilation of its defenders. As commander in chief, he could have simply ordered the army to take them out, but he didn't.

I have no idea how the planes flying support remained unscathed so long, but one was finally hit. The pilot was too low to parachute and crash-landed on the airstrip. In one of the most heroic acts of the war, standing out purely for its sheer spontaneity and altruism, Major Fisher, in the following plane, with no thought for himself and out of compassion for a fellow human being and pilot, trailed the crippled plane down and landed right behind it. He steered through the debris and torn metal on the runway, amid enemy fire, and stopped close enough for the other pilot to run over to his plane. Fisher then helped the other pilot board. Only divine intervention could have allowed them to make it out.

At 1:00 p.m., the camp sent out a final message: "Down to the last few rounds, no food or water." And they asked, finally, to be taken out. It had at last occurred to them that the command felt none of the loyalty toward them that they had shown the command.

Incredibly, even now, the command couldn't bring itself to admit defeat and remove the men. They waited for a few more hours before finally doing what should have been done right away when it became clear the North Vietnamese were going to assault the camp with overwhelming force. At last, the command ordered that the camp be evacuated.

But the command hadn't anticipated what a two-day battle would do to the South Vietnamese, and when the helicopters started landing a little more than three hundred yards north of the camp, the

South Vietnamese panicked and stormed them, ending any chance for an orderly retreat. The choppers couldn't take off and two of them toppled over, with one crewman dying. The commander of the helicopters, Marine Lieutenant Colonel House, was forced to order his men to fire on the South Vietnamese, seven of whom were killed. The remaining helicopters refused to land and returned to base, leaving almost everybody from the camp on the ground, stranded and virtually defenseless. They fled in small groups over the valley floor and toward the hills to the north. Some hid in the elephant grass. On March 12, the weather improved, and the choppers were able to get in and pick up the survivors.

Thus ended the fiasco at A Shau. Nine Americans and over a hundred South Vietnamese died in the battle. Captain Blair received the Legion of Merit and became a Special Forces hero; I was in awe of him when we met again in Nha Trang. Major Fisher received the Congressional Medal of Honor for rescuing his fellow pilot. Lieutenant Colonel House, who had ordered the South Vietnamese shot, received a decoration for bravery, all agreeing he had no choice; nevertheless, the Marines reprimanded him and forced him to retire for speaking to the press and giving the North Vietnamese propaganda. But all the heroism in the world couldn't make up for the unnecessary suffering the men of the A Shau camp endured at the hands of not just the North Vietnamese but also our Special Forces command.

Twenty

Twenty-five miles of jungle separated Hue from the A Shau. The first twelve and a half miles revealed a gray, heavily bombed and defoliated mass of dead trees and ghostlike vines. The Marines wouldn't set foot there. The next twelve and a half miles looked more promising from a recon point of view. This area was heavy jungle that ended in the A Shau Valley itself, so thick in places that our aerial photography couldn't read the contours and our cartographers had to dot them in on our maps. We would start in the east, nearest Hue, and work west.

Assionte kept the same roster at A Shau as at Khe Sanh, and so I had the first patrol. An old French road, Route 547, ran through the jungle from the coast to the A Shau, and a road like that had to have enemies all over it. My target, therefore, became a small clearing where the road broke out into the open, halfway between the A Shau and the coast, sixteen miles west of our camp. The road here looked as good as when the French had built it.

The clearing that the road ran through provided the only landing zone, but it looked like certain death, and I had no intention of landing there. The only alternatives were two craters on a ridge a mile west of the clearing, where somebody had tried to bomb the road and missed. The craters looked big enough to rappel into, and I doubted that the enemy would expect anybody to take that route or pay much attention to a helicopter hovering briefly over a bomb crater. I decided to set the world on fire by trying to rappel in, especially since Special Forces always bragged about rappelling but never actually used this technique on patrols. Moreover, I had rappelled a lot when mountain climbing, and you ran a lot more risks doing that than you did rappelling from a helicopter. I had trouble persuading the command, but Assionte and Allen finally agreed.

The mechanics of rappelling are as follows: Once in the helicopter, you make a loop in the rope and run this loop through two carabiners. Then you snap two other carabiners across this loop; the friction of the rope between these carabiners is your brake. You throw the loose end of the rope out of the helicopter, and two men get out on the skids on opposite sides, holding the end of the rope attached to the helicopter in front of them with one hand and the loose trailing end of the rope behind them with the other. Both men lean backward and jump at the same time, to keep the helicopter stable.

I figured that once I got everybody roped up and out on the helicopter skids, everything would work perfectly. The challenge was to make sure nobody panicked. I wasn't too worried about the two Americans, Brakeman and Shepard, but the Vietnamese were a concern. For their sake, I made our practice rappel particularly easy, from fifty feet and without packs, simply to get them familiar with snapping into the carabiners and to allow them to feel what it was like to get out on the skids and slide down. I was certain that once they got out on the skids, they would hold on for dear life. During practice, the Vietnamese hung on the rope at the bottom, and I had to help them off. My gloves got in the way, and for the actual rappel I decided to leave one glove off.

We were almost celebrities, and everybody seemed to jump on the bandwagon. Men steadied our ropes on the ground during practice, and Simpson volunteered to handle the ropes in the helicopter. The helicopter commander, a lieutenant colonel, insisted on personally piloting our aircraft. The news got around, and the First Corps C-Team commander flew up from Da Nang to take pictures of our practice to show to his friends in the States.

I realized I had more on my hands than I had bargained for when, at 7:00 on the evening of April 18, less than seventeen miles west of base camp, we inched over the treetops and I saw the gap in the canopy below me. Gallery after gallery of branches descended to a barely perceptible patch of brown dirt. Simpson threw out the rappel ropes, weighted with sandbags, and the ropes ran out their full length. I clipped onto my rope and ordered the Vietnamese point man out on his side. I nearly lost my balance when I climbed out onto the skid. I had never rappelled from this height before. We were 150 feet in the air, which was nothing like the fifty feet we had practiced from. I felt like I was about to fall off a cliff.

I jumped off and immediately plummeted out of control, wondering how I could have thought that practicing without carrying a sixty-pound pack resembled the real thing. I hurtled down faster and faster, the rope racing upward before my eyes. I pulled the braking rope around my body as tightly as I could with my gloved right hand, but this action made no difference, and if I hit the ground going this fast, I would be killed. One loop through the carabiners was nothing; if we had practiced with full packs, we would have realized that we needed at least two or three loops. I was about to get killed, not by the enemy but by my own carelessness and stupidity.

I panicked and squeezed the rope in front of me with my bare left hand. The rope cut into my palm, and I smelled burning flesh. But at least this worked, and I fell more slowly. The jungle on each side barely seemed to exist, and reaching the ground took forever. What had possessed me to take off one glove to help the Vietnamese? It was as stupid as practicing without packs. I could have just rappelled with both gloves on and taken one off at the bottom.

When I landed and unhooked, I saw that the skin of my left palm was shredded. There were two half-inch-deep gashes across the palm. As I looked to see how the Vietnamese man on the other rope was doing, he hit the ground with a thump, dangled on the rope, and swayed back and forth with the movements of the helicopter. He was dead, and I had killed him.

I looked into an abyss that I had just created. I had believed that I knew best and that everything I did was right, and all the attention I had received made my cockiness worse. I was incapable of seeing beyond my original assumption that once the Vietnamese got out on the skids for the actual rappel, they would be so scared that they would hold on for dear life. I had not considered that the Vietnamese might just take one look at the height and panic.

Then the Vietnamese man shivered and groaned. He was alive! I went over and cut him off the rope with my knife, to get him out the way of the others. I helped him to his feet; he staggered up and groaned again, but he managed to stay standing. He wasn't bleeding, and he didn't appear to have broken anything. If he could stand, he could walk, and if he could walk, he could gut it out on patrol like the rest of us.

The other four men had rappelled down by now, and Brakeman told me Simpson wanted me to leave the Vietnamese man on the rope so that he could haul him back up. "Bullshit!" I said to Brakeman. "We're going to keep going."

I didn't want to wait around anymore in that godforsaken crater; I wanted to get into the jungle before the enemy could find us. If we sent the injured man back, it would be an indication that I didn't know what I was doing. But if we kept going, I could show that rappelling worked *and* look indomitable as well.

I cupped my torn hand so that the others wouldn't see it and had Brakeman carry the injured man's pack. I picked up the sandbag I had cut off so that I could hide it in the jungle, and then we clambered out of the crater.

We kept moving until we couldn't see and then sat down for the night, the vast, hollow darkness descending on us—the interminable, awful night of jungle sounds, fireflies, and shape-shifting shadows that might herald our deaths. We were still close to the crater and the road was no more than 220 yards away. Every noise or shadow became the enemy. They could be anywhere. They certainly had to be on the road.

For safety, I put the injured Vietnamese man between me and Brakeman. He began to moan and writhe from pain, and each groan seemed to carry for miles. Somebody could hear him and be on top of us before we could be ready. To keep the Vietnamese quiet, I clamped his mouth shut and grabbed his arms to keep him from moving. He continued to groan, and I clamped harder until I was afraid that I might suffocate him. While I felt sorry for him, I couldn't show him any special compassion or mercy.

As I tried to keep the Vietnamese man quiet, I analyzed what I had done. He could be seriously hurt, and if I forced him to continue and anything happened to him, I would be responsible. I felt I had no choice but to reverse my decision and call the helicopters back in the morning to take him out.

If the choppers came back for the Vietnamese man, it would make no sense for me stay behind. My hand was mangled so badly that I would be a liability if we got into a firefight. But my departure would leave only four men, and having them continue without me was more than I could ask of them. The whole operation had originated with me, and if I came out, I didn't see how they could go on, so I might as well take out the whole team. Anyway, calling the helicopters back would eliminate the element of surprise we had gained from rappelling.

Nevertheless, I couldn't face the prospect of taking the team out. I had told everybody that compared to mountaineering, rappelling from a helicopter was a piece of cake, and now everybody was slightly in awe of me. I would do better by letting the injured man suffer and gambling that he wasn't hurt that badly, although this decision could possibly put his life in jeopardy and get me in a lot worse trouble than if I just took out the team.

All night I debated whether to keep the mission going and possibly destroy myself or take us out and ruin my reputation as a patrol leader. Then I began to see another possibility: I could take him out and stay in myself. Simpson had wanted to do that after the Vietnamese man got hurt. However, this option meant bringing a helicopter over the same place twice in less than twenty-four hours.

The Vietnamese man continued to writhe and moan. His injuries did not appear to be trivial. He could have one or more internal organs damaged, and any movement could make him worse or even kill him. I was deluding myself if I thought I could keep him going. As much as I hated the thought, I had to take him out.

I began to think more seriously now about taking him out and staying in myself. If I risked having a helicopter hover in the same place twice and still kept on going, I could do a lot more for my reputation than anything else I had done so far. As I was leading the first mission at A Shau, I could easily claim to have been compromised and ask to come out, but choosing not to do that would put me head and shoulders above everybody in the unit—not to mention that it would likely make everyone forget the botched rappel. I might not even run that much risk. If the enemy ignored a helicopter hovering over heavy jungle once, they might just do so a second time.

Staying in with my wounded hand would make me look even better. I could bandage it with a gauze packet and take antibiotics to prevent infection. Even with my hand in shreds, I could pick through vines, since we only used our fingers and moved very slowly. In a firefight I would be too pumped up with adrenaline to pay attention to my injuries anyway.

I decided that when I made radio contact in the morning, I would say nothing about my hand, and when we came back and they learned I had stayed in despite being wounded, I would have bragging rights over everybody. If I took out the patrol, I would likely lose a lot of credibility.

I had come up with a way to escape personal disaster. But I could have saved myself all this trouble in the first place if I had just followed Simpson's suggestion and put the Vietnamese man back in the helicopter after he got hurt.

In the morning, the crater looked the same, but somebody could have come down during the night and prepared an ambush. I had to wait there while the cable descended, the helicopter drowning out the sound of any enemies who might be in the area and the downdraft blowing the cable all over the place so that I had to drop my rifle to catch it. And I couldn't leave the crater until the Vietnamese man had made it into the helicopter.

As we left, I said to Brakeman, "I was sure he was going to give us away."

"I couldn't tell who was making more noise—him or you trying to keep him quiet."

"I could have killed the sonofabitch."

"A couple of times I thought you had."

We reached the ridge to the northeast, stopping every few steps to listen. The enemy was too smart to think that a helicopter would hover in the same place twice by chance. They could be on our heels.

Suddenly the treetops shook, and I feared the enemy had caught up with us. Branches bowed and sprang back up, the noise becoming louder until it was right over us. We glimpsed a black arm, a shoulder, and a patch of white fur. It was a troop of leaf monkeys that tore past us and was soon out of hearing.

By midmorning we hadn't heard anyone, and it looked like no one was on our trail. And so I claimed another victory. If a helicopter could hover in the same place twice without attracting attention, I had proved my theory that the enemy believed we landed only in open clearings and wouldn't pay any attention to a helicopter hovering over the jungle in the middle of nowhere.

On the evening of day three, April 21, we hit Route 547 exactly where I had planned. The light through the trees made me so excited that it took all my willpower to wait an hour before moving up. We had reached the enemy's primary route between the A Shau Valley and Hue, and while we couldn't just grab somebody out of a passing unit, we ought to be able to catch a straggler. I heard nothing and crawled up to the edge of the road.

The road's hard clay surface curved uphill out of sight around a bend to the west and downhill out of sight to the east. I observed the road for a while; then I got up and walked along it for several yards in both directions, kneeling to look closely. There were no footprints or tracks; the firm, packed surface was in as good shape as when it was built. Nevertheless, somebody had to be using the road for it to be in such excellent shape. In the tropics, roads deteriorate without ongoing maintenance. But maybe the surface was too hard to hold tracks, or perhaps the monsoons had washed any tracks away.

The enemy would only use the road at night anyway. We listened all night but heard nothing. Nobody was using the road, or at least it hadn't been used for some time. Maybe it was too obvious a bombing target. The whole area seemed empty. Our rappel had succeeded only because nobody was here, and we wouldn't have had a chance if the enemy had been present.

Feeling pretty disgusted, I got us up on the road. When the road emerged into the open, vegetation grew up over it, and it narrowed to a trail that showed occasional use, though not enough to give us much hope of catching someone. Still hoping to get a prisoner, I moved us into a thicket beside the road and waited. We stayed there all afternoon, but no one came by. The next day, we walked down the road and came out in the clearing that I had refused to land in five days earlier.

As the leader of the first team to go in at A Shau, I had to assume the enemy was everywhere and do everything possible not to land on them. How could I have known the place was empty? Even if we had failed to take a prisoner, at least we knew more now than when we started. Although I hadn't managed the rappel perfectly, nobody else would have tried it, and we could correct the mistakes next time, taking two loops through the carabiners and wearing two gloves.

Base camp seemed to share my view. Nobody paid the slightest attention to the fact that the patrol had come up empty. Instead, I was praised and admired for staying in with my torn hand, and everybody admitted that rappelling worked a lot better than they had thought possible. The Vietnamese man helped me the most, though, by not dying. As it turned out, he wasn't even seriously hurt.

* * *

While I was on patrol, we sent Carney and Sugzda for their first patrol into the south end of the A Shau Valley, three miles southeast of the A Shau camp and half a mile east of where the road vanished beneath the thicket of trees. We wanted to see whether the enemy had circled back north toward Hue from the south of the valley, although we might have tried to find this out without sending in two men with no recon experience.

Carney had experience only with picking landing zones for Ranger operations, in which you chose the easiest place a helicopter could land. In addition, Ranger operations landed in broad daylight, allowing you to see where you jumped, so that you didn't have to worry about stumps hidden in the twilight.

When Sugzda jumped out on April 22, sure enough, he impaled himself in the groin on a stake and had to be evacuated. It was night by then, and the recovery helicopter had to turn on its landing lights and reveal its location. As the helicopter pulled up, machine gun and antiaircraft fire opened up from every ridge, most of it .50 caliber, meaning several battalions, since we maintained .50 caliber no lower than the battalion level. We had to silence them before we could get Carney, who now had sixty to seventy enemies searching within fifty-five yards of him.

We called up jet fighters from Da Nang and "Puff the Magic Dragon" to drop illumination flares. While Puff circled overhead dropping flares, our command ship and the second recovery ship circled off to the side, and Miller (our FAC) flew into the uncertain illumination of the flares, fired his marking rockets, radioed to the

Miller, U.S. Air Force, one of our FAC's (Forward Air Controller), with whom I spent a lot of time in the plane and with whom I roomed in Nha Trang. He was astounded that I didn't wear socks because I didn't want my feet to get mold in the jungle.

jet pilots regarding where to hit, and tried to stay out of everybody's way. Assionte had flown out and radioed Miller to ask about the situation, and Miller told him, "Get off this frequency."

The fighters had to dive into the small lighted area and bomb. Our gunships flew into the same lighted area, fired, and flew back up, with everybody having to adjust his vision for the difference between the flares' pale light and the surrounding night, while red tracers crisscrossed the sky and explosions blotted out the jungle.

Not only did the pilots have to keep track of each other, but they also had to keep track of each flare, because once one burned out, the parachute continued to float down unseen, and they could fly into it. This situation lasted for two hours until we got Carney out.

Everybody was still in a daze when I returned. It was a miracle that nobody was killed and that we hadn't lost a helicopter. Those involved almost couldn't believe they were still alive. Brown became a celebrity for riding recovery. He said, "I told the pilots, if they shoot me in the balls, just throw me out of the helicopter."

Carney's patrol eclipsed mine, and he became the man of the

hour, which outraged me, because it lionized someone for not knowing what he was doing—landing in plain sight of all the surrounding ridges and showing once again our preference for drama over substance.

Twenty-One

After my patrol, they sent me down to Nha Trang for a few days. The day I arrived—April 24, 1967—the *Stars and Stripes* began reporting on the battle for Hill 861, four and a half miles northwest of Khe Sanh. It was the bloodiest battle in Vietnam so far that year.

Back when we were relaxing on the ammunition crates outside Khe Sanh and watching the FAC call in airstrikes on Hill 861, the sight had exhilarated us precisely because we didn't think that what was happening was particularly dangerous.

The Marines had gotten their first warning a couple days before the battle started, when the NVA killed four of five men who were on a patrol tasked with setting up an artillery observation post. Over the next few days, the lush jungle backdrop for the airstrikes we had watched became shattered black tree shafts and red chunks of clay as the Marines called in hundreds of airstrikes and artillery rounds that pulverized the hill. The Marines had counted on two of their platoons to take care of whatever enemies were left after the bombardment. Instead, the NVA hit them with extremely accurate rifle and machine gun fire from hidden positions, and the Marines staggered back, bringing with them sixteen dead and twenty wounded on makeshift poncho stretchers.

Whatever one might want to say about their tactics, the Marines came from a hard-charging tradition, and they were enraged by their defeat. The battle for Hill 861 now started in earnest. On April 26, the Marines mounted a full-scale attack.

The North Vietnamese yielded ground slowly, fighting with amazing ferocity, luring the Marines on and then springing out of camouflaged bunkers and spider holes and shooting the Marines in the back. The North Vietnamese were extremely well dug in and prepared to fight for every inch of ground. The Marines' artillery and

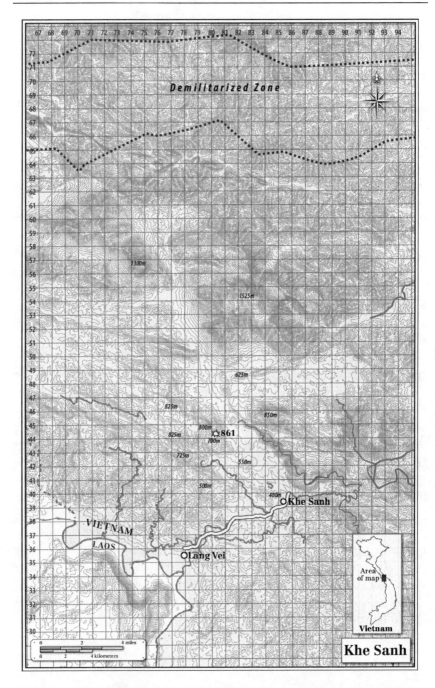

Khe Sanh map for the battle of Hill 861, when an American intelligence mistake saved my life.

bombing had had minimal effect, and they were suffering heavy casualties—sixteen dead (the same as two days before) and sixty-five wounded.

The Marines recognized the enemy's strength but believed they were unmatched when it came to taking bunkers, and now they knew where the bunkers were. They increased their attacking force by two battalions and believed anybody still on the hill was doomed. The Marines were approaching the crest and thought they were about to achieve their goal when, suddenly, the enemy popped out from dozens of hidden bunkers and pinned them down again. The battle raged for two more days before the Marines took the hill. They saved their honor but paid a very stiff price: 49 men killed and 156 wounded during the final two days alone.

The North Vietnamese had studied the Marines' psychology and knew exactly how they would react. The NVA began preparing well in advance for the battle and avoided contact with the Marines' perimeter patrols to lull them into a false sense of security. This approach gave them time to dig an elaborate bunker system and sneak several battalions onto the hill without the Marines knowing. Their goal was to inflict the highest possible number of casualties on the Americans and influence U.S. public opinion against the war.

The Marines had hesitated to send us to A Shau and had taken a day to decide. If they had kept us at Khe Sanh just one more day, I would have gone out on patrol and gotten myself killed. I never discovered why they opted to send us to A Shau. They might have decided on A Shau from the beginning, or the decision may have turned on something as trivial as a power struggle between officers, bureaucratic imperatives, or even what side of the bed someone had gotten out on that morning. Whatever the reason, the move saved my life.

* * *

While the battle for Hill 861 was raging outside Khe Sanh, at A Shau Sergeant Robinette was sent out with a Delta team to reconnoiter an area over thirty miles west of base camp. I checked on Robinette daily at the commo shack in Nha Trang, pretty convinced that he would make a mess of the patrol (and almost hoping that he would). I was not a fan of Robinette. He weighed about 250 pounds, which was just too big to move stealthily. He was stronger than any other man in the unit except Allen and barely concealed his contempt for anyone he considered an inferior, which included all young lieutenants. When interacting with us, he somehow couldn't form the word "sir" with his lips and had a hard enough time even addressing us as "lieutenant."

I had expected Robinette to create havoc in the jungle and get himself killed or, at best, require a rescue operation. But his patrol proceeded without incident, and by day three it looked to be a success. Then Robinette reported that he had ten to twenty-five enemies following him. As I had feared, he hadn't covered his tracks or paid attention to the niceties of handling vines and branches. The enemy had found him, and a rescue mission was on the cards after all.

The first recovery ship retrieved two of the Vietnamese members of the patrol before enemy fire forced it to pull up. When the second helicopter flew in for the rest of the men, a machine gun about 330 yards to the northwest shot it down; it crashed onto the treetops and hung there, settling deeper as branches snapped against the fuselage, with the men inside expecting to crash onto the jungle floor at any moment.

Sergeant Simpson, who was riding recovery, now took charge of the operation. Although the pilots, as warrant officers, outranked him, his rationale was that while the pilots commanded in the air, now that they were on the ground (or virtually on the ground), he commanded as the senior man from ground forces. In reality, Simpson didn't need a rationale. He knew more about what to do than anyone else and everybody knew it, and he went to work now to get the machine guns, ammunition, and all the men out of the helicopter before it fell from the tree.

In the middle of enemy territory, with the helicopter about to fall and the enemy about to surround them, Simpson gave calm, precise orders. He told the door gunners to get out on the nearest branch with their machine guns and directed them as they moved from branch to branch, carrying the machine guns by a relay system that Simpson directed. He told them to take their time and move carefully. Afterward, Simpson had the pilots retrieve the ammo for the machine guns in the same fashion.

Robinette and his two remaining men had reached the base of the tree just about the time Simpson got everybody down. There were eight men in total—three from the recon team and four from the helicopter crew, plus Simpson. Simpson ordered everybody to get away from the helicopter quickly, since it would attract the enemy.

He got the men to a ridgeline with a good view over a small clearing where Simpson expected the enemy would appear, since the fire that had brought down the helicopter had come from that direction.

Simpson ordered everybody into line, with Robinette and his men on the flanks; the pilots, whom he considered the least reliable, next to them; and the door gunners between the pilots and himself in the center. He gave a machine gun to one of the door gunners and took the other for himself, and then he told them all not to open fire until he did. He reminded the door gunner with the machine gun that when you shoot men moving in a file, you start at the ends and then move toward the center.

No sooner had Simpson gotten everybody ready than twelve enemy soldiers came into view about twenty feet away, walking in file along a trail and scanning the treetops for the downed helicopter. They resembled a bunch of Boy Scouts searching for a lost dog, apparently oblivious to the fact that a helicopter crew, if they had survived, would be armed. The troops wore bright green, newly issued khaki, unused web gear, and fresh jungle helmets, and they carried brand-new AK-4s. These were fresh recruits from North Vietnam, which was fortunate for our men.

The man who appeared to be their leader suddenly caught sight of the helicopter and pointed to it, and the other men raised their eyes in wonder, which explains why they didn't see Simpson on the ridge. The leader then caught sight of something (maybe a gun muzzle), lowered his eyes, and found himself staring at Simpson and his men. He actually gestured at them not to shoot.

Simpson had judged everything correctly down to the last detail. When the enemy leader gestured for them not to shoot, Simpson tapped the machine gunner's shoulder and then fired himself. Their fire converged on the center of the file, and the enemy melted into the grass as if they had never existed. It was right out of the manual and was far and away our biggest number of kills so far.

When the firing stopped, silence filled the clearing, and the men exchanged looks of wonder and disbelief. It had been such a clean, effortless victory. Simpson threw a grenade to kill any of the enemy who might still be alive.

When the rescue operation first ran into trouble, Assionte put sixty Vietnamese Rangers on alert and asked the Marines for two more CH-46 transport helicopters. When the second chopper was shot down, Assionte knew he would have to fly out there himself.

He had already done this once before, when Carney and Sugzda got in trouble and were being attacked by a substantial enemy force. On that night Assionte was a bystander, watching the red machine gun tracers flying through the night while the FAC ran the operation. A complete disaster was avoided, and the patrol rescued, but no thanks to Assionte. No one understood why he had gone out there to begin with.

In this case, we had a patrol that had gotten into trouble in broad daylight and in a hard-to-reach location; once the second helicopter went down, we had no choice but to send in ground forces. Assionte had to either command them or turn the mission over to Allen, which could have looked like buck passing or, worse, cowardice. Assionte put on a look of grim determination and marched out of the command bunker to one of the waiting CH-46s.

Assionte took off without his pilot's helmet and headset, and without waiting for any Rangers to board—a commander flying off to battle with no one to command. Allen watched this unfold and rolled his eyes. Then he grabbed his rifle and headset, distributed the Rangers among the remaining three helicopters, and flew off.

Once over the downed helicopter, which was still hanging in the trees, the CH-46s circled to orient themselves and find a clearing for the Rangers while our gunships flew diversionary patterns. The helicopters flew down, let the Rangers off, and then rose back up, continuing to circle, as the Rangers made their way up to Robinette and Simpson. Allen spoke on the radio with the pilots, the Rangers, and Robinette, peering back and forth between the ground and his map.

Assionte's CH-46 circled off to the side, Assionte not saying a word, although he could have used the Marine pilot's radio. Assionte probably wanted to project himself as a commander who trusted his subordinates but at the same time kept an eye on them. I was told (by Larrabee) that Allen would look over at Assionte's helicopter from time to time, shake his head, and mutter, "Jesus Christ!"

One of the helicopters had been shot down going in and crash-landed several hundred yards to the west. As its Rangers moved up to join the main force, the crew remained on the ground with it. Forty minutes later, Assionte suddenly broke out of his lethargy, and his pilot radioed for everybody to get out of the way as he flew in. I can only speculate on Assionte's thinking at this time. Had he needed forty minutes to build up his courage and make sure the downed helicopter hadn't been attacked? As Assionte's CH-46 settled in over the trees, Larrabee said Allen stared at it and toyed absently with his rifle.

As the downed crew boarded, Assionte stood on the ramp and helped them in, and the Marine pilots said afterward that they had never seen anything like this in their lives.

Twenty-Two

I finally saw the A Shau Valley from above on my first day with the radio relay. The valley's regular shape stood out dramatically from the surrounding jungle, and the dark green slopes mounting steeply from the flat valley floor made the area look so isolated that it seemed the only valley like it in the whole world. The blue-green mountains to the west formed the Laotian border, and flying near them made us nervous. The Ho Chi Minh Trail ran through Laos, and our FACs refused to fly over it—not so much from fear, but rather because being shot down in Laos could cause an international incident.

The mountains to both the west and the east descended to the valley floor in beautiful parabolic arcs and, amid the turmoil and chaos of this war, gave the valley a spirit of somnolence and peace. This impression was reinforced by the sight of the reddish-purple elephant grass swaying gently in the breeze and shimmering when the sunlight was on it.

The sharp yellow road running down the middle of the valley dispelled these illusions. The deep wheel ruts revealed the heavy traffic on the road at night; they were a disagreeable sign of human activity in the otherwise placid landscape. If we bombed the road, the craters would be filled in overnight, or a detour cut around to the side, which gave a good idea of the number of enemy soldiers waiting and hiding, able to erupt at a time of their choosing and turn the peaceful valley into a battleground. The stillness of the valley somehow seemed fixed on you, while the road resembled a wound, creating a unique combination of lonely beauty and simmering violence. At the southern end of the valley lay the remains of the A Shau camp, desolate and redolent of tragedy and death.

Aside from seeing the valley, riding radio relay was about as boring a job as you could get. Unless a team's main radio broke and they had to use their backup, I would spend a whole day flying around doing nothing. Once aloft, the pilot gave his crew chief the controls and read paperbacks all day, showing no interest in why I was there or what we were doing. He seemed as if he had been doing this job for a long time and would be delighted to do it for the rest of his tour.

At the end of the day, I went to the makeshift bar at the Montagnard training center. White paint peeled off the walls in flakes on the floor, and two doughy-faced American captains assigned to the training center stared out the window, saying nothing and ignoring the old Vietnamese bartender, the only other person there.

I asked, "How long have you been here?"

"Four months."

"Then in a couple of months you'll go into the field."

"Are you bullshitting? We've got to babysit these numbskulls for a whole year. If we were down in Saigon, we would get per diem. But up here they just give us cost of living."

A small incident that occurred the next day reveals a lot about the American war in Vietnam. As I drove back to camp, Marine MPs had the road blocked. Two Montagnard companies at the training center had gotten into a fight and were shooting at each other between their barracks. Americans sat parked in their jeeps; no one moved. Assionte had stopped all traffic out of our camp and cancelled our operations.

A crowd of Vietnamese civilian employees at the Phu Bai airbase, with no other route home, stood at the roadblock and looked toward the training camp, talking excitedly among themselves. Finally, an old woman with a huge sack on her back, in a hurry to get where she was going, hobbled past the MPs. She was followed by an old man with a bundle of wood; next to him was an old woman carrying a baby and suspending two cans of water from a pole over her shoulder. Eventually all the Vietnamese were on the move. The Americans continued to wait in their jeeps.

The MPs had their orders, and I could be waiting a long time before they got new ones. If a woman with a baby wasn't afraid of getting shot at, then I, as a Special Forces officer, shouldn't be afraid either, and I drove past the MPs while the other Americans ... continued to wait.

* * *

To a great extent, our lives depended on the relationship between Assionte and Allen. That relationship was fragile and subject to change. We couldn't tell for sure how much Assionte limited Allen's influence out of fear that Allen would completely overshadow him. Nor did we know to what extent Allen held back his advice, so as not to excite his superior's jealousy and suspicion. We had to tread between them, showing respect for Assionte as our commander while not overly demonstrating our respect for Allen, which was real and not feigned.

After Robinette's patrol, Assionte and Allen didn't get in each other's way as much. Allen probably suggested that Assionte couldn't possibly do everything himself and ought to rely more on his subordinates. Assionte had enough to do just getting the parts of the unit to work together; he didn't need to tell everybody how to do their jobs. Besides, he distorted his perspective by trying to do everything himself. Assionte should confine himself to broad strategy and let others take care of the details. This argument (assuming Allen or somebody else made it) seemed to work, and from that point on Assionte remained in camp and never went out on missions again, leaving Allen to run all operations.

Allen personally put in and took out every American and Vietnamese patrol, returning from one operation to go up immediately on another—taking out a recon team in the morning, setting in train a Ranger operation in the afternoon, and then rounding off his day by putting a recon team in during the evening. And that wasn't even counting the teams that got into trouble and had to be rescued. Allen logged as many hours as the pilots and wore his shoulder harness while in camp. He was lucky to have so much authority because most commanders assigned their deputies to administrative jobs. "Jesus, I'm glad Allen is running things," we all said.

To make this arrangement work, however, Allen had to convince Assionte that he had the best intentions and was simply working so hard in order to make the unit succeed. The better Allen made Assionte look, the better he himself would look, and he happily corrected or covered up any mistakes or lapses committed by Assionte.

Allen did all he could to ingratiate himself with Assionte, staying at his side and accompanying him everywhere, listening carefully and nodding gravely at Assionte's words. During meals, they talked heatedly at their table off to the side, and when Allen wasn't out on operations, you never saw one without the other. They conversed as peers, without hierarchy, understanding each other with a couple of words, Assionte calling Allen "Chuck" and Allen calling Assionte "Jim." Assionte seemed to pride himself on having a much better working relationship with Allen than Hoyez had had with him when Assionte was deputy commander.

Assionte, however, seemed to be the only one who believed this was an accurate assessment of their relationship. Just beneath the surface, you could discern Allen's contempt for Assionte. Allen couldn't stand Assionte for thinking that trying to act like a man actually made him into one. Light years separated the two men in everything but rank. And Allen's duty to Assionte didn't extend to acquiescing in his commander's fraudulent behavior and bad judgment.

Allen, therefore, did everything to show himself to be the exact opposite of Assionte. He represented a different world, a world where one held oneself to the same standards that applied for one's men, and Allen knew he was as good or better at this than anybody, although the contrast with Assionte made it easy for him. When Allen saw a group of sergeants, he immediately went over to talk to them, and in the mess tent he came over to our table to say, "You guys have all the fun. I wish I got to do what you guys do. You deserve all the support we can give you."

While the helicopters revved up down the hill, Allen would emerge from the command bunker, pulverizing the ground with his steps, his shoulder harness barely fitting around his massive body, his rifle looking like a toy in his hands. He bore the weight of the unit on his shoulders, picked up the pieces when something went wrong, and made Assionte look bad by contrast.

Assionte would trudge down the hill through the concertina wire and watch the men load and the helicopters take off, whether in the scorching heat of the day or during the cooler evening, the sky silhouetting his figure. His brow was always furrowed with concern as he tried to show how much he bore the weight of sending men out on missions. But he knew no one was convinced by the show he put on. When Assionte ate alone in the mess tent while Allen was on an operation, he chewed his food slowly and just stared at the empty space in front of him.

Twenty-Three

It's well known that a combat officer's efficiency diminishes over time. If he survives his first few weeks in the field, he gains knowledge and becomes a better, more capable leader. But eventually the strain takes hold. Combat officers who maintain a high standard of performance over a very long period are rare indeed.

I now saw that I had less reason to applaud myself than I had thought, as I began to do the things that I had condemned in others. I had held that, aside from the helicopter pilots, only recon really did anything. I couldn't perceive how somebody who hadn't carried a sixty-pound pack and picked apart the jungle all day with death at his heels could justify himself.

But getting up for patrols was beginning to wear on me—first the anticipation of going through the whole thing again, then the arrival at the landing zone, followed by the strain of the patrol itself. I didn't see how I could keep the routine up, with my life depending on so many things over which I had no control. Each patrol further depleted whatever strength I had left.

When Captain Briggs, our intelligence officer (S-2), rotated back to the States, Assionte made me the S-2 temporarily, and I suddenly found myself in the position of those I had looked down on as mere time-servers. I tried to make it appear that I had taken the job against my will, but I planned to do everything possible to make it permanent.

My first job as S-2 was to conduct a briefing for Marine Major General Hochmuth. I had never briefed a general before and rehearsed it to death. Assionte wisely sent Allen along for support.

I expected General Hochmuth to look for ways to trip me up. Instead, he greeted me outside his headquarters, bareheaded and without formality, like a kindly old gentleman. Once we were inside, he pulled his chair up next to the map, as if he simply wanted to learn the truth.

I kept to my script and did my best to highlight our accomplishments, going over them in detail. I emphasized the places where we had run into .50 caliber machine gun fire, pointing out that this firepower must signify the presence of battalions—that is, four or five hundred men. I based this judgment on the American practice of assigning .50 calibers at the battalion level, as well as the fact that the

North Vietnamese valued .50 calibers very highly, more so than we did. When I finished, I thought I had impressed the general.

Many moments in the Vietnam War affected me differently later in life, but this moment really stood out in retrospect after I read the *New York Times* accounts of fighting in the A Shau Valley when I was back at Harvard in the spring of 1968. When the briefing was over, Hochmuth looked at me and asked, "Are there any enemy in the valley?"

I couldn't believe it. I fought to think of an answer for this old fool who hadn't paid any attention to what I had just said. Fortunately, Allen intervened and prevented me from saying something stupid, and we returned to base unscathed. You don't make a major general look like a fool, even if he is one.

Hochmuth was killed that fall when a South Vietnamese artillery round hit his helicopter.

* * *

The North Vietnamese four-day defense of Hill 861 at Khe Sanh had fit into a larger plan. They were seeking to blood the Americans and turn sentiment in the States against the war. Once the Marines forced them off Hill 861, the North Vietnamese pulled back a mile to Hill 881 South and started the process all over again.

No one can question the courage of the Marines. They tackled the hill with grim determination, advancing slowly against stiff opposition. The enemy attacked from all sides and threw the Marines off balance. The Marines struggled to detect which tree or declivity up ahead the enemy was shooting from, risking death by just raising their heads to take a look. The enemy defenses had been skillfully laid out. Their bunkers were dotted unsystematically all over the hill, and you couldn't knock out one in order to take the next one farther on, as the Marines had been trained to do. Instead, they had to start from scratch each time, and as soon as they took a bunker, somebody would pop up behind them and start shooting.

The North Vietnamese believed the Marines would react exactly as they had on Hill 861, and they were right. When the Marines thought they had taken 881 South and secured a perimeter, NVA fighters emerged out of about two hundred spider holes and raked them with very accurate fire, using rifles with telescopic sights. The Marines were forced to go back over the ground they thought had already been won. It took three days to capture the hill. It was the worst fighting they had experienced so far.

The North Vietnamese now pulled back to Hill 881 North, and another brutal fight took place. By May 5, after four days of battle, the Marines finally took 881 North. Total Marine casualties in these battles came to 160 killed and 383 wounded.

On May 4, when the battle for 881 North was at its height, a Viet Cong battalion overran the Special Forces camp at Lang Vei. You would think that after listening to the artillery and B-52 strikes just six miles away at Khe Sanh, Lang Vei would anticipate that some of the action might spill over onto them. But no, and this lack of fore-sight (or should I just call it stupidity?) cost the lives of twenty-two South Vietnamese and two Americans: Lieutenant Stallings, whom I had met, standing guard, and the new camp commander, Captain Crenshaw, who was shot dead as he rushed out from his bunker.

Although the Marines claimed victory in the battles for Hills 861 and 881, a month later, General Walt, the Marine commander, was recalled before the end of his tour and given a desk job in the Penta-gon. This was generally interpreted as punishment for mishandling the hill battles. Walt had placed Marine pride above larger American interests, and his heavy casualties had caused outrage in the States and given the North Vietnamese a huge propaganda victory.

The Marines and Special Forces soldiers had fought when the time came and performed courageously, but you have to ask why we allowed ourselves to fall into such a trap in the first place. I sensed then, and I feel even more convinced today, that an underlying arro-gance was the cause. The Marines and Special Forces took it for granted that they had everything under control, but of course they didn't. This view indicates a belief that they just didn't have to try that hard, and if such slovenliness reigned in places like Khe Sanh and Lang Vei, it probably was endemic to the system—the system we had created in Vietnam, in the Pentagon, and perhaps in the nation at large.

Fundamentally, Americans felt as though we didn't need to try that hard because we would win no matter what. Our country had such an overwhelming military superiority that we just had to show up in Vietnam to be victorious. America had the best of everything, and therefore we always won and were always in the right, no matter what we did. That was an assumption that almost all of us believed at the time. We were smarter, worked harder, and did better than any-body else. All you had to do was look at the houses we lived in and the cars we drove, the outward manifestations of our natural superi-ority. We dealt in straight logic and hard facts, considered each man's

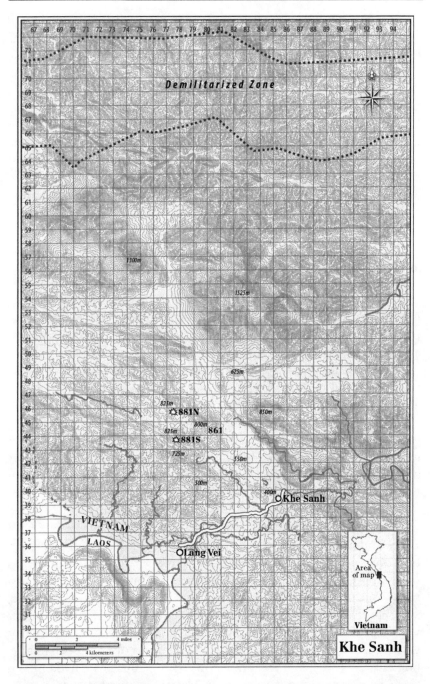

Khe Sanh map for the battles of Hills 881 South and 881 North, which revealed in all its glory the weakness of America's imperial assumptions.

labor his worth, fought for the ideals of the future against the superstitions of the past, and looked on others with more generosity and acted more altruistically than anybody else in the world. Our willingness to come all the way over here to save the Vietnamese proved this fact. Our moral superiority underpinned our military strength and entitled us to do whatever we wanted, no matter what that might be. We couldn't envision defeat, never even giving it a thought.

The battles for the hills turned out to be the first phase of the siege of Khe Sanh, which took place from late 1967 to early 1968. The Marines cowered in their trenches while the heaviest B-52 strikes had no effect on the besiegers, and the entire United States worried that Khe Sanh would fall. President Johnson feared a Dien Bien Phu–like defeat and humiliation.

Many analysts believe that the hill battles were fought by the North Vietnamese as preparation for the siege of Khe Sanh and formed part of North Vietnam's strategy to draw American forces away from the cities in the south before the 1968 Tet offensive, which was the turning point of the war—at least psychologically and politically.

Although the American military claimed victory in Tet, since we prevented the Viet Cong and North Vietnamese from taking any cities and inflicted heavy casualties on the attackers, the American public concluded that after years of war, we hadn't weakened the enemy's will to fight one bit. On the eve of Tet, General Westmoreland had told the American public that there was light at the end of the tunnel, that we were winning and victory was assured. Tet turned those promises to ashes. Whatever the facts about Tet, Americans saw nothing except continuing death and destruction, and they began to wonder whether the effort was worth the cost. Johnson's popularity plummeted, and after nearly losing the New Hampshire primary to an obscure Midwestern senator name Eugene McCarthy, he decided not to run for reelection.

Twenty-Four

Now I look back with a certain amount of shame at my efforts to remain as S-2, but this didn't stop me at the time, and I worked as hard to get out of patrols as I had previously worked to prepare and execute them.

The daily intelligence distributions we received consisted of reports of enemy activity that had nothing to do with us. I thought the other S-2 officers in the area might be picking up something outside standard channels, since their units had been here longer than ours. Visiting them also gave me an excuse to get out of the bunker. But they offered me the same meaningless intelligence distributions that we got, although I have to say they seemed happy to have someone to talk to. Thus, I decided to try the South Vietnamese army headquarters in Hue. This would also give me the opportunity to see the city for the first time.

Hue's massive, eighteenth-century French citadel seemed lost in time, as if the war didn't exist. Small boys were fishing in ponds bordered by deep grass, university students dressed in white strolled in pairs or lay on the grass reading, and girls with lavender parasols promenaded on the ramparts of the Imperial Palace. The palace and a lot more of the city would be reduced to ruins in the Tet uprising seven months later.

The Vietnamese army headquarters was located in an old French compound. Here, my efforts to garner better intelligence finally paid off. On the wall hung an old French army map that had a road coming out of the north end of the A Shau Valley, a road not on our maps. The geometrical lines left no doubt that it was a road, coming up one of the river valleys flowing into the A Shau from the east and descending to the east down another valley toward Hue.

Back at headquarters, I made sure everybody learned of my intelligence coup. After only two days as S-2, I had discovered a new infiltration route. My bragging finally caused Allen to call me aside and say, "Watch out what you say about Briggs. Assionte is writing his efficiency report, and you can hurt him. He was a good man."

* * *

The military provides the deepest insights you can get into the character of other men. I've already written about Sergeant Simpson and Major Allen in this regard. Captain Shelton made a strong impression on all of us, due to the atmosphere of wisdom and understanding he created and the feeling he gave us that he saw everything, knew everything, and would do everything he could to help us. This was not bluff or show; it was the real thing. Shelton's command style bore so little relation to what we had known until then that it took some time for us to adjust. We had a hard time believing somebody could actually command men the way Shelton did.

Shelton imposed his authority so effectively, I think, by showing his affection and respect for us. He would come in and catch us working on our equipment, or just back from patrol or about to go on patrol, and we could *feel* his sympathy for us, his admiration for our courage, and his fear that he might not see us again.

Shelton didn't personally give us the order to go on patrol, but he served in the hierarchy that did, and he acknowledged that he bore the same responsibility as those who actually gave the order.

You can't ask somebody to risk his life if you won't risk your own. Or at least you shouldn't. Shelton had no obligation to go on a recon patrol, and I don't think any of us would have thought less of him if he never did. But Shelton couldn't look himself in the eye if he didn't do exactly what the men under him had to do. As a measure of esteem, Robinette volunteered to go with him when Shelton went out on patrol. I remember Shelton fumbling with his harness when he was getting ready, not from nerves but because he had never prepared for a recon patrol before.

Livingston left a different impression. He had done as much as any of us (if not more) and yet took no credit for it and couldn't understand why we had made such a big deal about it. His attitude and behavior seemed to convey the question: *Why would you want to glorify something like this?* He had barely escaped with his life. That's all he saw, and he imagined having to do it again and again until, perhaps, he got killed.

Livingston showed no interest in our conversations and seemed not to listen to them. Why would we want to waste our time bragging and deluding ourselves into believing that going on recon proved our courage? Courage had nothing to do with it. If you went on patrol and survived, all it proved was that you had been lucky. If you got killed, that didn't prove you lacked courage—only that you had been unlucky. Livingston didn't really want to be associated with people who failed to perceive this distinction.

Livingston spent most of his free time lying on his cot, staring at the tent roof or out its side. If you came by to chat, he would joke with you for a while, but he clearly wanted to be left alone. The one exception to this rule was Ford. They became good friends, often talking together long into the night.

Their friendship came about partly because Ford felt the same way Livingston did about recon. He hadn't known how much he hated recon until he no longer had to do it, and he believed the rest of us went along out of a combination of conformism and misguided vanity. Now that he had freed himself from those illusions, Ford had become his own man.

Ford would stand in the middle of the tent and gesture enthusiastically, his eyes sparkling: "You won't ever catch me going out there like that again. I felt like I didn't have a stitch of clothes on. Now I've got eighty guys, and I stay right in the middle of them with as many around me as I can get. I'm the honcho, and they all take care of me. When we bivouac for the night, they cut everything down like beavers, and one of them clears a little space for me before he does anything else. You'd think we were staying there for a month. They're great kids."

Ford held up a letter he had just gotten from his girlfriend and kissed the thin blue paper. Then he suddenly looked as if he had seen a ghost. It had suddenly struck him that their separation could become permanent.

The rest of us kept busy preparing for our patrols. I was back in recon again. The S-2 slot called for a captain; I had been foolish to think I might get the job permanently. Once again, I was going into the jungle and playing with death.

Before a patrol, each man communed with himself as he attempted to get every detail right. Was this because we truly thought that doing so improved our chances for survival? Was it superstition, or possibly a coping mechanism? Perhaps a bit of all three. Certainly, our activity had a spiritual dimension that extended beyond the details themselves, a hope that the rituals we performed might please our Maker and tilt the scales in our favor.

You always saw someone's arm moving up and down and heard a cleaning rod scraping in a rifle barrel. Ford accumulated a small pile of used cleaning patches next to his cot as he tried to get his rifle barrel perfect. He put a new patch through the tip of his cleaning rod, ran the rod back and forth in the barrel, pulled it out, put his thumb in the rifle bolt to reflect light off his thumbnail, and, holding the barrel up to his eye, looked for specks in the rifling. He performed this routine over and over again until he achieved the result he wanted.

We sharpened our knives obsessively. Estenson rubbed his knife on an oil stone, his eyes six inches away from the blade, and then wiped off the oil with an old T-shirt and held the blade up to the light. He wasn't trying to get the sharpest edge possible; rather, he aimed to remove every visible imperfection. All of us seemed to sharpen our knives with this intent. The knives were made of low-grade steel that tarnished as soon as we put them back in their sheaths, and in fact we hardly used them. We were trying to obliterate something that wouldn't come out—to remove our own defects rather than anything on the knife.

Each of us had the irrational feeling that nothing affected our chances of survival more than how we arranged our shoulder harnesses and pistol belts. No two men did this alike, and each thought his way was the best. I took special pride in mine, having arranged to sleep with my harness on so as not to snore. If you slept on your back, you snored, so I arranged my belt so that I could undo it, roll over on my side, and sleep between my canteens. Normally you put your canteens behind you on your belt, but this arrangement put them too close together to sleep between them. So I first moved the canteens forward so that they were next to my ammunition pouches, but that put too much weight in front. I finally put my canteens directly on my hips, separating them enough to be able to sleep between them.

Each man communed with himself most deeply while he packed before going on patrol. Estenson handled himself best here, not mulling and hesitating over his equipment like the rest of us, but rather laying it out in neat piles on his cot, running his fingers over it, and then fitting each item right where it belonged in his pack.

A lot of our activity seemed designed to pass the time in the awful heat, with each day dragging on forever and the air so heavy that we fought to breathe. The heat dried the tent floor into a fine dust, which rose in puffs wherever we stepped. To keep the dust down, we sprinkled it with water, but this method worked only for a few minutes. The white sand outside blinded us when the sun was shining on it, and everyone tended to move in slow motion. We went outside so infrequently that the camp looked deserted.

The heat, though, was nothing compared to the fear. Fear hung in the air so thickly that you could almost see it, and each of us dealt with it in his own way. It was impossible to tell from a man's silence how he was taking the possibility of his life ending the next day. We tried to hold ourselves up with hope, but so much doubt accompanied it that hope became a fragile thing. We wanted nothing more than to get the mission over with. The more time you spent in recon, the more you knew it was indeed purely a question of luck, as Livingston maintained. The more patrols you went on, the more you felt your luck was running out.

I no longer wanted to prove myself. I just wanted to live. The abilities on which I prided myself had become like fantasies, and the glory I had dreamed of when I first joined the military no longer interested me.

I tried to gauge what lay ahead, running scenarios through my mind endlessly. Patrols here lasted a week, and after each patrol they gave you a week off, which meant two patrols a month on average. After my second patrol, I didn't see how they could give me a third one before everyone else had gone on two. The Marines had extended our operation for a month, and I had gone on my first patrol as soon as we arrived, so my third patrol wouldn't come around until our time in A Shau was ending. That, at least, was my hope.

*　*　*

Down at An Lao, whenever we wanted to send somebody up with the FAC, we had to first helicopter him over to the First Cav at Bong Son, ten miles away. This requirement had delayed getting an interpreter into the air when a Vietnamese team got into trouble, and Assionte refused to tolerate this inefficiency at Phu Bai. He wanted an airstrip right next to us to allow immediate air access.

However, the situation at An Lao hardly applied to Phu Bai. At An Lao, the flight to Bong Son could take half an hour; at Phu Bai, the one-mile drive by jeep over to the airfield took five to seven minutes, and any pilot coming in could radio ahead, so we could have somebody waiting. Also, the Phu Bai airfield was the best there was, a metal runway with lights for night landing, as well as a control tower.

There was so little need for the airstrip that I thought it served another purpose. The weaker Assionte felt, the stronger he had to look, and, with Allen handling operations, Assionte probably saw building the airstrip as one of his strategic responsibilities. It also gave him an opportunity to contrast himself with Hoyez. Hoyez had tried to scare everybody, but Assionte got things done, and the Seabees here would build the airstrip for free.

Assionte put Heddern in charge of building the strip, and

Carney in a jeep as we closed our camp at An Lao and drove to the First Cav's base at Bong Son.

Heddern leaped on the task as a means of rehabilitating himself. He bulldozed off the entire side of a hill for ten days—or, rather, the Seabees did, and he stood in the middle of the thick clouds of dust to show his disregard for hardship. Between the clouds we saw Heddern demonstrating his new mastery of a transit, bending over it and waving for men to move the sighting stake in one direction, changing his mind, and waving for them to move it in another. We couldn't imagine what he might be telling the Seabees, since they knew a lot more about building airstrips than he did, but the Seabees probably had a lot of experience with this type of situation.

Heddern not only stood in the middle of clouds of dust but also made the event a carnival. Only he was permitted to drive the truck, hanging his elbow out the window to show how much he was involved in his work. Every morning, and after pock time, Heddern drove right into the middle of camp, shouted for his Vietnamese to leap into the truck bed or onto the running board, and left with a flourish. During the day, he constantly drove back to camp to get something or to talk to someone, and he always had several men following him around. After meals, he hurried away, saying, "I have to get back to my airstrip." He would come into our tent so covered with dust that you could barely see his fatigues, and he made a point of ignoring the dust that clung to his eyebrows. Underneath, however, you sensed the same desperation and yearning for approval that we associated with Assionte.

Heddern's airstrip was finally completed, a flat red runway cleanly cut out of the hill, with beveled berms at both ends. Heddern had created this strip out of nothing, never having done anything like this before in his life, and he tried not to wilt under the spotlight, while finding excuses to drive over and look at his masterpiece. As a finishing touch, Heddern decided to run a strand of barbed wire around the strip, presumably to keep stray Vietnamese and animals from wandering onto it, although there was nobody inhabiting these desolate hills for miles around. I think Heddern set up his barrier more for aesthetic reasons. Such a beautiful airstrip had to have a framework, like a picture frame, and Heddern spent three days taking metal stakes from the back of his truck and pounding them into the ground. As a result, the stakes more closely followed where Heddern could drive his truck than the actual edge of the airstrip, and the strand of barbed wire resembled something like a cobweb, with the sun having to strike it before you could see it.

On May 10, Heddern's hour had arrived, and an army radio relay plane would attempt the first landing. Before the plane left Phu Bai, Heddern had already stationed his truck next to the airstrip with his Vietnamese workers in the truck bed, while the rest of us watched skeptically from camp.

The plane appeared out of the empty sky and headed straight toward us on schedule, its silhouette level with the sand hills. The plane grew larger and didn't deviate. This surprised us, because we had expected the pilot to circle the airstrip and negotiate with the ground or take one look and fly away. Nevertheless, the pilot kept on coming and brought the plane down in a flawless, graceful landing. This success completely vindicated Heddern, and he drove over to where the plane had stopped to pick up Bartlett and a Vietnamese man for radio relay.

After picking up the men, the plane taxied back up the runway for takeoff, and Heddern, in order to participate, accompanied the plane in his truck outside the barbed wire. At the end of the strip, the plane turned around to take off, and Heddern turned his truck around as well. When the plane started down the runway, Heddern kept up alongside, accelerating and taking off his hat and waving it out the window like a cowboy. The Vietnamese in the truck bed also took off their hats and waved them, cheering.

The plane and the truck with the cheering Vietnamese came neck and neck down to the end of the runway. At the end, the plane began to lift off and got up about six feet before hanging suspended in the air, with the sun glinting off a strand of barbed wire caught on the plane's left wheel. For a second the plane seemed about to break loose, but then it spun around and collapsed next to the runway, bursting into black and orange flames.

The pilot stumbled out, while Bartlett and the Vietnamese man seemed to levitate themselves out the door from behind the pilot's seat with a speed I have never seen since. As soon as the men got out, flames swirled against the plane's windows, a column of smoke and fire engulfed the whole craft, and the rifle ammunition inside began to go off.

Having gotten away from the wreck, Bartlett and the Vietnamese man were beating out the flames on their clothes. The pilot had gotten a head start and was not as badly burned. By now the plane had disintegrated, and black smoke drifted away from what remained of the wreckage. The medics' truck raced down the hill, and a sergeant next to me said, "Heddern sure got his airstrip off to a good start. Putting up that barbed wire sure was a good idea."

We heard the pilot was blind with rage. When he had tried to lift off, the truck, with its hullabaloo, had blocked his view, and since he didn't know what the truck was going to do, he had veered to miss it, not seeing the barbed wire. The pilot may never have noticed the wire in the first place, as a single strand of it would not have stood out against the dirt berm when he lined up the plane to land. Following this incident, pilots refused to use the strip, and it took us a week to persuade them to come back—that is, after we got rid of the barbed wire.

Twenty-Five

Our first patrols had found no enemies massing to attack Hue in the jungle near the coast, and in our next stage we patrolled the network of valleys and ridges leading to the A Shau Valley itself, moving up one valley at a time, trying to gain courage to take on the next, until finally we stood before the last barrier separating us from the valley.

This barrier was a thirty-mile-long ridge to the east that dropped directly into the A Shau. It seemed almost as terrifying as the valley itself and had a symbolic significance from the beginning. As we got closer, the dangerous nature of one of the most notorious sanctuaries in Vietnam seemed to pulsate in the air surrounding us.

Estenson took a patrol into the last valley before the ridge, almost twenty-two miles southwest of base camp, and stayed there from May 8 to May 14. While he was gone, I kept saying to myself over and over, *Just don't take any shortcuts or do anything stupid.* He didn't and displayed the spirit and courage on which we prided ourselves.

* * *

My next patrol changed my entire understanding of the war. Since I was the one who had discovered the existence of the road at the north end of the valley, Assionte wanted me to check it out. I had regretted being put back in recon, but I took pride in regaining my former prestige, because this patrol would take on the valley at its most strategic point, where the road came east on a narrow ridge out of Laos and turned at a right angle down the valley floor.

The road down the A Shau started here, the point where the enemy organized loads and scheduled traffic to make sure it flowed down the thirty-mile valley all night without a hitch and got under cover at the southern end before dawn. Troops in transit would also assemble here, and the enemy would protect this point with everything they had. Our aircraft always drew heavy fire here, and when I flew up with the FAC, Groth, to pick a landing zone, I got a good idea of what this meant.

Two streams flowed from the east into the A Shau north of where the road turned, and my path lay in one of them. The most northern stream, two and a half miles north of the road turn, entered the valley through a broad, shallow bend of rapids, with black rocks and eddies marking the surface. The southern stream, a mile north of the road turn, entered the valley through a narrow S-shaped gorge, hidden by trees, and looked less promising. Once again, I agonized over picking my landing zone, having to choose between a well-protected clearing south of the southern stream and a highly exposed clearing north of the northern stream.

The southern clearing seemed the better of the two options. Tall trees surrounded it, which would allow us to land out of sight of the valley floor, and the ridge to the east would screen our approach. Nevertheless, the dirt looked fresh, and I had sworn never to go in anywhere that looked cultivated.

The northern clearing appeared safer in this regard, but it lay on an exposed shoulder high above the valley floor. Anybody on the opposite slope could see us go in. Moreover, we had to approach from inside the valley itself.

Groth made one high sweep above the ridge, to appear as though he were looking for bombing targets, and I had this one sweep to make my decision. He then flew south, and the purple valley opened before us, with deep-blue mountains to the west. We flew over the road turn into the valley, the road here bordered by low dusty brush and stretches of rusty elephant grass, until we came to a stream ford, where Groth somehow spotted six machine gun emplacements. As he dove down at them to line up his marking rocket, pinpricks of light sparkled against the dirt. "You see those little yellow sparks down there?" Groth said over the intercom. "It means they're firing at us." Groth seemed to get a kick out of it. With him diving straight at the machine guns while aiming his rocket, I pictured him forgetting our altitude and flying within the enemy's range. If he got shot, I would have to try to land the plane on the road using the rear stick, and even if I succeeded, I didn't see how I could escape from the enemy once down. A sucking pop sounded from the right wing as Groth fired his rocket, and a waving trail of white smoke headed toward the ground. Groth pulled the plane up to evade enemy fire and threw it back and forth so brutally that I thought it might disintegrate. Groth craned to see the fighter-bomber above us, a black speck in the distance.

Groth radioed adjustments from his marking round, and the jet skimmed below us, over the patch of earth sparkling with machine gun fire, and left a geyser of black smoke behind. The smoke bulged into a black ball of dirt veined with gray, growing until it reached what must have been more than three hundred feet high, with huge brown nodules shooting out and scattering everywhere, finally falling to the ground after what seemed an unnaturally long time.

The bomb had hit off to the side of the machine guns, and Groth asked for another try. The second run did no better than the first, and Groth said, "They must have had a hard night." The strikes did, however, scatter tons of dirt and, and, even if they didn't kill anyone, they must have scared the hell out of everybody in the area. We saw no more sparks here, although afterward other jets met fire from different locations.

Groth flew north to the ridge with the road coming out of Laos, the line on its crest pure white from the heavy traffic that crossed every night. He called in an airstrike at this location. The bomb cratered the road right in the middle, and with the ridge's slopes nearly vertical on both sides, the enemy couldn't just drive around the crater to avoid it. The strike would take care of the road for some time to come.

The one pass over the ridge hadn't allowed me to decide on a landing zone, and I asked Groth to take me up again the next morning. After making a sweep over the ridge that contained my prospective landing zones, Groth again flew to the ridge with the road coming out of Laos, the same one we had bombed the day before. The crater had already been filled in, indicating how many workers the enemy kept ready under the trees to fix the road any time we bombed it.

I had to have something wrong with me to take so much pride in this patrol, which would show how far conceit and arrogance and the inability to envisage defeat can take anyone.

I always doubted the pilots would do what I wanted, and since I had chosen the northern clearing, I had to make sure they jumped over the eastern ridge into the valley at the last moment, to give us the best chance of getting in unseen. The ridge had several rock outcrops that looked the same, and I had to make sure the pilots jumped over at the right place.

We jumped over and dove down, and I started to count the six small ridges that led to my landing zone. The first one popped up, hiding the rest, and I couldn't tell for sure whether the next one was a ridge—the same problem I had encountered at An Lao. After what

I thought was the right number of ridges, a steep clearing appeared before us. We flew past it, and I yelled at the pilot to bring us back around.

The patrol consisted of me, Sergeant Smythe, and four Vietnamese. After we jumped into the clearing, we had to get as far up the ridge as possible before dark. Just as we were getting deeper into the jungle, the point man stopped, causing the rest of us to bunch up. He put his rifle under his arm, took a small white cone from his shirt, and stuffed it with black leaves. A match light flickered between his palms, and harsh smoke floated over us. We never allowed smoking on patrols, and I asked the Vietnamese team leader, "What's he doing?" The team leader gave me a pitying look. "He smoke," he said. And we waited for him to finish.

I seemed to have chosen a good landing zone, because nobody came after us during the first night or the next morning, and an hour after our first radio contact, I led the patrol up the ridge. The jungle became clearer, the trees were smaller, and the hunting trails looked old. We made it to the ridge top by noon, and I had achieved my greatest success so far—standing on one of the most strategic points in Vietnam, a corner of the A Shau I had only fantasized about conquering. I had become part of the A Shau myth, with the valley a mere stone's throw away.

I imagined the enemy battalions moving through the northern river valley. I pictured myself creeping down next to the road, watching the enemy's movements, waiting to choose the best time to jump out and capture someone, and then pulling back up the slope and calling in airstrikes to destroy the rest.

A week earlier, on the Cambodian border, a team from Project Omega (a rival recon group) had watched 480 men moving past from only fifty feet away. They let the enemy pass and then called in an airstrike, which was so successful that the enemy stampeded back over the team. Delta considered Omega upstarts, and so we had to get a battalion ourselves to keep up with them.

I got us to the point of rock above the northern stream by the third evening, right on time, and we listened to the road all night, hearing nothing. We started down the next morning, having done everything perfectly, tasting victory. The road was below us, which made each step a test of nerves, as we had to let ourselves down the slope by holding onto the trees to keep from slipping; each time a man knocked a rock loose, I thought we had had it. I also feared we would end up above a sharp road cut and it would be very hard to jump out and surprise someone.

All my perfect execution came to nothing when we suddenly found ourselves standing at the edge of a broad, shallow river, flowing peacefully in front of us and disappearing innocently behind misty bends. I looked at the slope on both sides to see whether the rocks and jungle were hiding something.

I had never felt closer to renown and glory, the prospects of which now evaporated before my eyes. I would never have such an opportunity again. Had my arrogance brought this defeat on me; had I invented a road in my mind in order to claim that I had found something? I didn't believe I was foolish enough or crazy enough to hallucinate what I had seen on the French map. A road like the one on the map couldn't simply disappear. And the French wouldn't have put an imaginary road on a map.

Had I confused this place with another location? Yet the road on the French map clearly came out of the northern end of the A Shau, and it went through a river gorge cutting the A Shau's eastern ridge at a sharp right angle. Only two rivers cut the ridge like that up here; the northern river was the larger of the two and more likely to have a road, with its northern bank being the best place for one. The enemy might have filled in the road to camouflage it, but the rocks and vegetation did not appear to have been disturbed.

In despair and humiliation, to save my honor, I hurried us across the river to the two-and-a-half-mile ridge we had to cross to reach the southern river. We should have watched the stream for a day and crossed at night, but doing so would waste a day that we could otherwise spend climbing the ridge (not to mention give anybody who had picked up our trail an extra day to catch up to us). Besides, the unbroken jungle on both sides of the river looked empty, and I saw no point in losing a day just to conform to the rules.

Having broken one rule, I decided I might as well break another. We were supposed to cross one at a time, but this approach would take all morning and increase our chances of being sighted, and so I decided to have us all cross together. As we stepped into the river, with the towering jungle walls hanging over us, it felt almost like walking on air.

I embarrassed myself here, too. After we crossed, I had one of the Vietnamese fill our canteens, and then I ordered a break before we started what would be a long, hard climb. The point man, a

Montagnard (the same man who had taken a smoke break on the first evening), shook his finger at me. Didn't I know better than to stop after we had crossed a river out in the open like this? He was right, of course. As empty as the jungle looked, someone could be watching from behind the leaves.

Now we had to climb up the slope. This southern slope was much steeper than the northern one, and it was harder to pull ourselves up by the trees without slipping and knocking rocks loose. However, we seemed to have succeeded when we reached the top without having heard anyone behind us.

I felt even better than I had previously when we saw a broad, well-packed trail before us on top of the ridge. Now I had a chance of catching somebody. The trail exhibited heavy use, and the dung on it showed that the enemy transported heavy arms and equipment down it by elephant, a throwback to ancient times. But on closer examination my chances appeared slim, since the mold on the elephant dung looked two to three weeks old. I consoled myself by basking in the fact that nobody else had walked this freely in the midst of the enemy.

I took advantage of the trail to move faster until the fear that somebody might catch us from behind got to me, at which point I moved us into the underbrush on the side.

The ridge put us through another test—namely, thirst, since it wouldn't have any water, and the water from the last stream (three canteens per man) had to last the three days it would take us to cross.

The heat was atrocious. Particles of dust and chaff hovered like mist around us, got into our noses and down our throats, and made our thirst worse. The heavy sweating reminded me of how little water I had left, and I drank barely enough to wet my mouth, the canteen's plastic tasting delicious. By the second day, my thirst had gotten so bad that I could barely concentrate on the vines. Thirst drives all thoughts except reaching water out of your mind, and it took extra willpower now not to become careless. Only my battle to maintain honor gave me the strength to keep some kind of patrol order.

Around midnight, while bathed in the familiar smell of the rotting jungle, with my head aching from thirst, Smythe suddenly whispered to me, "Sir, I don't have any more water. Can you spare a little of yours?"

"What did you do? Drink all yours?" Despite my anger, I couldn't put myself above a subordinate, and I handed him my canteen, although it took a lot of willpower to pass it over.

I listened to him drink. "How many canteens did you bring?"

"Two."

"Two?" I couldn't believe it. "You are supposed to bring three!" Bringing three canteens was so standard that I hadn't bothered to check and had asked Smythe only whether he had everything he needed. But then I suddenly saw Smythe in a different light, and I fell in my own self-estimation. If Smythe had brought only two canteens, he must have run out of water some time ago, and if thirst was driving me crazy when I had three canteens, it meant that he had actually persevered better than I had.

After that, I must have dozed off. Then, suddenly, the Vietnamese team leader shook my arm and whispered, "Look! Look!" Across the valley, among the trees on the opposite ridge, a row of lights shone. The flickering yellow-orange lights trembled for a moment, disappeared, and then reappeared farther south. The lead light darted ahead, as if trying to force the others to keep up. The lights moved steadily, bobbing up and down. From the way they flickered, they appeared to be torches.

The lights appeared to be moving very quickly, as if the people carrying them were running. They seemed far apart, judging by the distance between them—perhaps a torch for every ten men. There were so many torches that we could possibly be looking at a battalion moving down the Ho Chi Minh Trail by night, about to slip through our fingers.

I had heard of this, but I needed to witness it to understand just how much heart and will the North Vietnamese and Viet Cong possessed. Their spirit was more powerful, it seemed, than all of our modern technology. Even over on my side of the valley, I felt fear, and yet at the same time I had a curious feeling that I was violating their privacy by spying on them in this way. Still, I felt proud to be witnessing something few others had seen.

The next morning, I dutifully called in an airstrike on them and felt slightly ridiculous as anti-personnel bombs exploded ineffectively along the ridge, the men from the night before having moved beyond the area being bombed.

My head swam from thirst, and I barely saw the jungle around me. Then, by some miracle, we found a small pool of water halfway down the ridge. The jungle here showed no signs of activity. We had to plow on to get to our final objective, which was just a dotted line on the map south of where we were.

Around midnight, the sky suddenly started humming, followed by hissing, like the sound of rain, getting louder and nearer and growing into a roar, as if Niagara Falls were about to land on us: a B-52 strike. I didn't think the strike would hit us; B-52 strikes were not supposed to land within less than a mile of friendly forces, and with the command knowing our location, this strike was probably directed at the road turn out of Laos, about half a mile away. It was probably in response to my report about the torches. Loose bombs, though, were a different matter, and the whistles breaking loose from the main cluster and coming down separately scared me to death. These were probably bombs that had gotten stuck temporarily in the bomb bay. For some reason, I thought that hugging the ground and covering my head would do something to protect me.

Suddenly a green light illuminated the entire jungle, making the forms of tree trunks, vines, and the other foliage as vivid as in the day, all bathed in a hideous, sickly green light. Then the whole ridge gyrated as if it were about to rise up and then collapse. The sound engulfed me, and the shock lifted me a foot in the air. I couldn't tell whether I'd been hit until I struck the ground again.

This was as close as one could get to a B-52 strike without being killed. Bark, dust, bits of leaves, twigs and branches rained down on us. The air was filled with an asphyxiating dust.

I understood the enemy more clearly now than at any other time in Vietnam, even more clearly than with the torches on the previous night. If the enemy could endure B-52 strikes like this one and not give up, they possessed a level of conviction different from ours. You would expect that anyone who survived just one of these earth-shattering attacks would stumble over to the nearest South Vietnamese outpost and surrender. But not this enemy. I saw now that our cause was hopeless; we could never win.

We reached the dotted line on the map that evening, a flat leaf bed with fairly new tree sprouts, possibly once a lane if you used your imagination, but it gave little hope of finding anything, and I wasn't surprised when we heard nothing during the night.

I had one last scare the next morning, the morning of May 17. I went out to the elephant grass beyond the wood line to tramp down a place for the helicopter, feeling wonderful after finishing this patrol in this part of Vietnam. The helicopter arrived, and we took off without incident. As the helicopter lifted us out and we flew above the last ridge shoulder, though, I saw the barely perceptible valley floor below me with horror. I had stayed so far above the valley that I couldn't possibly have run into anything.

The door gunner on my side suddenly started firing at the wood line, I suspected out of jumpiness since we were close to the road out of Laos. "What are you firing at?" I shouted.

"Enemy fire!" he shouted back. Pilots reported fire from all over the ridge, which apparently was teeming with enemy troops. As at An Lao, my tactic of staying on ridges *seemed* to be justified.

I had considered this patrol my greatest achievement. But I shook my head in disbelief at my simple-mindedness, thinking that one quick look at a map in Hue had been enough, rather than returning to trace the road on the map and photograph it. Even more astonishing was Assionte and Allen's simple-minded trust in not telling me to do so. It wouldn't have taken much more than an hour.

Twenty-Six

Just as in the original A Shau battle, a lot of our heroism in Vietnam stemmed from making mistakes and then trying to recover from them. After Estenson's patrol, Sergeant Gleason went in about six miles east of the old A Shau camp. He picked a landing zone in an open valley exposed to high ridges on all sides. I think he picked the first place he thought he could get into and had thrown everything up to chance, since everything seemed to depend on chance anyway.

Gleason was the oldest man in recon, then in his early forties. The other sergeants looked up to him as their dean. I thought he was too old for recon and wondered why he had volunteered. Maybe he wanted to show everyone that he could keep up with the younger men.

On the evening of May 14, within seventy-five feet of the ground, enemy soldiers fired at Gleason's helicopter and hit its oil line. The pilot brought the helicopter down half a mile to the south, and a recovery ship was quickly on the scene, rescuing the crew and part of the team. As a second recovery ship came in for the rest, ten or twelve machine guns opened up from the hills on all sides and shot the helicopter down. It came down next to the men on the ground, and before we could get to them, all hell broke loose, with tracer and machine gun rounds zipping over the men's heads.

Two fighter-bombers came up from Da Nang for close air support while a Puff the Magic Dragon dropped flares from above and the FAC did his best to maintain order and keep planes from crashing into each other.

While all this was going on, the pilots had to remember where they had last seen muzzle flashes and then aim there, swooping down again and again while not letting the light of the flares blind them as they came out of the darkness. This chaos went on for two or two and a half hours. The pilots never lost their cool or put their own lives above those of the men on the ground. Pilots demonstrated such gallantry thousands of times throughout the war.

When the first recovery ship had settled in, the men on the ground (four helicopter crew members and the six team members) started to get on board. As they began climbing in, the helicopter tilted to the side, and Sergeant Markham, riding recovery, jumped out to lighten the load, to let the helicopter take out those already on board, just as he had on my An Lao patrol, except that tonight he had an awful lot of ordnance exploding around him. When Gleason tried to board, Markham said, "Let the Vietnamese get on this one. We'll take the next ship." Then, a couple of minutes later, the second recovery ship crashed right next to them.

For the next couple of hours, the men on the ground watched the bombing, hoping they wouldn't get hit but fearing that maybe they would. However, they could take some comfort in the fact that the tracers were now being shot at someone else and that the attacks from the air ought to keep the enemy too occupied to come after them.

Through all of these events, the men knew that Delta wouldn't abandon them and that they would eventually be saved. Markham had known this when he jumped out of the helicopter, his act as much cold calculation as altruism. He had more on his mind than the danger involved and knew that jumping out of the helicopter would set him up for life with Assionte and Allen, especially if everybody got out. Nevertheless, it took a lot of courage to make that calculation.

Everybody was still talking about Gleason's rescue three days later when I got back. We couldn't understand how no one had been killed or even seriously wounded. All the other sergeants were kidding Gleason about "trying to land on the whole North Vietnamese Army." Anyway, Gleason's patrol was a perfect example of heroism born of stupidity.

The two patrols after Gleason's had the same result. After failing in the south, we wanted to try in the north, testing the waters first with a Vietnamese team. We landed the Vietnamese in a small valley that was separated from the main valley by a ridge and cut by a meandering stream. The valley had a secluded air and seemed an easy place to start, even though it was less than a mile west of the road and only three miles southeast of the ridge coming out of Laos.

When the team landed on the open valley floor, machine guns opened up from the ridges to the east and west. One man was hit. The team managed to hide in the brush and called for gunships. Two gunships, two fighters, and a Puff the Magic Dragon spent three hours in the air attacking the enemy before we got the team out.

After these two failures, I couldn't understand why the command then put Sergeant Simpson in on the open valley floor, two miles south of where the Vietnamese patrol had been attacked. That patrol had telegraphed our intentions to the enemy, and they had demonstrated that they would do everything they could to prevent us from getting into this area. Simpson's patrol seemed more like bravado intended to prove our fearlessness rather than a serious attempt to achieve anything. We were putting men's lives at risk for prestige purposes.

In the military, harebrained projects challenge men's honor, and when the idea first surfaced of sending someone out on the most difficult and dangerous patrol so far, Simpson would have considered it a personal affront if he didn't get to lead the mission. He probably dropped some hints around the command bunker about the importance of picking the best man, and the decision went in his favor by default.

As Simpson started in, he sighted seven men right there at the landing zone, so close that he saw one's gold tooth, and he knew many more had to be close. The enemy started firing immediately, and Simpson aborted before getting in. As he pulled up, about a dozen .50 caliber machine guns started to fire from the north and south, but somehow they got out of there.

Afterward, I saw on the map where Simpson had tried to land, and his choice of landing zone was enlightening. Simpson had picked the single hilltop in a vast valley of open elephant grass, overlooked by high ridges to the north and south and highly visible, much more so than the spot Gleason had chosen. Simpson had the coldest judgment in the world and had to know exactly what this option meant. The choice therefore was not an accident, and the chances of running into the enemy here were 100 percent.

Whether Simpson planned it that way from the start is debatable. I suspected that the closer Simpson got to going into the northern end of the A Shau, just south of the ridge with the road coming out of Laos, the more he would have pictured gun barrels pointing at him from every direction, and the more he would have wanted a landing zone that he was sure to get shot off of immediately.

Harebrained projects became almost like a craze at this point. We had been here too long, and it was beginning to affect our minds. When I came back on May 17, I found the main topic of conversation (aside from Gleason's assault on the entire NVA) was parachuting into the old A Shau camp, with Larrabee being the strongest advocate. A few days earlier, a Special Forces unit in Four Corps (the far south of Vietnam) had made a "combat jump" into the Seven Mountains area—the first Special Forces "combat jump" of the war. A combat jump was something you wore on your sleeve for life, and Delta felt we had to keep up with these upstarts.

The idea of jumping into the A Shau camp probably originated with Allen, although I question whether he really meant it. However, once something like that gets started, it tends to gain momentum very quickly. Jumping into the A Shau bore no resemblance to jumping into the serene landscape of the rice paddies around Seven Mountains. Somebody could shoot you as you came down, or you could impale yourself on a piece of the rubbish in the camp. I don't think anybody had the faintest idea of what we would do once we got there. The idea, though, took on a life of its own, and anybody who was anybody felt he had to volunteer.

* * *

The patrol I had just been on saved me from having to volunteer for the prospective combat jump because Assionte sent me to Da Nang as liaison with the Marines to impress them with the man who had led it.

Da Nang itself was fun. I didn't have much to do, so, rather than listen to squelch over the radio all day, I looked for excuses to get out and see the city. This task required some stamina. If we had sent everybody stationed in Da Nang into the field, we might have won the war. Men crowded the boardwalks in dress khakis like it was midday in Honolulu or even Manhattan, and you had to wait in line if you got caught in the middle of them. It took two hours to drive to the airfield two miles away and half an hour to cross the fifty-five-yard bridge connecting the airfield to the city. Traffic rules had no meaning since you never got anywhere unless you broke them (which I became very good at).

The Marines proved as hard to navigate as the city itself, with desks in their headquarters organized according to which man had staked out which desk first. No desk had anything to do with its neighbors. To get anything done, you had to go from a desk on one side of the room to another on the opposite side, and everything moved at a snail's pace. The people at Marine headquarters had settled in for the duration. There were colonial ceiling fans turning slowly overhead and coffee cups on the windowsills with men's names on them.

My crowning moment at Da Nang came when I took my beer over to join a couple of sergeants at a free table in the C-Team bar, which had no distinction between ranks. I still felt awkward around sergeants, knowing they considered lieutenants a sorry excuse for soldiers, but now I planned to take my revenge. I started off gently, preparing the ground by asking the sergeants about their units and how things were going. I wanted them to ask me the same thing, and when they did, I offhandedly said that I had just finished a recon patrol at the northern end of the A Shau. It worked like a charm. Incredulity spread over their faces, and I saw fear lurking in their eyes.

Twenty-Seven

The valley floor on the western side of the A Shau Valley had always stood as our final challenge, and we had put off facing it as long as possible, because it lay within gunshot of the mountains on the Laotian border and because the peacefully waving elephant grass here looked more suspicious than elsewhere.

We could have claimed that going in on the open valley floor had nothing to do with checking routes out of the A Shau toward Hue, but we felt we had lorded ourselves over everyone we had come into contact with so far, and when Radio Hanoi said they looked forward to meeting us in the A Shau camp, we had smiled to ourselves about how sorry they would be if we actually took them up on it. Now we were beating our chests about parachuting into the camp. We had been everywhere else—the eastern ridge, the south, and the north—and if we didn't try the valley floor to the west, it could look like we had chickened out.

As usual, we sent in a Vietnamese team first to test the waters. Landing a team two and a half miles northwest of the A Shau camp would alert the whole valley, and we should have picked a stronger team, as this team had come out in heavy fire two days earlier and was not yet fully recovered. But for five days, from May 17 to May 21, the team moved smoothly and ran into nothing more interesting than a few abandoned huts and bunkers.

Most crises have innocent beginnings, and on the fifth day, May 21, the team asked to come out because one of their men had gotten sick. The team picked an opening in thick brush at the base of a ridge overlooking a stream, brush so thick they had to stand on roots and push aside the branches with their rifles to signal the helicopters. The helicopter pilots begged the team to find a better place, the slope being too steep to land and requiring that the men be hoisted up by cable, which exposed the helicopter to clipping the slope with its rotors, as well as offering a perfect target for anybody on the ridge.

The Vietnamese said finding a new place would take too long; plus, their sick man needed help. As the men on the ground and in the most danger, they had the final say. You sensed that they also resented the Americans telling them what to do and couldn't have cared less what the pilots wanted, figuring the helicopter would get in somehow. The pilots begged the interpreter to argue with the team one more time, but the team still refused, and the pilots had no choice but to go in.

Sure enough, as the helicopter hovered, a machine gun on the top of the ridge opened up and hit the helicopter's instrument panel. Plastic and metal sprayed throughout the cabin, and a piece hit one of the pilots, Montoya, in the eye. He began bleeding profusely, the control stick became too slippery with blood to handle, and if the co-pilot hadn't pulled Montoya's hand off it and kept the helicopter up, they would have crashed.

Stanley, riding recovery, unfastened Montoya's seat belt and dragged him to the rear of the chopper to stop his bleeding. He gave Montoya first aid and probably saved his life, and the co-pilot succeeded in bringing them all safely back to Phu Bai.

As the helicopter pulled up, machine guns opened up from the surrounding ridges, and we had to call in bomb strikes and strafe the ridges to suppress the fire before our helicopters could try again. That afternoon, during a gunship run, the enemy hit one of the gunships in the tail boom, causing the pilots to lose control and crash more than five hundred yards north of the Vietnamese team. The helicopter landed on its skids and then bounced up and spun over three or four times as it went down the slope before landing in a gully upside down. A minute or two later, it exploded.

We focused on rescuing the survivors, and our helicopters circled out of machine gun range, dipped down briefly to scan the wreck, and flew back up to escape the machine gun fire. We called in an Air Force "Jolly Green Giant" from Da Nang—a large crane helicopter used for hoisting out wrecks. It hovered over the wreck for a moment, but the pilot didn't dare remain exposed for long to such heavy machine gun fire and pulled up. As the Jolly Green Giant pulled up, the pilots saw a signal panel downhill from the wreck, but they were afraid to go back for the man and rescued the Vietnamese team instead. Now, with the American crew still on the ground, the Vietnamese team, which had caused the whole mess to begin with, was rescued.

Pilots believed being on the ground meant certain death, and in this case, it seemed just a matter of time before the enemy got the survivors of the gunship crash. Late in the afternoon, one of the Marine CH-46 helicopters braved the machine gun fire long enough to hover over the spot where the Jolly Green Giant had seen the signal panel earlier and managed to hoist out Szwed, the left door gunner. As the CH-46 pulled up, the pilots spotted two more men waving from the gully but couldn't go back for them because of the intense enemy fire.

As darkness fell, one of our slicks went in for the two men the Marine CH-46 had spotted in the gully. The helicopter got in over the men and prepared to winch out each one separately, because a Huey lacked the power to haul out more than one man at a time (and even one man tended to destabilize it). In any case, the loop in the cable was big enough for only one man.

The two men on the ground saw the lowered cable, but neither believed that the helicopter could hover long enough to lower the cable twice and haul both of them out. They both leaped for the cable at the same time and tried to get into the loop together. The loop didn't stretch wide enough, and each man only got it under one armpit.

As the helicopter struggled to remain aloft, the machine guns on the ridge opened up, and Gallagher, the uphill door gunner, was hit in the chest. To avoid the fire, the pilots let the helicopter slip downhill and forgot about the men on the hoist. The chopper dragged the men through the brush and knocked them against the trees, and the friction dragged the helicopter lower, the pilots battling both to get away from the machine gun fire and to avoid getting dragged down by the men on the cable. Hall, the gunship's right door gunner, hit a tree and let go first. Cochran, the pilot, held on a little longer, but he then let go, too. This action saved the helicopter, and the pilots got it back to Phu Bai, with Gallagher dead on arrival.

The helicopter had come so close to rescuing the men that another helicopter was sent out when it was already dark, at about 8:00. As the helicopter got close, a tiny flame flickered in the elephant grass, like a cigarette lighter. However, it was too dark to go in closer with the enemy machine guns about to open up, and the pilots didn't want to risk losing an entire helicopter crew for one man. As a gesture of solidarity, they flicked their landing lights on and off, to let the man know that they knew where he was and would come for him in the morning, showing our confidence that he would make it, although I'm not sure we were all that convinced he would survive until morning.

The command hadn't sent in the Vietnamese Rangers right away, as they hoped the Jolly Green Giant or the Marine CH-46 would save the day. As the day wore on, though, this hope pretty much vanished. When the Jolly Green Giant failed get the job done, we should have realized that there was no choice but to put troops in on the ground. I think we should have seen this outcome from the beginning.

That evening Assionte and Allen finally decided to send in the Vietnamese First Ranger Company right after dawn broke. Livingston would command them.

We prepared ourselves as best we could for bad news. But to our surprise and joy, the next morning the helicopters reported a small piece of pink paper (which turned out to be a pay slip) fluttering in the elephant grass. Our man was still alive and free! They dropped a bundle to him with a rifle and a radio, letting him know about it by loudspeaker.

Operations usually look a lot better on paper than they do in practice. When the Rangers landed, the enemy shot up one of the rear engines of a CH-46, which crashed. The Rangers had to wait until another helicopter could pick up the crew. Then a sniper shot one of the Rangers, and they had to wait an hour until we took out the wounded man before they could start moving again.

As long as the Rangers moved fast, the operation looked to be fairly straightforward. The Rangers knew where the man was, and if they fanned out, they should find him easily enough. Furthermore, the man would have heard the Rangers come in and would naturally come down to meet them. So I couldn't understand what was taking so long.

When the Rangers finally reached the top of the ridge, they set up a perimeter and sent a platoon down to check the wreck. The men found pieces of the helicopter scattered everywhere. Fearing booby traps, they searched very slowly and deliberately. They broke the breaches of the helicopter's two machine guns to keep the enemy from getting them. However, they found no traces of anyone and refused to search beyond the wreckage for fear of being ambushed.

Livingston chose to sweep the slope to the east, which proved to be fortunate because around 5:00 he made radio contact with Hall, the gunship's right door gunner. After the linkup with Hall, who was stressed and exhausted and could barely stand, the question remaining was whether the other two men from the gunship, Cochran and Wrobleski, were still alive and hiding somewhere.

We would never have asked the Rangers to spend a night in the valley if finding Hall hadn't raised our hopes of finding Cochran and Wrobleski. Now we had to face our own responsibility for attempting the valley floor in the first place. Guilt over this decision now weighed on us almost as heavily as the danger to the men. The enemy had had twenty-four hours to assemble a regiment of two or three thousand men who could attack the Rangers and overwhelm them.

Our worries were relieved the next morning when Livingston radioed that the Rangers were all right, but the longer Livingston stayed out there, the more time he gave to the enemy. Livingston got the Rangers moving again and got them to the top of the ridge, but they didn't find anybody and no signals were seen from the air, so Assionte ordered Livingston to send the Rangers back down to the wreck. We had found Hall and seen Cochran, but there had been no sign of Wrobleski, the co-pilot, and we began to think Wrobleski had crawled into the brush to hide, perhaps too badly hurt to put out a signal panel. If not already dead, he would be suffering terribly from thirst.

The exhausted Rangers refused to go down to the wreck again, and Livingston lacked the power to compel them. If the enemy hadn't set up an ambush the first night, no power on earth could convince the Rangers that they hadn't done so by now. Livingston did manage to persuade them to try slightly farther to the west, and a little more than a hundred yards from where they had spent most of the last two days they found Cochran, who had fallen off the cable with Hall. The Rangers had missed Cochran while going up the first day and then missed him again while coming down, when they found Hall.

After the Rangers found Cochran, the command thought we had pushed our luck far enough and wanted to get the men out of the valley. Assionte now ordered sixteen CH-46 choppers from the Marines, four times as many to take out the Rangers as we had used to put them in. We bombed the surrounding ridges and tried to land the helicopters halfway down the slope, but the enemy shot them off, and the pilots agreed to take the Rangers out only on the valley floor.

After the helicopters got shot off on the first try, the Vietnamese lost all discipline. Livingston tried to maintain some kind of order, but he couldn't prevent the Rangers from taking the same route down that they had used going up, with predictable consequences: at the bottom, the Rangers ran into the enemy waiting for them, and three men were killed. Panic ensued, and then it was every man for himself. The Rangers ran for the helicopters through the chaff and dust thrown up by the downdrafts; some of them barely missed being turned into mincemeat by the tail rotors. No one stopped to help any man who stumbled and fell—such was our fear of the valley.

* * *

I wanted Livingston to tell me what it had been like out there, and while he showed little inclination to go through it all again, he somehow enjoyed laughing about it.

"When we got off the choppers, they just stood there looking at the elephant grass. I had to run up and down behind them, yelling, and chase them in. I had to do this all the way up the ridge. If they'd gone any slower, they would have been standing still." He grinned at the memory.

"There were machine guns shooting at the helicopters all the time, but the snipers were the worst thing. Every time a round went off, I was certain it was aimed at me."

I asked him about trying to get the Vietnamese to go down to the wreck again. "Are you kidding?" he said. "They looked at me like I was crazy. I would have had to shoot some of them first. Hell, then they would have shot me."

Larrabee later gave me his version of the decision to send in the Rangers. After the Jolly Green Giant had failed to rescue the downed crew, everything had fallen on Assionte, and his responsibility grew heavier with every minute he gave the enemy.

Major Tat made things worse. Assionte might have had four men out there, but if we sent in the Rangers, Tat would have almost seventy, and Tat would not pretend that sending the Rangers onto the open valley floor remotely resembled a normal operation. He refused to go along unless we made it worth their while by paying them double. All Vietnamese recon members got double for each day on recon (which I found disillusioning when I learned about it). The Rangers, Tat felt, deserved the same thing.

According to Larrabee, Assionte almost turned purple when he heard this demand. Everything he had always known about the Vietnamese was likely running through his mind—their venality, corruption, and lack of ideals. We were risking our lives to bring the Vietnamese democracy and free them from oppression, seeking nothing for ourselves, but the Vietnamese saw the war only as an opportunity to shake us down. The pilots had been shot down while altruistically trying to rescue the Vietnamese, and now the Vietnamese wouldn't do anything for us unless we submitted to their blackmail. This view was not entirely accurate—the Americans weren't seeking only freedom for Vietnam—but regarding the Vietnamese themselves, it was pretty much on the mark.

According to Larrabee, Tat read Assionte's thoughts. It was as if Assionte had said them out loud. Tat stiffened, no doubt recalling decades of colonial humiliation and oppression by the French and now by their successors, the Americans. If his soldiers lacked the Americans' supposed altruism, it was because they lacked Americans' high salaries.

Assionte tried to trap Tat with army budget rules. The Rangers' salaries were a line item, and Assionte couldn't just move funds around any way he wanted, nor could mere mortals change budget rules, whether on the fly or otherwise. Assionte thought he had Tat, but Tat knew the Americans had cash coming out of their ears and could find the money anywhere in the budget they wanted, like anyplace else in the world.

They were in a standoff all afternoon, with Assionte barely able to look at Tat and wanting to report him to Nha Trang. Tat, however, knew he had all the cards, and Assionte lost his last bargaining chip when the Jolly Green Giant took out the Vietnamese recon team. This development freed Tat from having to worry about his own men, while Assionte still had Americans out in valley and at the mercy of the North Vietnamese. Moreover, Tat knew from the beginning that Assionte would lose, because if Nha Trang believed that Assionte couldn't get along with his South Vietnamese counterpart, that would ruin him. So, when Hall and Cochran fell off the cable and we lost hope of retrieving them that day, Assionte had to capitulate.

* * *

The next day, Assionte ordered me to accompany the helicopter commander, as Delta's representative, on his visit to Montoya, the wounded pilot, and I got a better understanding of what it had been like out there in the valley. The helicopter commander brought along Cochran, and as we flew out to the hospital ship in Da Nang Bay, Cochran stared half-consciously at the helicopter floor. A beautiful cobalt-blue sea spread out beneath us, small sparkling white waves breaking the surface with large freighters moving across it. The harbor's measureless activity lay below, cranes swinging pallets out of ships onto the docks until no empty space was left and front-end loaders hurrying to get everything into the right warehouses on time.

We landed on a painted white circle at the stern of the hospital ship, a sailor guiding us with stiff, pretentious hand signals. As we got out, Cochran gripped the door tightly to stand up, and the helicopter commander had to help him. Once on the deck, Cochran stared at the commander's heels and struggled to keep up with him, as if he were still out in the middle of the A Shau.

A cheerful nurse, white and spotless, escorted us into the ship, seemingly unconscious of what we were thinking about her. She might as well have been taking us through the Taj Mahal, with the ship resembling conditions we were not used to at all, a marvelous universe of immaculate corridors, polished brass railings, and stainless-steel locks.

When we reached Montoya's room, the nurse peered inside and, smiling gently with the pleasure of bringing us together, said, "Here are some friends to see you." We clumsily stumbled in over the raised threshold. Montoya sat upright in bed with a thick bandage over one eye and several layers of adhesive tape running from his nose back to his ear. A piece of metal with the velocity of a bullet hitting anywhere near someone's eye had to crush it, and we thought Montoya might not want to talk about his injury, so we stared awkwardly at the bandage for a few seconds, until the commander said, "How are you doing?"

"Fine. Fine," said Montoya cheerfully. "How's everybody back at base?"

He began to explain where on the ridge the enemy had fired from and showed no resentment toward the Vietnamese recon team, except to say, "That LZ had high brush and it was killing our lift." He said nothing about his eye, and I began to think he might still have it.

Finally, the commander, lowering his voice, asked delicately, "How's your eye?" And Montoya's answer sticks with me as much as anything I experienced in Vietnam, and I have heard similar answers from others who were wounded in Vietnam a lot more seriously than Montoya.

"Oh, I lost it," said Montoya lightly. "Some piece of the instrument panel blocked the round. An edge must have caught it. You'd think it would go right through it. Hell, I'm lucky I wasn't killed."

The commander tried to lighten Montoya's spirits by telling him about Cochran: "Cochran here was shot down, rolled over inside his chopper four times, and has just spent two nights out in the A Shau Valley." And he turned to the nurse to impress her too. She smiled at Cochran with admiration, and Cochran tried to oblige by twisting his lips into something that he hoped might resemble a smile.

* * *

How we handled the case of Wrobleski provides a good example of how much we conducted the Vietnam War for show. Szwed,

Hall, and Cochran had no idea of what had happened to Wrobleski. One of them thought that he had glimpsed Wrobleski, still strapped in his seat, when he had climbed out of the helicopter, but all were too absorbed in getting themselves out to register what might have happened to anyone else. With the helicopter upside down and the transmission burning, they had to open their seat belts without falling on their heads and then get away before the helicopter exploded. They saw nothing of what went on around them, and by the time Hall and Cochran had joined up, they had moved too far from the helicopter to see anybody who might still be around it.

We didn't know how well the Vietnamese had searched the wreckage the first time. With the enemy having had one night to set up booby traps or ambushes, we would have taken the same care they did, and, on the second day, our decision to ask the Vietnamese to go back down to the wreck raises the question of whether we were asking them to do something we wouldn't have done ourselves.

If the enemy had captured Wrobleski, we should have run into them nearby, but we hadn't, which seemed to rule out that possibility. Wrobleski had to be out there somewhere, either dead or too wounded to signal; otherwise, he would have signaled already. If dead, he could not have died in the wreck, because the Vietnamese would have found him there. Unlike the other men, he might have failed to get out of the helicopter before it exploded and crawled away afterward to die or find someplace to hide. In the latter case, he would now be lying out there, slowly dying.

Since we couldn't prove what had happened one way or the other, we had to carry Wrobleski in our records until we could confirm him as dead. Assionte wanted to make our records look as good as possible. He said he wouldn't stop looking for Wrobleski as long as we were there "if we had one chance in a million" of finding him. Therefore, every day, Assionte had a loudspeaker plane circle this part of the valley and call for Wrobleski to show himself, and he put in our records, "Search for MIA WO Wrobleski continued."

Although this action might look good on paper, it didn't look good in practice. If Wrobleski had been hurt too badly to get up and show himself the first couple of days after the crash, how in the world did anyone expect that, after lying out there for several more days, bleeding and dying of thirst, he could get up now? The loudspeaker plane did, though, allow us to appear as if we were doing something without actually having to do it. If we had really intended to take action, we would have had to send somebody in to look for Wrobleski on the ground, and if the Vietnamese refused to do so, we would have to send in Americans, and Assionte would no more have dared to ask Americans to do this now than he would have dared to ask the Vietnamese.

After the operation, we felt very proud that we had gone into the western side of the A Shau, though we certainly didn't want to do it again. Now everybody at base camp seemed to collapse and the camp as a whole slowed down. The old urgency was gone. We had three more weeks here, but the operation seemed already over, and nobody mentioned parachuting into the A Shau camp again.

By going into the western side of the valley, we had done a lot more than we had set out to do (and much more than the Marines had dreamed possible). We had disproved the notion that you couldn't get into the valley with anything less than a full American battalion.

Assionte benefited the most. Somebody showed up almost every day to pay homage and learn the secret of how we had done it: the American Special Forces deputy commander, the American Special Forces officer in charge of psychological operations, the Vietnamese First Corps commander, the Vietnamese Special Forces First Corps commander, the American Special Forces E Company commander, American Special Forces First Corps commander, and so forth. Assionte explained to them what we did well, what we did less well, and what we needed to do to improve. His guests were invited to lunch, and he conversed with them politely as he escorted them up to the mess tent, handed them their trays, and gestured magnanimously for them to go through the chow line first.

Assionte took advantage of the slower pace to correct aspects of our life that he felt had become lax and to show that he ran as tight a ship in the field as he had back in Nha Trang. He had the mess sergeant put four card tables in the mess tent for officers, complete with pink-and-white checked tablecloths, salt and pepper shakers, silverware, and napkins. On Assionte and Allen's table, the sergeant placed a glass vase containing a plastic flower. Meals, as a result, became unbearable, with the sergeants a few feet away barely concealing their contempt. The tablecloths made the mess sergeant's life miserable. The wind knocked over the salt and pepper shakers and vase and blew the tablecloths all over the place. The mess sergeant was constantly running around, putting them back on the tables. He tried lowering the tent flaps to keep out the wind, but doing so caused the tent to become unbearably hot, and the wind blew in anyway.

Twenty-Eight

While I questioned the effectiveness of our bombing campaign, I have to say I enjoyed participating in it when I flew up with Groth to pick a landing zone for my next patrol. After flying over my area, we flew to the south of the A Shau camp to see whether anything had changed since the last time Groth had flown over this place.

This area had the most bomb craters of anywhere in the valley; the trees had wilted and turned brown, and most seemed to have died. Yellow bomb craters broke up the ground. The road, however, wound steadily around the craters and through the shattered forest; the bombing had not made any real difference.

We believed the enemy stored what they brought down the valley at the point where the road began to disappear under the trees, until they distributed it farther south. Looking down on a narrow strip of trees at a bend in the road, Groth thought that something had changed from the last time he had been here; possibly a storage area had been created. I didn't see anything, but I never questioned anything Groth said he saw.

We dove down for the marking round, the plane bouncing and the clump of woods dancing in front of the cabin window, and I hoped we wouldn't have to deal with sparks of machine gun fire this time around. Groth steadied the plane and fired, and a white cloud of phosphorus smoke blossomed at the southern end of the clump of trees. Groth twisted the plane up to a safe altitude, and the silver wedge of a fighter-bomber raced underneath us, passed over the tree clump, and executed the strike, which caused tons of brown earth to bulge up and then come cascading down. However, the strike didn't quite hit the target, so Groth tried again, with the second run coming closer. Groth had let the enemy know that we knew what they were up to, but he didn't want to waste more bombs on such an insignificant target and said, "Let's try to get something over at A Shau."

I had never seen the camp this close up before, which allowed me to experience its full desolation: the ugly twisted metal and rusted corrugated roofing, the wrecked plane sprawled across the airstrip, and the triangular walls so overgrown with brush that they were almost invisible. The lifelessness of the scene said it all.

Groth perceived an invisible line running through the elephant grass to a couple of corrugated metal sheets east of the camp. He took this to be a trench leading to a bunker and called in a strike, which scored a perfect hit. Suddenly, he exclaimed, "Look! Look! Look at them down there!" He brought the plane lower and started to fire his rifle out the window, operating the plane with one hand and shooting with the other.

I saw nothing until I picked out three black figures sprinting along the edge of the trench, stumbling and falling, getting to their feet and running again, moving through the grass surprisingly fast, too scared to worry about running out in the open. One jumped into the trench, disappearing for a moment, and then leaped out and started running again.

This was the first time I had seen the enemy in the flesh, and I had to do my part. I leaned as far as I could out the rear window and started to fire, unable to get off a good shot because the men kept tripping and falling and the plane bounced all over the place as Groth concentrated more on firing than piloting. First, I tried to aim in front of the running men while fighting the plane's movement. Then I pointed my rifle in the men's general direction and held down the trigger, hoping that by spraying the area, I would have a better chance of hitting something. I got off a second magazine as one of the men reached the end of the trench and seemed to dive under the corrugated metal, but I couldn't see whether we had hit anyone. Neither could Groth, but that didn't keep him from reporting afterward, "Three KIA (prob)."

Challenging the enemy in one of the most dangerous places in Vietnam and flying within the range of their machine guns produced an extraordinary feeling of exultation and invincibility. I felt like I could do anything and wanted to come back and do it again. As we flew up to head back to base, Groth said, "How'd you like that?"

* * *

I had come up pretty dry on all my previous patrols, but now I saw the possibility of doing something big. Previously, I had gone into the unknown, but this time I would be heading into the known: a pinpointed, active target. Almost nineteen miles southwest of base camp and nine miles northeast of the valley, the Vietnamese Rangers had found a camp that appeared to be a command center of some sort, equipped with a mimeograph machine for printing propaganda. Assionte wanted me to see whether the enemy had come back. He believed they wouldn't think that we would check the same place twice, and therefore they might have come back.

The interrogation of a Montagnard prisoner had revealed that the Montagnards could tell the size of our operations by the sound of our helicopters. If they heard the rotors of CH-46s, that meant a company-size operation, while the sound of the smaller, one-rotor Hueys meant recon teams. Consequently, they left our company-size operations alone and only came after the recon teams.

Assionte and Allen considered this a major discovery, although I didn't see why we needed a prisoner to tell us something so obvious.

We would use Livingston and Simpson's An Lao format and put in a twenty-man platoon, this time in Viet Cong clothes and armed with AK-47s and landing in four Hueys to sound like a recon team.

I took being given this patrol as another sign of my prestige, largely because it had originally been assigned to Shelton. Anything associated with Shelton was prestigious; the patrol passed to me when Shelton left to command an A-team. The prospect of a big success seemed to open before me. We could pinpoint our objective, and I didn't see how I could miss, especially with the luxury of going in with a platoon.

This would also be my final patrol. Your final patrol in Vietnam reminded you of what we had all heard since we first arrived in country: men got killed right after they got to Vietnam or right before they left. This wasn't entirely true, of course, but there was enough truth in it to keep you up at night. When guys first came in, they hadn't built up their guard, and then they dropped it just before they left. I now had patrols down cold; the original terror had left me, and so I might get careless without realizing it. I felt this possibility more strongly than ever now because I hadn't yet gotten shot at.

The patrol started on June 8. A couple of the Vietnamese ran in the wrong direction, and I had to grab them and turn them around. On entering the jungle, we ran into the worst thicket I had ever seen; to get through, we had to grab the brambles with our bare hands and bend them out of the way. All the beer I had drunk in Da Nang now caught up with me, and I was drenched in sweat in no time.

As the ground rose and we began to get out of the brambles, a couple of muffled pops sounded up ahead, not much louder than distant bird calls, yet clearly gun fire, and I dropped against the ridge and signaled for the Vietnamese to move up beside me. The Vietnamese looked to the sides for escape but found themselves blocked by the brambles. I had put Strick and Ward, the other two Americans, in the middle of their file to control them, and they now prevented the Vietnamese from running away. Having no other choice, they scrambled up beside me, grateful to be told what to do. My head remained clear. I kept well below the ridge and barely glanced above it, seeing a gray tree root with a spider on it, yellow grains of dirt, and a patch of sunlight on a leaf farther on. As the smell of gunpowder wafted over me, I congratulated myself on reacting so well under fire.

But then this moment turned into one of my most humiliating experiences. When I dropped down behind the ridge, Lieutenant Ninh, the Vietnamese recon platoon commander, did the exact opposite and ran forward to see what had happened to the point man, showing infinitely more courage than I had. Ninh reemerged holding the point man, who stumbled back with blood running down the side of his face. Ninh stopped to examine the man's head, tenderly, as if he were a child.

I now tried to erase the shame I had brought on myself by running up to them, as if taking charge, and to give the man first aid, although if he had been shot in the head, I didn't see what I could do for him. Ninh told me that the man had nothing more than a slight flesh wound from his head hitting his rifle when he fell.

When the point man had entered a small clearing, he found himself facing two Montagnards, who stood looking at him for a few seconds trying to figure out who he was, confused by his Viet Cong clothes and AK-47. Once they realized he was an enemy, they had fired. The point man had dropped to the ground to avoid getting hit and cut his head on his rifle.

I hoped that I had muddied the water enough to save my reputation. Now I raged at losing the best chance I'd had so far to achieve something big. If we had killed the two Montagnards coming off the landing zone, I would have become a recon leader without equal. Instead, the nitwit point man hadn't even thought to shoot when the Montagnards were at his mercy.

I called the FAC to report being shot at but couldn't get him, and I gave up after a few more tries for fear of radio interception. I had never known a FAC to be this sloppy before, and I felt betrayed. The FAC was always supposed to stay up until dark in case something like this happened, and if the point man had been seriously hurt, we would have been in real trouble.

I consoled myself with the prospect of taking revenge the next morning when I radioed that we had been shot at coming off the landing zone but that the FAC hadn't stayed up. Better yet, it would show everybody that I didn't even need their help and could do everything on my own—spending twelve hours under threat of attack without radio contact would be quite a contrast with every other patrol that had gotten shot at and had radio contact immediately.

Even more important, however, was the fact that I would now be able to claim that I could take getting shot at as well as anybody else. Getting shot at was my reason for coming to Vietnam. It may not have been much of a firefight, but it met the specifications and gave me the right to claim I had been in a war. I hadn't experienced a moment of truth or felt any different after being shot at than I had felt before, but I would milk this encounter for everything it was worth, especially as the shots passed within a few feet of me. As the jungle night began to settle in, I felt grateful.

Our strategy worked perfectly. The Montagnards had come down thinking we were a recon team and backed off when they sensed a larger force, failing to come after us that night, although since I had a platoon, I almost hoped they would.

I saw the enemy camp as an easy target and didn't see how I could possibly miss. I planned to dupe the enemy by heading north for two days and then turn east to the ridge that led to the scorched spot in the jungle I had spotted with Groth. This was where the Rangers had burned the camp. If the Montagnards followed us, they would think we were off on some wild goose chase and after a couple of days would lose interest and give up.

This patrol also meant a lot to me because of my relationship with Ninh, and my admiration for him grew as I watched his conscientiousness and care for his men, Vietnamese relationships differing qualitatively from ours. Ninh understood each of his men deeply, knew their emotions and anxieties, and cared for them almost like a father. He seemed to guide them by telepathy and knew exactly what each man was doing even if he couldn't see him.

I didn't interfere, except occasionally to remind Ninh of our direction. When we stopped for the night, he went to place each man on the perimeter. He judged each man's angles of fire, checked his rifle and ammunition, and weighed his water. Ninh didn't return to begin his own meal until each of his men had started theirs. After watching him, I felt like selfishness incarnate.

On the second day, we turned east, crossed a stream, and reached the ridge that led to the camp, not having run into anybody or sensed anyone following us, and by the third night we had moved down the ridge far enough to attack the next morning. After three days, the sound of our helicopters would have become a distant memory and the camp would no longer be on the lookout for us.

On the morning of June 11, we approached the camp from uphill and could see light through the trees. It was a steep, muddy descent, with men slipping and making noise. I had to count on the enemy being unprepared for our approach and less than on their guard. We got down to the level of the camp, where large fallen trees and mats of vines blocked our path, and the going became very difficult. I asked Ninh to go ahead to take a look, since he moved even more nimbly than I did and could read the signs better. He took a long time to get to where he could see something, and when he reappeared, I tried to read his face but saw nothing. He had in fact found nothing.

Impossible! I climbed over the logs to look for myself and saw only a sea of burned trees all toppled and tangled together, the wood smelling in the hot sun and flies swarming around the knots. It had been like this for a long time. A ways off, a metal canister from a napalm strike glinted in the sunlight. This was a misjudgment on my part, because I should have known that no one could possibly burn a hole this big in the jungle by setting a small camp on fire.

I had performed perfectly. But now I faced the same awful sense of failure I had felt on my last patrol when I failed to find the road. I blamed it all on the lieutenant who had led the Rangers and didn't deserve to be a lieutenant if he couldn't plot his own map coordinates.

I didn't give up, though. If the Air Force had napalmed this ridge, they must have seen the fires from the camp, so the camp had to be around here somewhere. I asked Ninh to have his men scour the slope for it, expecting him to balk at sending his men all over a hillside to look for something so vague. His men might make it over only a few logs before calling it a day or get so lost that we would have to go out and look for them. Yet Ninh undertook this task as wholeheartedly as he did everything else, and so did his men. While I wondered whether I would see them again, they searched every inch of the slope and found their way back in an hour—unfortunately emptyhanded.

Suddenly, a man hurried up to report a trail by the stream below us, and we descended to take a look at it. The man led us a hundred yards along the creek bottom to a bend in the stream, where he pointed at the jungle to indicate that we had come far enough. This part of the jungle looked no different from any other, and I didn't understand what he was trying to tell me. Then the man went over and swept aside a branch to reveal a well-packed trail behind it. No American would have found it.

The trail's incredible camouflage displayed the skill of those who had lived their entire lives in the jungle and whom we considered inferior. You would never have suspected the presence of a trail here. Those using the trail could approach up the stream bed without leaving tracks and disappear into the jungle without anybody having the faintest idea of what had happened to them.

I took the risk of having us walk on the trail. If we moved through the jungle alongside the trail, we would make noise and move too slowly to surprise the camp, and I trusted the Vietnamese to sense the presence of any sentries before we got there.

We moved quietly under the jungle arches and looked nervously around us. Suddenly, the Vietnamese near me froze, whispered among themselves, and then advanced even more slowly, the men spreading out and getting ready to fire. The thatch of two low huts appeared among the leaves, and we stopped, although we needn't have, as the huts were empty. They smelled strongly of sweat, probably from the Montagnards who had shot at us the first day. It was not much of a command center.

The huts, nevertheless, represented remarkable craftsmanship, with thatch a foot thick, perfectly aligned, and strong enough to withstand any monsoon, as well as two symmetrical hardwood posts, six inches thick and polished like mahogany, at the entrance. Inside, the lattices supporting the roof were beautifully lashed together, and the crossbeams connecting the walls sleeved neatly into each other. It must have taken the Montagnards a long time to build these structures.

Before I knew it, the Vietnamese started taking out their

frustrations by demolishing everything inside the huts, and Ninh made no effort to stop them. Then they lit the thatch with cigarette lighters. The fire spread quickly, and the ammunition inside began to explode.

This development, of course, meant that setting an ambush was no longer an option. The smoke from the burning huts would give us away. I should have stopped the Vietnamese when the first cigarette lighter came out, but I hadn't. Without consciously thinking it through, I had allowed the chance of ambushing the enemy to slip away. I would be coming out the next day, and a successful extraction would mean I had survived Vietnam, barring some strange mishap or accident. I saw no real reason to bring unnecessary danger on myself at the last minute.

We left the huts and went to watch the clearing where we would come out the next day, doubting the Montagnards would come after us. The next morning, June 12, the sound of the Marine CH-46 turned the clearing into a theater of glory, bravery, victory. I had finished my last patrol, survived Vietnam, beaten everybody else in recon, and finally been shot at to boot. I hadn't really done much of anything, but, like many men who served in Vietnam, I knew that when I got back to the States, everyone would believe that I had been a courageous warrior.

As we waited on the edge of the clearing, Allen radioed that the pilot wanted us to check the clearing for booby traps.

"What?" I asked.

"Roger. Check it."

I didn't know whether I was dealing with a traumatized pilot or some new, ridiculous Marine rule. The enemy had no reason to booby trap a clearing like this one. We were far behind the normal fighting lines, and the enemy would never expect a helicopter to land here. Furthermore, I had sent patrols around the clearing the previous evening and again in the morning, and they had found nothing.

I spread the men out, we searched the clearing, and I radioed to Allen that it was clear. Allen answered, "He wants you to pull up all the roots and bushes."

"What?" I said. "Say again."

"He wants you to pull up all the roots and bushes."

"That will take an hour!"

"Pull up all the roots and bushes. That's an order."

It took a special kind of pilot to have us pull up the roots and

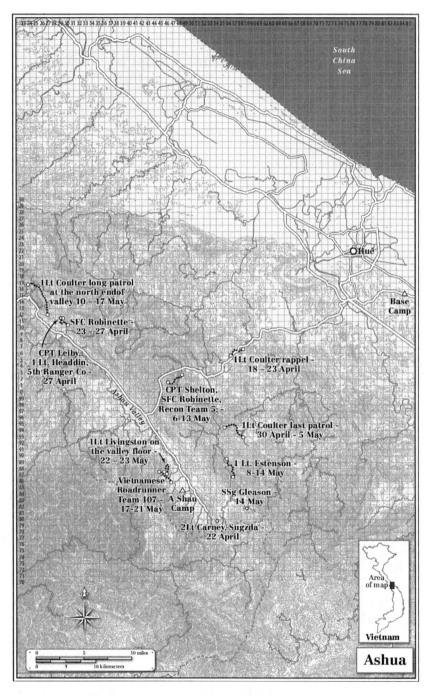

A Shau map. All our major patrols during our greatest operation.

bushes like this, out in the open and deep in enemy territory, while he flew around in a large armed helicopter. The roots and bushes were well grown in, and we had to use both hands to pull them up and, obviously, put down our rifles while we did it. This idiocy or madness of the roots and bushes encapsulated everything we in recon had always felt about everybody else, and I burst out laughing at how easy the Marines made it for us to show how much braver we were than them.

Twenty-Nine

When Shelton left to become head of his A-team, I became the new recon platoon leader. The promotion depended strictly on seniority, and since I had the most time in grade in recon, it went to me. I flattered myself, nevertheless, that I deserved it. I had finished all my patrols without losing a man and had spent more time on patrol than anybody else. At the same time, I knew I couldn't achieve Shelton's level of authority. I just didn't see how I could fill his shoes. The sergeants in particular were not going to give me the same level of respect Shelton had achieved.

I also feared what every officer fears when he takes command of his equals—that I would become one who forgets the men he has worked with, while they in turn would think all the power had gone to my head. In their careers, the sergeants had already experienced this development at the hands of young lieutenants more times than they cared to remember, and they probably wouldn't do something I asked them to do as readily as they would for Shelton. I didn't dare give them anything resembling an order.

The issue came to a head on one of our last nights at A Shau, when Assionte called a practice alert. The recon platoon had responsibility for firing the mortar to light up the area with flares, and the sergeants took charge immediately, with Simpson sighting the mortar. I feared to say anything that might show I knew less about this task than they did and stood off to the side. At the same time, I feared that if I didn't take charge, the sergeants would think I was afraid of them, and so I tried to look as if I knew exactly what I was doing but, like a good commander, wanted to show my confidence in my men by giving them responsibility. I'm pretty sure, though, that the sergeants saw right through me.

I don't know how long this situation might have continued if it hadn't been for the incident on our last night. We had taken down the tents and gone to sleep behind the remaining sandbag walls, while several sergeants took the jeep over to the Marine Enlisted Men's Club at Phu Bai. Around midnight, a jeep screeched to a stop on the other side of the sandbags two feet from my ear, and I heard Brown and Stanfield shouting, "Those goddamn motherfuckers! We're going to blow the shit out of them! Put the rifles and the M-79 under the hood."

I pretended to sleep, not wanting to spoil their fun, until my responsibility dawned on me, and I got up. The light from the jeep's headlights reflecting off the sandbags revealed Brown and Stanfield weaving unsteadily around the open jeep's hood, with a couple of rifles lying across the engine.

"Okay," I said. "What's up?"

Although he could barely stand, Brown tried to explain. "Those goddamn motherfuckers said that one of them is worth three of us, and we're not going to take any of that shit. We're putting the rifles under the hood to get them past the gate."

"Okay," I said. "Take them back." They sheepishly took the rifles off the engine and stumbled back to where their tent had been.

My position was unassailable, and even as drunk as they were, they knew it. In reality, they hadn't really wanted to go through with the attempt and were just as happy to have me stop them. Most important, I had my first opportunity to show that I wasn't afraid of sergeants and to impose my authority without looking as if I was throwing my weight around. I thought I had handled the situation well.

Thirty

After A Shau, we knew no one could match us; nobody could do what we did. We lived by our own laws, others stepped aside for us, and when Assionte threw us a party after the last elements returned, it allowed us to revel in these feelings as never before.

Assionte cleared out the mess hall, filled several trash cans with iced beer, and hired a German stripper who had come to Vietnam for the U.S. military market and had already taken Nha Trang by storm. He probably used up all the discretionary funds in the budget. We started off in the usual separate groups, with Assionte, Allen, and Larrabee at the head table, but Assionte got up and mixed a bit with his troops, asking us, "How do you like the party?"

After the beer had warmed us up, distinctions of rank dissolved, and we gravitated to the men we had gone on patrol with. We knew each other inside out, each of us having proved his worth to the others, and we imagined no higher privilege than being among such men.

We were pretty drunk. Brown climbed up on a chair, holding the back carefully, and stood on it, swaying back and forth, saying several times, "I want to say something." He screwed up his face, trying to remember what it was, but couldn't, and several men had to reach up to help him down.

Nothing makes you feel better than being told you are as good as you hope you are, and the sergeants now treated me as an equal and even seemed to want to listen to me. There was no greater compliment that could come from these men, who looked for nothing except whether you had guts, men impossible to hide from or deceive because you lived together twenty-four hours a day.

Even Markham and Robinette came up to tell me I had done a good job, and that meant a lot coming from them. Simpson, however, paid me the highest compliment of my life. Drunk and barely able to stand, he said, "Sir, I'd follow you anywhere."

At this point, the German stripper appeared on a stage that had been set up in a corner of the mess hall, dressed in a green, transparent halter that barely reached her thighs. Her large breasts were visible beneath it. Besides the halter, she wore only thin green panties. She began twirling around to the music, swinging the halter above her breasts, and the helicopter crewmen started shouting and whistling until it hurt our ears, stamping their feet and pounding the tables with their beer cans.

After twirling around for a while, she reached down and slipped off her panties. She then proceeded to twirl them around on one foot. This move created absolute pandemonium in the mess hall, with the crewmen losing all control and several falling over backward in their chairs. Then, when the noise could not have reached a higher crescendo, the girl called for a volunteer, and the crewmen chanted for the gunship commander. The gunship commander normally wore a red bandana, leather vest, and shoulder holster, and three days earlier he had been leading gunship runs at tree level. He resisted, smelling trouble, but the crewmen's shouting gave him no choice, and he came forward slowly, clearly wishing he was someplace else.

Once he got up on the stage, the girl unbuttoned his shirt and took off his pants, undressing him down to his shorts. She took off the gauze halter dress, so that she was now naked, and put it around the major's neck. Then she took his shorts and peeked inside, feigning shock and giggling for the audience's benefit. Finally, she took the halter off him and twirled in circles around him, while the major stood looking at the ceiling, wishing this would end as soon as possible.

It remains a mystery to this day why the crewmen didn't take off the mess hall roof. They fell into each other's arms laughing and crying, pounded on the tables, and hit each other on the head with their beer cans. Someone shouted, "This sure beats the hell out of Charlie!" The girl chose this moment to slip out the back, and the gunship commander sourly picked up his clothes and got dressed.

We drank until the beer ran out around 2:00 in the morning, went to sleep and got woken up at 4:30 to make sure we got to the Vietnamese compound on time for an awards ceremony. Everybody had a massive hangover. No one knew what the medals were for except that they had something to do with An Lao, now so long ago that nobody remembered what had happened. We assumed the Vietnamese had put together something as a courtesy—one that we were to discover came with a heavy price.

We had breakfast at 5:00, but the truck to the Vietnamese compound wasn't leaving until 7:30. We spent the next two and a half hours trying to stay upright by leaning against the barracks walls. If we had sat down, we never would have gotten up.

When we got to the Vietnamese compound, twenty minutes away, we found it empty except for helmets in formation on the ground. One of the sergeants said, "I'm glad they waited around for us." Arriving this early, however, gave us plenty of time to practice, and we began to understand the genius with which this event had been organized. The Vietnamese wanted us to run out and form a line in front of the helmet formation. This wouldn't have been so bad except that doing so involved running over the compound's egg-sized rocks. The rocks made for bad footing even in the best of circumstances, without hangovers, and the sergeants took one look at them and said, "Holy shit!"

The ceremony didn't start until 10:00, so we had time to see whether we could actually run across the rocks. It turned out that one Vietnamese soldier had been waiting for us—the bugler, whose job it was to sound the call to let us know when to run out. His bugling was hardly better than our running. "I hope he doesn't die in the middle," said Simpson.

The morning grew hotter, and the rocks began to burn through our boots. Meanwhile, the beer from the night before began to make itself truly felt. We hobbled over the rocks, swearing under our breath, and improved only out of terror at the thought of having to keep on practicing. When none of us could take it any longer, they let us take a break beneath some trees, although they didn't let us sit down. Simpson said, "Don't anybody breathe on him when he gives you your medal, or he'll get alcoholism."

As the morning sun approached its scorching peak, the Vietnamese emerged from their barracks and took up their positions. The bugler managed a bugle call, someone shouted "Ugh" for "attention" in Vietnamese, and we managed to make it across the rocks. General Quang, the Vietnamese Special Forces commander, drove up in a French Citroën, accompanied by two pretty girls holding our medals on red pillows. As Quang came down the line, he stopped in front of each of us, pinned on our medal, and shook hands. Out of the corner of my eye, I caught sight of men rocking back and forth and struggling not to fall down.

When General Quang finished, the bugler bugled again and somebody shouted "Ugh, Ugh" for "parade rest." Finally, we could hobble back over the rocks to the truck. But suddenly the bugler bugled once more, somebody shouted "Ugh" for "attention," and they began to play a tape-recorded speech in Vietnamese over the loudspeakers, and not a brief formality either, but a major treatise.

The sun was no joke by now, and the air of the compound shimmered in the heat. We could barely hold ourselves up any longer. Each time the taped speech seemed about to end, the speaker broke forth with a new flow of words. I fought hard to think about something else but could focus only on trying to make it through the next sentence. The tape finally stopped, the bugler bugled, and again, thankfully, we heard "Ugh, Ugh." Surely our ordeal was now at an end. But then the bugler bugled yet again, someone shouted "Ugh" for attention, and they played the other side of the tape.

When the bugle called us to parade rest again, we were sure this was just one more diabolical hoax and waited for whatever they would come up with next. When it appeared that we had actually been dismissed, we couldn't believe it at first and stood there motionless. When we discovered that it truly was time to leave, Livingston said, "Jesus Christ! I don't know what the hell I did before to get this medal, but I sure as hell earned it today. They couldn't get me to do this again if they paid me."

Thirty-One

A few days after the party, Estenson came into the barracks and said, "What did you do wrong? Assionte wants you in the orderly room on the double."

As I entered, the sergeant major looked right through me. Captain Craft, the S-1 (personnel), jumped up from behind his desk and followed me to Assionte's office, swinging his arms dramatically. I knocked on Assionte's door, and he bellowed, "Get in here!" As I went inside, Craft grabbed a chair from outside, shut the door, and sat back against the wall to watch.

Assionte's voice quivered with rage. "Who do you think you are, Coulter? Who told you that you could trade men around to other units behind the sergeant major's back? What do you think? That we all sit around here with our thumbs up our asses?"

"Sir?"

"Stanley told the sergeant major that you gave him permission to transfer to Shelton's A-camp!"

All became clear. A couple of days earlier, Stanley had come to me and asked whether I minded if he transferred to Shelton's A-team. Stanley looked on Shelton as a god and seemed to have gotten Shelton to agree to put Stanley on his team if Stanley could get out of Delta. I knew Stanley didn't like recon and had done all he could to avoid going on patrols, and it made no sense to have somebody in recon who didn't want to be there (and who wasn't much use anyway). So I told Stanley it was all right with me as long as he checked with the sergeant major first and got somebody from Shelton's team to trade places with him.

Stanley had obviously come to me first, believing that I was a softer touch, in order to sandbag the sergeant major by telling him that I had given my permission. Now I understood why Craft had followed me in.

We had called Craft a "strap-hanger" for coming up to Phu Bai when, as S-1, he had no business there; he had come simply to jump on our bandwagon and bask in our glory. He flew on a couple of reconnaissance flights over combat areas in order to qualify for a Combat Infantryman Badge, and you can probably imagine how we took that. I have no doubt that Craft got wind of this development and would have resented my supposed actions the most. I had already sensed that he hated me, because as S-1 he knew that I had gone to Harvard, while he had not gone to college and had worked his way up in the army on his own. For me to succeed in his profession was more than he could take.

"No, sir," I said. "That's not true. I didn't give Stanley permission. I told Stanley I didn't mind as long as he asked the sergeant major first."

Assionte had primed himself to bring fire and brimstone down on me, but now he realized what Stanley was trying to do. His face clouded over, and he said quietly, "You did, huh?" I could actually feel Craft deflate behind me.

"Yes, sir."

"Don't ever let it happen again. Now get out of here!"

"Yes, sir." I saluted and left, having prevailed in office politics as well as recon, with the extra pleasure of knowing that Craft had to take his chair back outside.

My next victory lacked this drama but ended my oldest battle. One evening before chow, while Estenson and I were leaning on the sandbags in front of our barracks and chatting, I asked him, "Who started the rumor that I was a spy for Assionte?"

I had never thought that this story was a brainchild of Heddern's. While I didn't like Heddern, I also didn't think he would pull this type of thing on his own; he was a follower rather than an instigator. However, the whole business had been so hurtful that I had just tried to put it behind me.

With the passage of time, the situation had changed radically in my favor. The issue of my supposedly being a spy had lost any possible relevance it may have had when the accusation was first made by Heddern. I had proved myself beyond any doubt, and everybody had observed me long enough to know that I had integrity.

Estenson said simply, "Larrabee."

I had to be as dumb as the day I was born not to have figured this out. Of course, it was Larrabee! He had been doing this kind of thing for as long as I had known him, probably for his whole life, a gift from birth. Nobody else in Delta came close to Larrabee as an intriguer and spreader of slander, and everybody in recon except me had known that Larrabee had tried to stab me in the back.

* * *

As recon platoon leader, I intended to seal my reputation by instituting some reforms, using my authority to inspire the men and instill a new focus on nuts and bolts. I hoped to revolutionize recon and change it irreversibly.

I had more authority than anybody else, because no one had been out there and knew what it was like better than I did or had reduced recon to such a fine art. The key was picking an obscure landing zone and staying lost for three days. Once you knew how to do this, you knew everything.

I started by calling everybody together at the beginning of training, looking them in the eye and speaking to them as equals. I told them they were the best men on the planet, so that they would idolize me and want to live up to my expectations. I also wanted them to believe in their competence because I did. I then added that the entire unit revolved around them and that I was there simply to serve them, so that they would feel they were the most important people in the world. When I looked into their eyes, I saw trust and admiration.

* * *

My friendship with Ninh meant as much to me as the sergeants' respect; I hadn't met a finer man in Vietnam, Vietnamese or American. Although I could have figured out a lot of what I learned from Ninh on my own, this didn't stop me from believing that while other lieutenants might invite their Vietnamese counterparts into the barracks, none possessed the deep insights into Vietnamese life that I had gained from Ninh.

I attributed a lot of this understanding to my French. Ninh

Lieutenant Ninh at A Shau, just before we left on our Roadrunner Operation; one of the finest men I have met in my life.

spoke French fluently, having studied at the Dalat French officers' school. French was more natural to him than English, and French allowed us to understand each other in way that would have been impossible in English. The other Americans couldn't understand us, and Ninh could express thoughts in French that would have been impossible to convey in English. Speaking French also freed us from the clichés Vietnamese and Americans used about each other, which on both sides simply boiled down to "That's the way they are."

I let the sergeants run the training and spent much of the day in the platoon room with Ninh, learning how the feelings of the Vietnamese differed from ours and how personal relations played a great role in their units.

One morning, one of his privates came in and began to talk to Ninh without the slightest deference in his voice or mannerisms, in a way that no American sergeant would have done with me. The man poured out his confidences, and Ninh bowed his head and listened carefully, interrupting a few times to ask questions. The man talked for quite a while, and when he finished, Ninh let him go with a couple of words. After the man left, Ninh said to me, "His grandmother is sick and he wants a couple of days' leave, so I gave it to him. I always listen to my men when they want to talk. Even a stupid man can give an intelligent man good ideas."

Ninh invited me to a coffee house in the center of Nha Trang, right on the edge of one of the town's busiest streets. I hadn't known there were coffee houses in Nha Trang or that Vietnamese frequented them. This one must have had a special standing for Ninh to choose it; yet it seemed like an unremarkable cookie shop and, in any case, would be of no interest to most Americans, since it didn't serve beer.

The owners had crammed the shelves with boxes and jars in no particular order, and the dusty glass cases beneath the counter were filled with cookies and cakes. I couldn't see how they could sell so many. Four small, unsteady iron tables stood in one corner with equally unsteady iron chairs beside them.

Ninh ordered black coffee and a plate of Vietnamese cookies. He brought the saucers with coffee and cookies over and watched intently as I tasted the cookies, worried that they might not be acceptable. The strong black Vietnamese coffee was delicious, although the cookies didn't impress me.

Ninh had put all his feelings into this gesture, considering it an obligation and a privilege to show hospitality to a foreigner who had come to his country, and I made sure to show him that I appreciated it.

A few days before we started training patrols, Ninh invited me to his home to introduce me to his wife, the highest compliment he could pay me, showing that I had won his trust and that he was convinced I didn't look on the Vietnamese with the condescension typical of Americans. As far as I knew, Vietnamese never invited Americans into their homes. I attributed this to their feelings of inferiority—feelings that sprang from the fact that they were poor in comparison with us.

Ninh, his wife, and their child occupied an eight-foot square concrete cubicle, open in front, in a row of similar cubicles. A frayed hammock was in one corner and a small, blue propane stove in the other. This was government housing for married officers, one cell per family—a humbling contrast to our luxury, yet immeasurably more luxurious than the Vietnamese enlisted men's quarters.

Ninh introduced me to what he cared for the most in his life: his young wife, pretty and demure, holding their very young, naked son. She stood in the opening shyly, watching with wonder and barely daring to smile when I said, "Hello."

Ninh invited me to take a walk, which was the purpose of his invitation. Children were playing on the trash-littered stubble in front of the cubicles, and delicious odors and the sound of talk and laughter filled the air as families prepared dinner. The air became cooler as day started turning into night.

As we got up to where the concrete cubicles ended, Ninh took what for him was a fateful step and honored me with a trust I will always remember. "I just don't know what to do ..." he said, his voice trailing off.

He didn't need to finish. I understood immediately what he meant. Ninh didn't know what he was fighting for anymore. He was taking a big risk in confiding this problem to me.

For the first time, I saw the great difference between the Vietnamese and the American view of the war, although I should have seen it much earlier. Americans saw the war as unambiguous right versus unambiguous wrong, righteousness against evil, no subtleties. From our perspective, it was the straightforward issue of stopping the communists, drawing the line, keeping communism from spreading one more inch. It was our world against theirs, freedom against oppression, the battle America had fought throughout our history, and we couldn't have conceived it any other way.

We assumed that those who had sent us to war were wiser than we were and knew what they were doing. The overwhelming scale of our enterprise by itself made us right. We wouldn't go halfway around the world and make such an effort unless it was the right thing to do. The black-and-white nature of military life leads you to no other outlook anyway. When you spend every second considering the other side your enemy, you aren't going to go back and reexamine the underlying premises. Of course the enemy is bad, and you are good and right; otherwise you wouldn't be doing this.

Ninh, however, saw this situation very differently and had to ask himself whether he was fighting for his people or for the Americans. The war had become an American war by now, run by Americans, no matter how much we tried to pretend to cooperate with and consult the Vietnamese. From our point of view, so much was at stake that we couldn't possibly worry about whether we were humiliating the Vietnamese or violating their sovereignty. The Vietnamese were too underdeveloped to know what they should do, and we had to guide them, being much better qualified to decide what was best for them than they were. There was, of course, more than a bit of racism in this thinking.

As much as Ninh might like the Americans, and maybe even sympathize with us, he couldn't avoid facing the possibility that he might not be fighting for the Vietnamese or for Vietnam, or even defending his own honor as a soldier and a man. Instead, he was serving a foreign power and had become the tool of another country's foreign policy, possibly having nothing to do with him, no matter how fine the American justifications for being in Vietnam sounded.

Ninh hated the Viet Cong and North Vietnamese, but he recognized that they fought out of genuine patriotism and weren't somebody else's puppet or surrogate (Soviet and Chinese help notwithstanding). They put national aspirations and patriotism above themselves, and I'm sure that on one level Ninh admired them for this.

At the same time, however, Ninh hated their ruthless ideology and dreaded to think of what would happen to Vietnam if their side won. The Viet Cong and North Vietnamese carried their dubious theories down to the smallest, stupidest details and terrorized anyone who refused to conform; they would kill their own sisters if they had to. Ninh couldn't support them, and if he tried to change sides, he would be killed by one side or the other—by the South Vietnamese government as a traitor or by the communists as a provocateur or spy.

Ninh had no illusions about his own side. The American war effort gave South Vietnamese generals and officials a spectacular opportunity to enrich themselves under the cloak of good intentions, and they certainly went ahead and did so. Ninh found himself fighting not only for the Americans but also for the corruption-riddled South Vietnamese government.

Amid contradictions that touched him vitally but didn't affect me at all, Ninh had to force himself to go out on patrol, month after month, year after year, something that would go on long after I left, and Ninh put his heart into it, because he was a sincere man and not a mercenary. Besides, he had to earn his living, had no other profession, and had probably considered the military a noble calling when he had first joined.

We continued walking in silence, and I struggled to understand how I could have been so insensitive to the view of the war held by so many South Vietnamese. As we turned to go back, Ninh said, "I had a chance to transfer to a regular unit, but Major Tat asked me to stay."

This revelation brought out again how differently Ninh saw things. For him, everything depended on personal relations, and if somebody he looked up to asked him to risk his life, he wouldn't think twice about it. With a broad smile, Ninh added proudly, "Major Tat always puts the right man in the right place."

Thirty-Two

When I was working in Secret Documents, Kim Chi used to sing three times a week at the headquarters officers' club, and between songs Tom Patterson and I would go over to buy her a Coke and sit with her. She was very pretty and seemed flattered by our attention. Nevertheless, she held herself aloof, and I attributed this stance to her conviction that all Americans only wanted to sleep with Vietnamese women. I hadn't seen her since then and wondered what had become of her.

One time while we were at A Shau, they sent me on leave down to Nha Trang and, after lining up a bar girl for the night, I went to drink at a ramshackle Vietnamese bar on the beach. No one came here except Vietnamese. They danced to deafening music while the sound of the pounding surf filled the night outside.

During one of the breaks, Kim Chi appeared on the lighted floor, a vision of streaming black hair and graceful beauty, and began to sing the most beautiful Vietnamese song I had ever heard, better than anything I had heard her sing at the officers' club.

I hesitated to approach her during the break. Vietnamese bars were less prestigious and paid a lot less than the officers' club, and Kim might not want me to see that she was now singing here. Also, she might not want the Vietnamese to see that she and I, an American, knew each other. Any Vietnamese woman who knew an American was immediately assumed to be a whore.

Yet, somehow, I couldn't resist going over to her. To my delight, Kim's face lit up, and she rushed over, grabbed my hand, and said, "I am so glad to see you. I am afraid I never see you again. I think you are killed or go home." My initial joy, however, was clouded over by the thought that Kim might want to gain status by showing that she knew an American or perhaps to cultivate me for favors I could do later.

When the lights went off, she led me to a small table and pulled me down to sit beside her. We sat on small stools, our knees touching in the dark and Kim's neck smelling of perfume. I offered her a Coke, and she smiled with pleasure. I was at a loss for words at first, but then I asked her why she wasn't still singing at the officers' club.

"The sergeant there not hire me if I don't sleep with him."

"He tried to blackmail you into sleeping with him?"

"Blackmail?" The word was unfamiliar to her.

"A threat. A bribe."

"Yeah," she said softly. "I have to look for Vietnamese bar. But Vietnamese bars bad if I try to get into good clubs," she explained, widening her eyes for emphasis. "Best for me is go to Saigon."

"Are you going to Saigon?" I asked apprehensively.

"Mother, brother, sisters here in Nha Trang. I don't want to go. Once I stay in Saigon for a month, and I miss them very much. I am only one with a job, and I have to give them money."

"Wouldn't other clubs hire you?" I asked.

"Sergeant tell all the other sergeants. And I just learn new American songs, too."

She accepted my offer to dance and, after her next song, returned to sit with me at the table. I hadn't felt this way for so long that I had forgotten what it was like. I never expected to find it in Vietnam. Bar girls were not the same thing—not even close.

I didn't want to miss what I saw as my one chance and overcame my shyness to ask Kim to have lunch with me at Le Fregate, the best restaurant in Nha Trang and much frequented by high-ranking American officers and the cream of Nha Trang society. Kim beamed with pleasure and said, "Thank you. You so nice."

I asked where we could meet, expecting her to suggest some street corner so as to keep from revealing where she lived. But without hesitating she said, "You pick me up at my house," and wrote her address on a slip of paper. I hoped this meant what I thought it did.

The streets were clear at noon the next day, and it took me a while before I found a couple of old men who could tell me where Kim's street was. I found the house, number 11. I rang the bell and heard footsteps, and when she answered the door, I found myself face to face with a beautiful woman in a lovely *ao dai*. We stood for a moment in the courtyard, where chickens pecked among weeds, broken crockery, and twisted pieces of metal. Inside a wrinkled old woman with betel-stained teeth sat on a concrete bench next to a smoldering cooking fire, staring at me as if I had arrived from another planet. With her was a naked, soot-covered little boy. Kim paid no attention to them, and I couldn't figure out how the three of them were related. The boy certainly seemed much too young to be the old woman's child.

Kim flew in and out of the house over last-minute details, her light green *ao dai* billowing around her, and glanced at me happily from time to time. After she made sure everything was all right, she gave the boy a piece of candy and said a few words to the old woman, and we left. Outside I held her hand as she climbed into the jeep, to impress her with my gallantry.

Le Fregate produced the desired effect, and Kim looked around wide-eyed at the opulence, trying to figure out how she should behave. Large wooden ceiling fans turned overhead. A pastry table and a cheese tray, covered with glass to protect them from flies, dominated the middle of the room. The owner hurried over to escort us to a table. Kim seemed impressed by the immaculate white tablecloth, sparkling wine glasses, and glistening silverware, and she caressed the tablecloth to get the feel of it. Everything now seemed to be falling into place. I urged Kim to order the roasted lobster, while I took the filet mignon, so tender it barely needed to be cut. We had salad with a vinegar and oil dressing, thin (and very hot) French fries, and Rhone wine, the bottle leaking around the cork, but the wine glowing in our glasses and tasting of the earth. Behind us chicken wire protected us from grenades, and in the distance, we could hear artillery and bombing.

I tried to read Kim's face for signs of progress, and every time she looked cautious, my spirits fell. Nevertheless, I felt her warmth growing, and when I helped her into the jeep, she put all her weight on my hand. When I left her at her house, before I could ask, she insisted on meeting again.

Back at Phu Bai, I thought about Kim constantly, of her thighs beneath her *ao dai* next to me in the jeep, and planned to give her all my attention when I got back to Nha Trang. We were both adults, and Kim had to know what warm smiles from a grown woman meant to a grown man.

I planned everything out in detail—first getting a jeep, followed by lunch at Le Fregate, after which I would take Kim to the French hotel on the beachfront.

Kim happily agreed to lunch, and the next day after breakfast I asked the sergeant major to reserve a jeep for me. During the morning break, I drove to the hotel and rented a room in the back annex. I was sure the Frenchwoman handing me the key knew exactly what I was up to, as the back annex allowed me to drive up to the room without being seen. The second our training ended at noon, I drove down and picked up Kim, and at Le Fregate she smiled with her usual shy delight and asked me to get her new scores for American songs. At one point she lowered her eyes and told me I wasn't like other Americans she had met.

Nothing had gone wrong so far, but the real test came after we left the restaurant and hit the beach road. To take Kim home, I had to take a left, while getting to the hotel required a right turn. If I turned right, Kim might suspect something, and everything depended on how she reacted. Would she go along, or would she freeze?

I made the right turn. Kim's dress moved as her leg stiffened and she drew in her breath, but she didn't object, which surprised me a little because I hadn't expected her to give in so easily. I still had to make the turn into the hotel's rear courtyard, though, and now I was holding my breath.

I turned into the shadowy alley. Kim again said nothing, and I felt like a gambler who has staked everything on one throw of the dice and won. Once we reached the back of the hotel, however, I ran into an unexpected obstacle. Pots and pans clattered from the kitchen window facing the hotel annex, and this could ruin my plan, because Kim wouldn't want anyone in the kitchen to see her. But I was too committed to stop now. Everything depended on whether Kim would take the chance that nobody in the kitchen was watching.

I stopped at the annex boardwalk, got out of the jeep and up on the boardwalk, and headed to the room without looking back, hoping to give Kim no opportunity to object and guessing she would prefer to jump up and follow me rather than have people in the kitchen see her sitting in the jeep. I walked a few yards in silence, and then I heard Kim's high heels hit the boardwalk behind me. She entered the dark, hot room and went over to turn on the ceiling fan. I had survived Vietnam, gotten shot at, succeeded in recon, and was now about to do something that no one in Nha Trang dreamed possible— have a woman for free.

Kim was quiet when I drove her home. However, she seemed to recognize that we had entered a new phase and agreed to have lunch with me again. A couple of days later, I reserved a jeep, rented the hotel room during morning break, and at noon drove over to her house to pick her up. I rang the bell, but for a long time no one answered. Finally, the old woman opened the door a crack, handed me a note, and then shut the door again. On a page from a child's notepad Kim had written neatly in pencil that she couldn't come today because she had crashed her "Lambretta" and needed sixty dollars.

I stood next to the jeep, hollowed out from the humiliation and certain that passersby knew exactly what had happened. I took the key back to the hotel and drove back to our compound.

I didn't believe it. I had never heard of a Lambretta, and I wondered why Kim thought I would fall for such a story. She was no different from the bar girls, with no inkling of the feelings she had given me every reason to believe she had for me. Kim held to the bar girl principle that if we slept together, I had to pay, while I held to the opposite principle and refused to base our relationship on anything but genuine sentiment, real feelings, even if those feelings wouldn't amount to love.

I put it down to Kim's lack of sophistication. She probably had never been in this situation before and didn't understand my feelings on the subject. She had tried this to see whether it worked. If it didn't, she wouldn't lose sleep over it.

I tried the beach bar several times with no luck. I tried her house in vain. Finally, one night, Kim appeared at the beach bar again, as beautiful as ever, singing with the same lovely voice. I stepped into view to see her reaction, and although she looked a bit ambivalent, she graciously came over and sat with me during her break.

I was direct. "Where were you the other day when we were going to have lunch? I don't believe the story about the Lambretta."

She listened quietly and then said with poise, "Yes, there was," her denial giving me no leverage. However, she didn't become angry or try to tear me apart, as an American woman might have done, which seemed to support my view that she hadn't placed too much weight on this relationship.

She became her usual warm and graceful self, and I fell under her spell once more and invited her to lunch. She seemed overjoyed, and all seemed right with the world again.

Thirty-Three

Our lunch had to wait because the men had just finished classes and I had to run training patrols.

I had made a point of focusing our training on the nuts and bolts, such as looking where you were going when you jumped out of a helicopter; not panicking at fireflies, jungle sounds, or anything else during the first night; and handling each leaf when you moved it as if it might explode. Nobody can understand what this process is like until he does it; these physical and psychological demands are what recon really is about, and if our six new men didn't experience what it was like to jump into brush at twilight, watch fireflies and listen to the jungle all night, and pick apart leaves all day so quietly that someone six feet away couldn't hear them—in other words, learn how fundamentally recon differed from everything they had done so far—I wouldn't have trained them properly. I also had to give the new team leaders (Brown, Bartlett, Kerley, and Stanfield) practice at picking landing zones and not getting lost while flying in.

To make the patrols more realistic, rather than send them across the mudflats, we would put the teams in twelve and a half miles southwest of Nha Trang, an area that was still relatively safe, with no recent reports of the enemy. Besides, we had the Nha Trang airbase at our disposal and no reason to take the same precautions we would for a real patrol.

I had a low opinion of past practice and was convinced that I could get much more to the heart of things; I wanted to use this opportunity to display my genius again. In the past, we had put in two patrols, waited three or four days for them to finish, and then put in the next two patrols, which meant that the second two patrols hung around doing nothing while the first patrols finished, and the first two patrols hung around doing nothing while the later patrols finished. I considered this practice awfully inefficient. We had little enough time to prepare and could save a lot of time by putting all four teams in at once. Nobody had tried this approach before, and once again I could show that I knew how to run circles around everybody else.

Given a flight of fifteen or twenty minutes each way, if we started a little earlier, around 6:00 p.m., we could get the first two teams in around 6:15, have the helicopters come back for the other two teams by 6:30, and still have plenty of time to get them in before dark, at 7:00. The first two teams might not go in exactly at dark, but they would come close enough, and I couldn't understand why nobody had thought of this plan before.

Before the men went in, I called them together and told them that Delta was all nuts and bolts and they had joined one of the toughest units in Vietnam. I emphasized my trust in them again, to make them want to live up to it, and looked closely at Brown, Bartlett, Kerley, and Stanfield, wanting to convey my expectations to them most of all. I felt certain that Brown wouldn't let me down if it was the last thing he did.

You would think that, after seeing it so many times, the sight of men with knives taped to their web gear, grenades and ammunition pouches on their harnesses, green taped rifle barrels, and radio antennas woven into rucksacks wouldn't affect me. Yet I felt a sense of regret and guilt. I would not share their danger this time. I would instead stay back and do nothing, and as they got into the deuce-and-a-half to go to the airfield, while Simpson, the radio operator and I followed in the jeep, I felt almost like a traitor.

Brown and Stanfield would go in first, and the helicopters would then return for Bartlett and Kerley. Brown and Stanfield boarded, and, as their helicopters rose and got smaller over the mountains, all the brotherly love I had felt watching teams go in at An Lao and Phu Bai expanded into a sensation of total power over the men under me and their blind faith in me. No other emotion is able to carry you away so much, fulfill you more—or cause more damage. I felt as if the sky itself was under my power.

Small clouds dotted the pale sky above the mountains and began to turn rose in the sunset. The radio operator had the static turned up, and it broke to announce that Stanfield had gotten in. Then it broke with a report that Brown's helicopter had lost power and was returning. "What?" I said to the radio operator. "Why?"

"Didn't say."

"Is he trying the alternate?"

"No. Just coming back."

This couldn't be true! I had never heard of something like this happening on a training patrol. They had plenty of light, no enemies for miles, with just a hop, skip, and jump over to the alternate site, and it was no more dangerous out there than back in the barracks! How could somebody not get in? Any idiot could do it.

I watched the helicopter reappear and dreaded going up to it when it landed. Brown sat in the door, swinging one leg insolently back and forth and staring down the airfield. "What happened?" I asked.

"The pilot just headed back," he said sullenly.

"Why didn't you try the alternate?"

"Just didn't." He sounded almost belligerent now, not looking at me and basically telling me to go to hell.

I suspected that the reason Brown hadn't gotten in was not because he had lost his nerve but because the sight of the jungle and the thought of spending the night in it had made the thought of spending the night downtown with a bar girl too irresistible.

Brown's behavior destroyed any illusion I had about my authority. I had thought the men would consider my telling them they were the best men in the world the highest compliment they had received in their lives and that they would die before letting me down and proving me wrong. Instead, they saw it as a trick to get more work out of them, and my disillusionment was made even worse by the fact that I thought Brown and I had a special relationship. Now I saw that Brown couldn't stand my authority over him any more than he could stand the authority of other officers.

In my despair, I forgot about Bartlett and Kerley, Bartlett having already left on Stanfield's helicopter and Kerley standing next to me waiting to get on Brown's. The weight of their presence suddenly dawned on me. If I didn't give all of the men the experience of jumping out of a helicopter at dusk and spending the first night in the jungle, I wouldn't have trained them, and I had to send Brown back out to his alternate site and make him spend the night in the jungle, whether he liked it or not, while making sure Kerley spent the night there, too. If I sent Brown back out, though, we might not have enough time to put in Kerley.

I tried to gauge the sky for how much time we had left. Sending Brown back out, having the helicopter come back, and then taking Kerley out meant three trips. The helicopter would be able to return in the dark, and the sky looked light enough to make it, but shadows descend fast in the tropics, especially in the deeper valleys where the teams would land, and I had the disadvantage of always going in on patrol and never having to judge twilight like this before.

I couldn't tell from the sky how much time we had left and now froze in place, just as when I was sighted by the old women at An

Lao. If I gambled on putting Brown in and it didn't work, I would look like a fool for wasting time on Brown that I should have used on Kerley. But if I didn't try with Brown while we still had a chance, I would look like I was letting an enlisted man undermine my authority. With Kerley standing nearby and Brown just sitting in the helicopter swinging his leg back and forth, the pressure on me increased.

Suddenly Assionte appeared as if out of nowhere, in a jeep that came to a screeching halt beside me. He had monitored us on the radio and rushed over the second he heard a team hadn't gotten in. He stepped out of the jeep and approached within a few inches of me, like a sergeant in boot camp.

"What's going on out here, Coulter? Why did you let that goddamn chopper come back?" He was livid, the veins on his neck standing out. He began to pace back and forth next to the jeep. "What are you going to do about it, Coulter? Who's in charge out here? Don't just stand there! Do something!"

Assionte knew perfectly well that I couldn't control whether Brown got in, but he had to get mad at somebody. This incident was happening at the end of his tour, in full view of Colonel Kelley's office, as Kelley prepared to write his efficiency report.

Assionte's tantrum had no effect on me. I had no friend in the world and prayed to the sky for a solution. If I failed to get Brown in, all my plans would collapse, and I would lose my reputation. Yet the longer I took to decide, the less chance I had to put in Brown while still leaving time for the helicopter to come back for Kerley. You would think shame alone would force me to do something, but instead it paralyzed me.

You can probably imagine the effect on me of Simpson standing right there, no doubt thinking, "Now we're going to see what Coulter's made of." Assionte, by comparison, meant nothing.

Finally, Simpson asked, "Sir, why don't we just put him in in the morning?" His coolness and logic, so quick and simple, cleared up everything. Of course, we didn't have enough time to put in Brown and come back for Kerley, something so obvious that I felt even more stupid and ineffectual for not thinking of it myself.

Now I had to do everything possible to maintain an appearance of authority; otherwise, the men would think Simpson had decided for me. "Yeah," I said. "Okay. Let's put him in in the morning," trying to make it look as if I had welcomed a subordinate's good advice and been about to say the same thing myself.

Brown jumped out of the helicopter, and Kerley scrambled on. The sky had faded, and by the time Kerley's chopper had diminished to a small dot, it was almost dark. The helicopter disappeared behind the mountains, and we waited in suspense. The squelch broke, and we heard that Kerley had seen a fire at his primary landing zone, and by the time he got over to his alternate, the pilot couldn't see well enough to get in and aborted.

So much for my training and all my talk about nuts and bolts! It never occurred to me that I had never done this before and had no real idea of what I was doing. I had taken so much pride in fitting everything together tightly and calculating it down to the last minute that I never considered that my plan might not work. Just as bad, preserving appearances had remained my top priority. To make it look like I was springing decisively back into action, I asked Assionte for helicopters at 5:30 a.m.

By the next morning, I hoped everyone's memory had faded, and I tried to act as if everything would have worked perfectly but for Brown.

To strengthen this impression, I volunteered to ride recovery for Kerley and had Simpson ride recovery for Brown, to show how well I used my manpower and how willingly I did the same work I assigned to others. In broad daylight, we didn't have to worry about the dark or stagger the flights, and, anyway, Simpson and I would look silly standing around on the airfield doing nothing.

I'd never watched a team being put in before, and that morning I had my first sight of the jungle at dawn, a view you can only get from a helicopter at 6:00 in the morning, and worth coming to Vietnam just to see. First, there appeared the pearl-gray rice paddies on the outskirts of Nha Trang. Then the sun hit the mountains, the orange stripes creeping down their eastern slopes while the intervening ravines were still hidden in shadow, and then, finally, as we rose, the deep blue western valleys beyond.

It was so beautiful that I forgot about Kerley, and I had to remind myself to pay attention. His olive-drab helicopter blended in with the jungle; to keep it in view, I lay down on the floor of my helicopter and struggled to catch sight of the rotors. Kerley's clearing lay in a small valley among sharp hillsides, and it looked fairly easy to land in, with plenty of room, the only obstacle being a dead tree over in one corner. His helicopter advanced slowly, looking for a good place among the logs lying in the clearing. It seemed to skirt the dead tree, but suddenly a large red-orange spark flashed from the rotors and the helicopter sank down to the ground.

This happened in such slow motion that I thought it was part of the landing and expected the helicopter to fly back up again. The helicopter seemed to land too gently on the logs to have crashed, but my pilot told me it had, and the men below us got out and scrambled over the logs, seeking to get away before the helicopter exploded.

I tried to think of what I had done to deserve this outcome. One could argue that my too-rigid planning had led to Brown's failure, but the helicopter crash was caused by pilot error, for which I could not be blamed. This had never happened on a real operation, with tougher landing zones and a lot more to worry about than a dead tree. Now we would have to spend so much time dealing with this problem that we would have no time to try again with Kerley, which effectively meant the end of the operation.

At the same time, I felt joy. The pilot's error was much bigger than mine from the night before, and blame would now shift to him. As the recovery ship, we had to pick up the downed men, which meant I actually had something to do.

As we descended, the air lost its coolness, and we hit the cloying jungle heat with all the associations that become part of anybody who went on recon. The clearing looked a lot worse up close than it had from above, a mass of tangled logs piled on top of each other with no helicopter able to set down on them; we had to balance on top of the heap and have the men climb up to us.

Everyone seemed unhurt except Kerley, who had a bloody lip. The men crowded around to get on, Kerley and the other two Americans looking as if they had suffered a lot worse than a fall from a few feet. The three Vietnamese scrambled into the helicopter before I knew it, while Kerley and the two other Americans waited for permission. I doubted a Huey could carry eleven extra men—myself, six recon team members, two pilots, and two door gunners. I thought I should tell Kerley and his men to wait. The two pilots and two door gunners, however, had climbed on without our pilot's objection, and Kerley and the two Americans looked so pleading that I couldn't turn them down. This was one of the most fateful mistakes of my life. I reasoned that the pilot ought to know how much his helicopter could carry, and it was his responsibility to object if he thought he couldn't take Kerley and the other two men.

Everyone piled in on top of each other, the most men I had seen in a Huey, and the helicopter struggled to rise, got up a few inches, hung in place and floated back and forth on top of the logs, as if about to topple over, until it suddenly sprang up. One of the helicopter's skids had caught a log but now freed itself. However, catching the log broke its momentum, and the pilot had to gun the helicopter straight at the trees at the bottom of the clearing to build up speed and get over them. The jungle wall came closer, we rose no higher, and the pilot fought with all his might, his face as white as a ghost.

We began to rise, inch by inch, and the dip in the treetops got closer, but we weren't going to get over it. I prayed that we would at least stay above the heaviest branches and hit only the smaller ones, although even a small branch can cause slight nicks in a rotor that create vibrations capable of shaking a helicopter apart.

The fuselage plowed into the trees. I don't know whether all my experience had made me cooler or I simply had no choice, but I watched us crash with detached curiosity, wondering whether I would survive the fall by grabbing a branch and shinnying down a tree or whether I would fall too hard to grab anything and get killed.

I pictured the sky above laughing at me for dying in a simple training accident after surviving some of the most dangerous patrols in Vietnam. So it was true that men got killed either right after they got to Vietnam or just before they left! And I had brought this on myself. I hadn't had the courage to forbid Kerley and the two Americans to get on, which, as the senior ground officer, I should have done, even though the chopper pilot hadn't objected. Worse, I hadn't shown the initiative Markham had and jumped out of the helicopter to lighten the load. If we all died, I would be responsible.

Then the sky suddenly opened around us, and we made it over the last treetops. A small sunlit valley with a winding river extended below, and the pilot tilted the chopper's nose down to pick up speed. We reached the main valley, the morning sunlight streaming down its slopes, and I drank in its brilliance with gratitude. A few inches lower, and we would have had it.

I had never seen a man perform better than the pilot, and yet I cast everything to my advantage when we got back, leaving nobody in any doubt that I had nearly gotten killed after magnanimously volunteering for recovery, providing yet another shining example of the risks we ran all the time. "The pilot was white as a sheet. Hell, he was more scared than I was. There were vines hanging off the machine gun barrels. I figured this was it."

When Kerley's helicopter crashed, we had aborted Brown's patrol and now had only half the teams in. We couldn't go back and try again, since doing so would throw everything off, and now half the men would go on the next operation without any field practice.

Assionte was so mad he couldn't see straight. Two machine guns with their ammunition and the helicopter's radio with our frequencies remained out there, and Assionte wanted to send a Nung platoon out to guard the helicopter until a "Jolly Green Giant" could haul it out. The CH-46 pilots, however, refused to land until we had cleared off the logs, and Assionte reasoned, "You guys caused this, so you two can go out there and take care of it," and ordered me and Simpson to go back out to recover the helicopter's machine guns and radio and clear the logs. Although disappointed at how little sympathy Assionte felt for me after my close call, I saw this as an opportunity to show Assionte I was capable of taking anything he leveled at me.

The helicopter let us off in the clearing with our rifles, two chainsaws, and a gas can. The silence was, in its own way, overwhelming; the only sound came from the flies buzzing around our heads. The wrecked helicopter lay off to the side, hidden somewhere in the brush. We had to find it, and somebody had to go first. I couldn't ask Simpson to go first after he had told me he would follow me anywhere, so I pushed into the brush ahead of him.

The flies were whirling all around me, and I felt more exposed than I had ever been on recon before. The blank jungle walls bored into me, following all my movements. Anybody behind the leaves would be able to pick us off with ease. An hour had passed since the crash, giving anyone who had heard it plenty of time to come over and wait for us in ambush.

I instinctively adopted all my caution from recon and moved one piece of brush at a time, ready to drop to the ground at the first shot. This process continued for a while until Simpson couldn't take it any longer and pushed past me, disgusted with me for wasting his time. He knew what had to be done and didn't want to play around. There were no enemies for miles, speed was our best defense anyway, and if anybody had actually gotten here first, they would already have opened fire.

Despite my humiliation, I couldn't force myself to move faster. Fear of shots coming from the brush acted on me like a physical impediment. Simpson had reached the helicopter and was on his

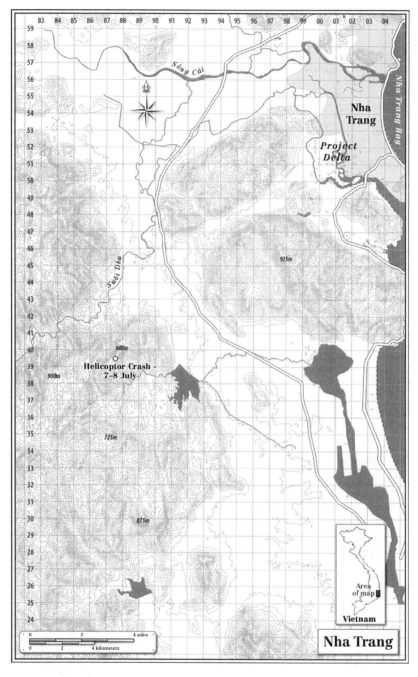

Nha Trang map. Showing the needless helicopter crash during our practice operations.

way back with a machine gun by the time I got there, and once I brought the second machine gun back to the clearing, he had already returned with a belt of ammunition.

We got everything to the clearing and had to start on the logs, which were chest high and badly tangled. As usual, the chainsaws wouldn't start, and when we finally got one of them going, it jumped off the dried logs as if they were rocks. I had no better luck with our backup hand saw and told Simpson, "We'll just have to tell them we can't get the logs off."

Simpson climbed out onto the pile of logs and began to heave them up in his arms by their butt ends and hurl them off to the side, daring the jungle to shoot at him (and probably also acting for my benefit, as Simpson liked to grandstand). I had heard the tales of Simpson's contempt for danger, and now I was witnessing it for the first time.

As much as I told myself to get out on top of the logs like Simpson, I couldn't do it. Fear of the jungle walls held me back. I had nothing to hide behind if somebody started to fire, and the logs were packed so tightly that they left no space for a man to hide under them. I tried to imitate Simpson but stayed at the edge of the clearing, as close to the jungle as I could, and kept my eyes on my rifle, staying behind Simpson's back so that he couldn't see me and hoping that he was too busy grabbing and tossing logs to turn around and look. I reassured myself that Simpson knew he stood head and shoulders above everybody else and couldn't possibly expect me to equal him, officers being more delicate than sergeants anyway, but none of this rationalizing helped. I hadn't gained a thing from Vietnam; I hadn't learned to act like a man.

Thirty-Four

We got back without incident, and I could turn my attention to Kim and our upcoming lunch. I reserved the jeep, rented the room, and went to her house. Kim looked as beautiful as ever, her white *ao dai* flowing sensually around her legs.

At Le Fregate, the white tablecloth and the glistening wine

glasses framed Kim as bewitchingly as before, and she held the same power over me. We had an idyllic, sultry meal. Kim talked about her family and handed me a list of things she wanted from the PX, asking sweetly, "You buy me?"

After we left, I made the turn to the hotel, and Kim didn't stiffen. I turned into the back courtyard, where the sound of pots and pans came from the kitchen, and then got up on the boardwalk and headed for the room, expecting to hear Kim's high heels behind me. When I reached the door, I turned around to look. Kim was still sitting in the jeep, staring angrily at the windshield, indifferent to anybody in the kitchen who might have been watching. This response was meant to humiliate me, because the whole kitchen staff had seen me fail to get a woman to come into a room with me. I drove her home in silence, let her get out by herself, and returned the key to the hotel.

Kim considered me a hopeless child for believing she would fall for me or think of me differently than she would other Americans. I, however, believed that she would innocently take me at face value, which was the technique behind my seduction.

I had never considered that Kim might be the same as other Vietnamese women, thinking only in terms of the money I had to offer. She was like a bar girl, perhaps a notch higher, but intending to get as much as she could from me in the short time that she knew we would have together. Kim knew the going rates in the bar girl economy and that if I saw her, I avoided paying someone else. Being a lot classier than the average bar girl, she saw no reason why she shouldn't get three times what I would pay for one of them. I now had to go back to bar girls, and one night at The Streamer a girl told me that she had been at the beach bar when I danced with Kim and had burst out laughing because Kim's husband was sitting in the audience.

* * *

The following Saturday, the Vietnamese intelligence officer, Thanh, slipped out from behind his desk in the orderly room and, in a low whisper, asked whether I wanted to go to a party the next day. I barely knew him and had never heard of anybody in our unit being invited to a Vietnamese party, and I took this offer as another sign of my good reputation among the Vietnamese. Ninh probably had told the others that I treated the Vietnamese as equals and didn't look down on them like other Americans did. I sensed the party didn't involve our unit and that I should attend in civilian clothes.

The next afternoon, Thanh drove up with a delicate old man sitting next to him in the jeep, a man so slight the seat cushion stuck out on both sides of him. "This is my old professor from Saigon. He has come up for a visit," Thanh said. The man gave me a weak handshake and immediately started speaking French, saying that he had spent a year studying in France.

The professor looked pretty bland and uninteresting, and I foresaw a long, slow afternoon of clichés about France while I struggled to find something to say. Thanh apparently hadn't invited me because of my reputation among the Vietnamese; rather, he wanted to show off the fact that he had an American in his unit who could speak French.

I got into the back of the jeep, and we drove over to the orderly room, where Thanh picked up a .45 pistol. This was unusual because none of us went downtown with weapons, and I assumed it related to the professor's prominence. We didn't stop in town but drove to a high promontory to the north, a place I had never visited before. It was clearly the most beautiful spot in Nha Trang, and we came here as a way to honor the professor.

The sparkling blue bay became dark purple closer to the horizon, and gentle waves made their way toward the beach, ending as white foam on the shoreline. To the west, the city spread out in neat squares, a patchwork of red roofs separated by green foliage, projecting a sense of harmony you would never have guessed from the disorder in the town below. Two hundred feet below us, waves smashed against the black basalt base of the cliff we were on, fell back and tried again, sending geysers of spray up through cracks in the rocks.

There was a small shack that sold coconut milk, but no beer—a sure sign that no Americans came up here. We sat at a small wooden table shaded by a thatch roof, and Thanh brought us large glasses of sweetened coconut milk, placing the pistol on the table at his elbow. The professor spoke slowly, without expression, in a whisper I had trouble hearing over the wind. We had exhausted niceties about France, and keeping up my side of the conversation became more and more difficult.

Did Vietnamese throw parties like this? Sitting with an elderly professor sipping coconut milk might work with a mild-mannered academician who liked to speak French, but Thanh should have known better than to subject a young American officer to this tedium. I had taken in the place's beauty and now thought only of getting back into town, hitting the bars, and drinking all the beer I could hold.

The professor, speaking so quietly that it didn't register at first, told me the following: "I don't teach anymore. I am an inspector for the Ministry of Education. Some students have killed a teacher, and I have come up from Saigon to investigate." The teacher had caught six students cheating on a mathematics exam and failed them; they then followed him into a coffee house and stabbed him to death. All of the city's teachers had panicked, fearing that any time they disciplined a student, he would kill them, or try to, which would of course wreck any attempt to teach students anything. Apparently, the whole education system in Nha Trang was on the verge of collapse. "I have come to calm the teachers down. The students have been condemned to death, but the teacher's family has asked for clemency."

This story changed the nature of the "party" and explained the .45, which Thanh had brought in case another student tried to attack the professor. I should have felt honored, but instead I felt insulted, because Thanh had invited me not because of my reputation or my French but as a bodyguard. Students would presumably think twice about attacking the professor if he was accompanied by an American.

While I sympathized, I had trouble taking the murder of a teacher that seriously. We were, after all, in the middle of a bloody war. On top of that, it looked increasingly as if this "party" would last forever and that we had come up here just for "cocktails" and were now going elsewhere for dinner with an old friend of the professor, a former instructor at the Vietnamese NCO academy.

We drove from the promontory down to the town's northern outskirts. Here small houses stood on stilts in hedge enclosures, their courtyards pecked bare by chickens. The NCO instructor waited by his gate, glowing with pride, every last speck swept off his courtyard and a card table set up in the middle. To prevent the meal from consisting entirely of male guests, he had invited two very pretty, very shy high school French teachers. The bottle of cheap whiskey on the table interested me most. Finally, we were getting down to business.

An old woman, who seemed terrified of making a mistake, began to serve us, first rice rolls, then noodle soup, changing dishes between courses and rattling the bowls with trembling hands. Two small boys fanned us with palm fronds to keep away the flies, their eyes wide with awe, and the NCO instructor held the whiskey bottle as if it had cost him a fortune, filling our thimble-sized glasses for us, as if we were royalty.

I have noticed how the humble efforts of others to please us tend to make us feel even more important, and now I turned the dinner into one in honor of me as much as the professor, which in turn required me to meet everyone's expectations and become the life of the party, especially with the high school teachers, whom the NCO instructor had obviously invited for my benefit. How else could he hope to entertain a young American officer?

The teachers kept their eyes demurely on their food and reddened at my attention, doubtless having heard all about American men, which made me work even harder to impress them with my French and my sophistication. These were the first "respectable" Vietnamese women I had met and, fueled by the whiskey, I soared to greater heights.

I suddenly realized that I had gotten carried away at a dinner in honor of an older man in a country that reveres age, and I shut up out of sheer embarrassment. The professor, the NCO instructor, and Thanh had been talking among themselves in Vietnamese, but as soon as I looked over, they switched to French. They were discussing responsibility for the murder, with Thanh blaming the students and the professor blaming society. The professor argued that youth had no models or standards to look up to anymore; their families had failed to teach them a sense of right and wrong, like families in Germany after the Second World War. And try as teachers might, if families failed to teach their children values, nothing a teacher did would make any difference. Vietnamese society had become so engulfed in violence and the youth so brutalized that larger morals and principles had lost all meaning. In a collapsing society, the professor asked, looking at us for understanding and raising his hands in helplessness, with youth not listening to their parents and parents having lost their authority, how could you expect anyone to defend principles for their own sake? Even when parents tried to enforce values, children no longer paid the slightest attention to them.

I hadn't believed that people sitting in a dirt courtyard with chickens pecking all around them could hold abstract intellectual discussions or that this was possible anywhere in Vietnam. While I liked the Vietnamese personally, I (like most Americans) considered them backward.

I had three reactions. The first was to marvel at my discovery that material inferiority doesn't mean inferiority in every respect and that the poor can have thoughts just as elevated as anyone else. At the same time, I felt proud of my ability to understand Vietnamese culture and win their trust. Finally, I felt superior to Americans who couldn't do these things.

I looked on myself as more virtuous, too. While I had seen how much our bombing and artillery disfigured the country and how much our money distorted the economy, I hadn't paid much attention to the suffering of the Vietnamese people. I spent too much time and effort trying to stay alive to waste time thinking about them, and since I was responsible only for my own conduct and duties, I felt no responsibility for what we were doing to Vietnam and its people. Now I enjoyed the pleasure of sympathizing with someone else's sorrow and recognizing my own guilt.

The evening did not end here. We were also going to visit the military court judge responsible for trying the students, one of Nha Trang's highest officials, and we left the NCO instructor happy at having gotten through the dinner in one piece.

The judge graciously invited us into his bare wooden house, with no furniture except for an aluminum lawn chair and a worn couch. The judge placed a Coleman lamp in the middle of the floor, while he sat in the lawn chair and we sat on the couch. The judge's presence filled the room. He had a strong face with penetrating eyes that seemed able to read you instantly, and Thanh treated him with the deepest respect.

He and the professor entered a long discussion, Thanh watching them apprehensively and periodically translating for me into French. The judge had a hard accent (which I assumed was North Vietnamese) and a very direct, almost blunt manner. Nevertheless, he treated the professor with great deference, bending forward to listen to the other man's opinions, as if they were equal or superior to his own. The Coleman lamp's filaments quavered in the darkness, and moths batted against its glass, as if in time to the discussion, their shadows bouncing around us on the walls.

The judge and the professor were debating whether to execute the students. In their minds, the issue was not a question of law and order but a concern for the welfare of society. If the court failed to execute the guilty students, other students might think they could get away with anything and lose their values still faster, leading to swifter and deeper social collapse. But if the court executed the students, all other students might see authority as increasingly evil and repudiate still more the side the judge and the professor wanted to win them back to, and society would thus become even more cruel and violent.

I had never heard a discussion about life and death like this before, and the two men's faces, illuminated by the Coleman lamp, seemed to contain all the wisdom in the world. The two men drew closer together, but their faces showed that they had come no closer to a decision. By the time we had to go, they still hadn't decided, and they parted with expressions of sadness on their faces.

Thirty-Five

The next day, Assionte called us into formation, the red and yellow South Vietnamese flag flying overhead like a toy, while its rope banged against the flagpole. Our feet bounced on the burning sand, the heat off the backs of the men in front reflecting into our faces, as Assionte called Larrabee forward. Larrabee stepped up, snapped his heels, saluted, and held his chin tightly against his neck, while Assionte read orders off a piece of paper that fluttered in the breeze and pinned captain's bars on him.

We hadn't known Larrabee had this much seniority. And we could see what lay in store for us. After the formation, we all swore never to salute him. Larrabee must have sensed this resolve, because whenever he came out into the compound, he stuck closely to Assionte and Allen, so that when we saluted them, he could pretend we were saluting him as well.

A few days later, Delta gave a farewell party for Assionte, and I learned for the first time the depth of the abyss over which I had been hanging ever since I had asked to quit when I learned the other lieutenants thought I was spying for him.

Nobody really wanted to give Assionte a farewell party, but the army has done this since time immemorial, and it at least gave us an opportunity to drink as much as we wanted. Assionte gave the usual speech and received the usual round of applause. I spoke next; I had been tacked on to the program because I was leaving at the same time as him. I knew Assionte would give the standard speech and decided to break the mold, feeling strongly that justice required me to recognize those who did all the work. Every man in recon takes on the jungle by himself, independent of hierarchy, and succeeds on the basis of his own courage and fortitude. Delta's success depended entirely on those in recon.

I mentioned every member of recon by name and said that each one had opened my eyes to a new category of men whom I respected more than anyone else and that I considered my association with them the highest honor. My departure from convention left the men perplexed for a while, but when my words took hold, their ovation grew until it far exceeded what Assionte had received.

As we drank and congratulated ourselves afterward, the sergeant major approached me, which I found surprising simply because he rarely paid any attention to me. I attributed his approach to the men's applause for my speech.

His words surprised me. "You remember when you asked to leave Delta?" he asked. "Hoyez wanted to court-martial you for cowardice, to make an example of you for trying to quit before a big operation. He even opened a file. Then he had second thoughts. He figured that Headquarters might not want him to attract this much attention before a big operation. So he decided against a court-martial at the last minute."

It was impossible to decipher the sergeant major's motives. Maybe he wanted to praise me by contrasting how low I had been with how high I had risen. Or perhaps he wanted to tarnish me by reminding me of how low I had once fallen (a double-edged compliment being not uncommon among sergeant majors), and I couldn't tell now whether I should feel delighted at my narrow escape or horrified at how close I had come to being court-martialed.

At the time, I had believed my motives to be pure and had no concept of what I was doing, coming within a hair of destroying myself. I would have had absolutely no defense in a court-martial because nobody would have taken my word against Assionte's. I had told him in so many words that I couldn't take it, and Assionte couldn't have understood this statement differently. Even if I had managed to prove that the other lieutenants had accused me of being a spy, a court-martial wouldn't have considered this much of an excuse (and certainly not the real cause of my desire to leave). If the court had somehow failed to convict me, the trial itself would have ended my career in Special Forces, and for the rest of my life people would suspect that, on some level, I had been a coward.

* * *

When we returned to the States, we had to make sure that everybody thought what they were supposed to think about us, and for me this problem boiled down to two issues. First, those of us who had spent all of our time in the jungle hadn't gotten a tan, but everybody back in the States would think that anyone who had spent a year in the tropics had to have a tan and, if not, he hadn't been out in the field and in combat. Therefore, I spent the two weeks I had left in Vietnam getting as tanned as possible. After the unit left on a new operation, nobody cared what I did or where I went, and every day I took the jeep to the beach and had the whole place to myself.

The second issue presented a greater challenge. As a Special Forces officer in a beret and wearing jump boots, I had a heavy burden on the plane back. Everyone else on the plane would be regular army enlisted men who would look at me first to see how many medals I had. To look like somebody, I had to have at least two rows, three medals to a row. I got three medals in the top row just for coming to Vietnam. Then there were three medals in the bottom row that I could claim I had truly earned: my Good Conduct Medal, an Air Medal for having flown forty hours over enemy territory, and my Vietnamese Silver Star. However, no American enlisted man would think a Vietnamese Silver Star meant anything, even if he knew what it was, and my two rows of medals meant nothing without an American medal for valor, at least a Bronze Star.

I took a calculated risk. I would wear nothing but a Combat Infantryman Badge, a blue rifle in a silver wreath, which you received for having been under enemy fire and put on the right side of your uniform. I gambled that the other men on the plane would assume that a Special Forces officer had to have seen all sorts of combat and gotten all sorts of medals but didn't want to make a big deal of it or go to all the trouble of putting on all his medals for a simple flight back to the States.

* * *

The day before I left Vietnam, Ninh and Thanh came down from base camp to say goodbye, a mark of their affection and respect.

They took me to a small shack at the entrance to the airbase for breakfast, where Vietnamese sat crammed at long wooden tables and a woman in the center aisle gave bowls to those at the ends to pass along to those in the middle. A wonderful aroma of hot peppers, chicken broth, herbs, and hard wheat rose from the bowls and engulfed the tables.

We squeezed into a place, and Ninh ordered coffee and noodle soup, passing the bowl to me carefully to keep it from spilling. The soup looked amazing—brilliant red and green peppers, bright yellow lemongrass, and ivory noodles swimming in broth. Ninh watched me take the first bite of it to make sure I liked it, which I did. I had never tasted anything better in my life and couldn't understand how a little shack like this could produce something so wonderful. No wonder they had such a crowd.

As Ninh watched me, I had the feeling that he wanted to test the degree of my friendship. By coming down here to say goodbye, he showed the importance he attached to our friendship and what it meant for him to have known me. I sensed, though, that he feared I might not feel the same way he did and, by showing his feelings for me in this way, he, on one level, wanted to make it awkward for me not to reciprocate.

When we finished, Ninh paid with a stern, dignified expression, and then he and Thanh began a long discussion. Finally Ninh said, "We have decided to give you a present."

We drove to an unfamiliar Vietnamese compound on the other side of town, and Ninh disappeared into a low white building, remaining inside so long I began to fear something had happened to him. He reappeared at last, beaming in the sun and holding a pair of fatigues in his arms, made of fine-textured cloth in reddish, iridescent camouflage that I had never seen before. Ninh said, "These are the new Vietnamese jungle fatigues. They have just come out but haven't been issued yet. They are very hard to get." It had obviously cost him a lot of time and work to obtain them for me.

Besides the touching nature of this gesture, it captures so much about the Vietnam War. While, on one hand, Ninh's gesture moved me, on the other, I thought I deserved it. At the same time, however, I felt very uncomfortable looking Ninh in the eye, given that our futures, our fates, were likely to be vastly different. Ninh would fly back up to base camp the next day and go back out on patrol again and again for years until he got killed or badly wounded, while after less than a year and paying hardly any price at all, I would fly down to Saigon the next day and then go on to Oakland, where I would get out of the army and return to Harvard.

Yet I reacted as we all did during the war. I had no obligation to sacrifice myself for the Vietnamese and no legal requirement to serve more than one tour. If I extended, I would probably get killed for no purpose; I disliked even having to defend myself. It boiled down to nothing more than the fact that I had lucked out in life and Ninh hadn't, and while I didn't particularly like to think about this situation, I wasn't going to lose much sleep over it.

Afterword

The Vietnam War led to a profound change in how Americans saw their country. Before the conflict, trust in government was high and we saw government as a force for good. The war shattered that image because of the horrors we imposed on Vietnam: napalm, Agent Orange, the Phoenix Program, B-52 carpet bombing, massacre of innocent civilians at places like My Lai. Our carnage was captured in the words of the army major who ordered the burning of the village Ben Tre: "We had to destroy the village to save it."

More than two million Vietnamese died in the war, as did nearly sixty thousand Americans. Our actions also led to the largest genocide since World War II. We overthrew Cambodia's King Sihanouk, installing an incompetent general who paved the way for a takeover by Pol Pot's murderous Khmer Rouge regime, which exterminated 3 million of their fellow Cambodians. The only domino that fell during the Vietnam War was the one we pushed over.

That said, our involvement in Vietnam was probably inevitable given our anti-communist stance at the time and the backdrop of the Korean War. (Secretary of State Dean Rusk considered the Vietnam War a continuation of the Korean War.) But once we saw that we had taken on more than we could handle, we should have emulated good businessmen who claim that success depends not on getting into good deals but on getting out of bad ones. Robert McNamara's recognition years later that the war was one of national liberation, not communism, came many days too late and many dollars too short. The unification of Vietnam was going to happen anyway; there just would have been less bloodshed had we gotten out of the way. There are no perfect solutions in human affairs, making it even more important to correct mistakes before it is too late.

When you first return from war, you are still intensely loyal to your fellow soldiers, and it took me about three months to turn irrevocably against the war. I was among the first to join George McGovern's anti-war campaign for the 1972 Democratic presidential nomination.

Our leaders didn't get us out of Vietnam; the American people did. The majority of Americans turned against the war in October 1967, three months before Tet, but we didn't leave until 1973, six years later. The draft ultimately ended the war. I attended a conference for dairy farmers in Kansas City in 1972, while working for the McGovern campaign, and met a farmer, the fingers of his left hand all cut off by machinery. He told me that two of his sons had been killed in Vietnam, and when his second son was killed, he took his shotgun into the local draft office and told the manager that if he drafted his third son, he would kill him. Therefore, I support a draft army. If American families had faced their sons being drafted for Afghanistan and Iraq, I believe we would have gotten out sooner or, better, never even gone.

After returning from Vietnam in 1967, I was readmitted to Harvard, although there was a policy not to readmit anyone who had left twice. I graduated Phi Beta Kappa after taking a heavy course load plus summer school. I felt I needed a graduate degree, so I chose to go to INSEAD (Institut Européen d'Administration des Affaires) in France; this program required English, French, and German, so I had to learn German. I was the only American student there. It was a one-year course, and I got an MBA. It was a fascinating experience that allowed me to learn about the different psychologies among Europeans.

I needed an American degree, so I went to Harvard Business School and graduated from there as well. At this time, American politics was very intense, mainly because of the war, and after I graduated from business school, I walked into the campaign headquarters of Senator George McGovern, who was running for the Democratic nomination for president, and volunteered. That was the start of my career as a professional political organizer.

I was McGovern's first advance man and worked for a year and a half on his campaign across the United States. I slept on people's floors and survived on petty cash. Those of us who were involved in his campaign from the beginning loved McGovern like a father. After he won the nomination, I worked in New York and California during the general election campaign, which we lost to Nixon in a landslide.

I continued to work as a political organizer for Democrats such as Henry Howell when he was running for governor of Virginia in 1973. Because of the reputation I had from the McGovern campaign, Jimmy Carter's campaign asked me to run their general election campaign in Indiana. In need of a deputy, I hired a young attorney who had made something of a name for herself as a staff lawyer during the Nixon impeachment inquiry—Hillary Rodham Clinton.

We lost Indiana, but Carter thought I had done a good job and appointed me a federal commissioner on the newly created Copyright Royalty Tribunal, which was designed to resolve the copyright issues that for over a decade had been blocking the development of cable television in the United States. I was not a lawyer, nor did I know anything about copyright or communications law, but I won every vote during the seven years I served on the tribunal. The strategy I developed for the tribunal led to many disputes being resolved by mutual agreement of the parties involved, often avoiding lengthy and costly litigation. As a result, the role of the tribunal has been diminished, saving taxpayer money. I believe I am one of the few government officials ever to have worked to *reduce* their agency's role, as opposed to building it up at taxpayer expense.

After my term expired, I taught expository writing at Harvard. Then I became fascinated with what was happening in the Soviet Union: *perestroika* and *glasnost*. With considerable difficulty, I obtained a job teaching business English at the Plekhanov Russian University of Economics in Moscow. I became fluent in Russian and then got a job teaching business and finance at Moscow State University. I also worked with those supporting Boris Yeltsin's campaign for president of Russia in 1991, making me probably the only person who has worked with both the McGovern and the Yeltsin campaigns. I was present in Moscow when the putsch occurred in August 1991 and Yeltsin stood on the tank and defied the coup leaders.

In Moscow, I met my wife and the love of my life, Lena. I had been married and divorced in the 1970s, but when I met Lena, we both somehow knew that it was meant to be. We have three children, Eliot, Holley, and Douglas. Eliot is a first lieutenant in the 82nd Airborne Division and has served in Kuwait. Holley is a college student studying at the Higher School of Economics in Moscow. And my younger son, Douglas, attends Peking University's affiliated high school.

Beijing? Yes. In 1997, I decided that China was now the most interesting place to be. We took the Trans-Siberian Railway across Russia on our way to Beijing. Job-wise, it was Russia all over again: I started out teaching business English and then was invited to teach finance and accounting at Peking University's Guanghua School of Management in Beijing, where I've been ever since. My children all speak fluent Russian, Chinese, and English and speak Chinese among themselves. I also am fluent in Chinese. At home, my wife and I speak Russian.

*   *   *

I visit the States briefly during most summers, staying at Chocorua, New Hampshire, where my sister Jean still lives. When I moved to Russia in 1989, I felt somewhat optimistic about America. I thought the elder Bush was not a bad president, and I believe Bill Clinton, whom I know, will be judged by history as a good president. His administration looks pretty good compared to those of his successors. But the current profound divisions in our society, the violently politicized media, and intransigent ideologies have entirely changed that picture, and I find it now very hard to be optimistic.

Appendix

New York Times, Monday, April 29, 1968
U.S. FORCES BEGIN MASSIVE ASSAULT ON ASHAU VALLEY
Airmobile Division Copters Enter Jungle Stronghold of the North Vietnamese
ENEMY'S FIRE IS HEAVY
10 Aircraft Lost in a Day—Security Is Tight in Drive Started 10 Days Ago

By Bernard Weinraub

THE ASHAU VALLEY, South Vietnam, April 28

Waves of helicopters, sweeping through intense antiaircraft fire, have landed on the northern fringes of the Ashau Valley in a massive, allied assault on this vital enemy stronghold along the Laotian border.

The United States command hopes in this major offensive to thwart the sizable infiltration of troops and supplies through the Ashau Valley into the northern provinces. The North Vietnamese are believed to have great strength in the northern provinces and last week some officers expressed fear of an attack on Hue or Danang.

"Militarily the Ashau is one of the most important pieces of real estate that the enemy has occupied in the I Corps area," said Maj. Gen. John R. Tolson, commander of the First Cavalry Division (Airmobile). "It's certainly one of his top logistical support bases, as important to him as Camranh Bay is to us."

Westmoreland Gives Rules

The progress of the operation was wrapped in tight security.

Gen. William C. Westmoreland's headquarters announced that details of only the first three days of the operation—April 19, 20, and 21—could be disclosed. The United States command added that newsmen on the scene could not write dispatches about further details "for several days."

The valley's scenery is magnificent—a riot of rust browns and purple. Streams weave through it and double-canopy and triple-canopy abound. The thickly shrubbed treeless peaks are crowned with clouds.

Whirring into the valley at dawn on the cloudy, drizzly morning of April 19, the United States helicopters came under repeated North Vietnamese antiaircraft fire from gunners hidden in the valley's thickly camouflaged ridges.

On that first day, 10 helicopters of the First Cavalry Division were shot down and a number of others damaged. Nine soldiers aboard the helicopters are listed as missing in action. Four others were killed.

"Roughest Reception"

"It was the roughest reception we've ever had in Vietnam," said an officer with the division. "They've got quite a force in there."

The major question among American military commanders was whether the enemy would fight the American and South Vietnamese troops in the valley or retreat into the thick jungle in the hope that the allied reconnaissance force would soon leave.

Five thousand to six thousand North Vietnamese troops have held the valley for two years. This apparently includes two antiaircraft and three engineering battalions.

Army intelligence officers estimate, however, that the North Vietnamese have a massive mobile force that can easily strike the valley. This was estimated to include 10,000 men around Hue, 35 miles away, as well as 8,000 men just north of the valley.

"Big Ditch" Among Hills

"This valley is one of the weirdest pieces of terrain I've ever seen," General Tolson said. "It's a great big ditch among a whole bunch of hills. The valley floor is 2,000 feet deep. He has a lot of troops in there and I look forward to taking him on."

The jagged valley is a 25-mile maze of fog-shrouded peaks. Within the valley are choke points, as narrow as 600 feet in some spots, as wide as five miles in others.

Along the hills and ridges, the North Vietnamese have bulldozed a 30-foot-wide road and a tangle of routes that lead to Hue as well as to Danang, 50 miles to the southeast.

The importance of the valley to the North Vietnamese was underscored by the intensity of their 22-mm, 37-mm, and 57-mm antiaircraft fire—which was called the heaviest antiaircraft fire of the war in the South.

"It's Bad Down There"

That was emphasized by Maj. Charles Gilmer, the executive officer of the helicopter reconnaissance outfit for the First Cavalry Division. "I'll tell you this," he said, "if you fly over that valley you have a good chance of getting killed. It's bad down there, very bad."

Hampered by the antiaircraft fire as well as by fog and rain, the combat operations limped in the opening days. Hundreds of soldiers sat for hours, even days, at staging areas near Camp Evans. Supplies, C-rations and ammunition went undelivered. Several wounded waited 24 hours for evacuation.

Slowly the operation gathered momentum. As clouds broke and the lush ridges of the valley became dappled with sun, Chinook helicopters thundered over the valley hauling 105-mm and 155-mm artillery onto landing zones overlooking the valley floor.

Infantrymen, many still exhausted from the division's drive into Khesanh three weeks ago, began moving into the valley. Flying from Camp Evans into the northern fringe of the valley, a brigade of nearly 2,000 infantrymen opened up a series of critical landing zones for helicopters.

The landing zones had been carved out earlier with blasts and B-52 strikes on selected peaks, some as high as 6,000 feet.

Problems accompanied the opening of the first three landing zones. At one near the heart of the valley, a helicopter blade tangled in a tree and the craft crashed. The presence of the debris and poor visibility delayed the air assault of three companies for 48 hours.

At another landing zone in the northwestern tip of the valley, the first wave of helicopters was hard hit by North Vietnamese .50-calibre machine-gun fire as well as by antiaircraft fire from surrounding ridges.

Four helicopters were destroyed.

Lights Go By at Night

At a third landing zone, where four soldiers were killed by sniper fire, Sgt. Henry D. Williams of Brooklyn squinted into the sun to watch a tractor churn up dirt near the make-shift landing pad.

"It's scary, man. It's scary here at night," the 29-year-old noncom said. "You see the headlights of their trucks all over and you hear their engines going. I've been in a lot of bad things but I'm a little scared of this one."

Possibly the most treacherous moment for the American troops occurred when a battalion assaulted a landing zone that turned out to be too small, too low on a ridge and too thickly grassed.

The First Cavalry Division battalion, led by Brooklyn-born officer, Lieutenant Colonel Joseph E. Wasiak, was ordered to march three miles to open a new landing zone.

Crawling through jungles and forests, the battalion met only sporadic sniper fire and stumbled on the first prize of the operation: two bulldozers, one with Soviet insignia. Both were destroyed. The battalion reached the new landing zone three days after starting out.

In the first days of the operation, the Americans suffered 20 dead. The North Vietnamese were reported to have lost 50 men.

Since the North Vietnamese overran a Special Forces camp in the southern part of the valley in March 1966, the valley has been under total North Vietnamese control.

A principal reason for the timing of the big American move appears to be the availability of the First Cavalry Division, which was based in the Central Highlands until January. Last month the division played a major role in breaking the siege of Khesanh.

Another reason—linked to Khesanh—is the belief that the North Vietnamese 325 C division, which was based near Khesanh, has moved into or near the Ashau Valley.

A third reason was expressed by one officer of the First Cavalry Division. "It finally reaches a point where he starts building his roads outside the Ashau towards the cities," he said. "He has moved too damned fast for us."

The allied force in the valley is under the over-all command of Lieut. Gen. William R. Rosson, the commander of American troops in the I Corps Tactical zone, in the north of South Vietnam.

New York Times, **Friday, May 3, 1968**
ENEMY ROUTE CUT BY ALLIED SWEEP IN ASHAU VALLEY
Drive on Supply Base Held Successful So Far—
U.S. Ends a 4-Day Silence HELICOPTER LOSS HEAVY
Casualties Are Increasing in Fight Near DMZ—
Terror Blast in Saigon Kills 3

By Bernard Weinraub

SAIGON, South Vietnam, May 2

The United States command, breaking a four-day silence on the massive sweep into the Ashau Valley, said today that the assault had cut off a major infiltration route for the North Vietnamese.

"Right now we are sitting right on their supply lines for everything south of the Khesanh and Dongha areas," said Lieut. Gen. Robert Cushman of the Marines, the commander of United States forces in the critical northern provinces.

"That valley is not a fortress, but almost a highway for logistics," the general said at a news conference in Danang....

In Saigon, Brig. Gen. Winant Sidle, chief of information for the United States command, said, "The drive to clear the Ashau has been successful so far. There's an awful lot of stuff in there and we're going to find it."

Although ground action in the lush valley has been sporadic since the assault began on April 19, American casualties have mounted steadily.

From April 19 to April 30 there were 63 Americans killed and 363 wounded. The official estimate of the enemy death toll is 377.

Copter Losses High

The number of allied helicopters destroyed or damaged is unusually high. On the first day of the operation 10 helicopters were shot down by antiaircraft fire. Since then a total of 50 are believed to have been destroyed or damaged by North Vietnamese gunners hidden in the valley's ridges.

The 25-mile-long valley, in the northwestern part of South Vietnam, was overrun two years ago by the North Vietnamese. Within the valley, the North Vietnamese have bulldozed a maze of roads and infiltration routes that lead into Hue, 35 miles to the northeast, and Danang, 50 miles southeast.

Since the start of the assault by 12,000 to 15,000 allied troops, the headquarters of Gen. William C. Westmoreland had imposed unusually tight security rules on the operation. Military officials have said that continual disclosure of information about the operation would endanger American lives.

"If the enemy is provided specific information about units, locations, casualties, and material losses this could aid him in his efforts in this operation," said General Cushman. "The location of this operation and the drive for maximum success is the real reason General Westmoreland has embargoed the operation."

General Cushman reported that allied forces had uncovered large amounts of North Vietnamese arms and ammunition, including several 37-mm antiaircraft guns that are mounted on four-wheeled carriers and hand-operated by two-man crews. It was the first time such weapons had been captured in South Vietnam.

Tank Is Captured

The allied troops, including a South Vietnamese airborne task force, also captured more than half a dozen trucks, a Soviet-made tank, thousands of artillery rounds, Soviet-made flamethrowers, communications equipment, mine detectors and rockets—as well as stacks of ammunition and demolition material.

General Cushman said that most of the North Vietnamese in the valley appeared to be engineer troops and security forces and antiaircraft crews. Military sources estimate that 5,000 to 6,000 enemy troops are in the valley, and that 15,000 to 29,000 North Vietnamese are within striking distance of the Ashau Valley.

At the start of the operation, units of the First Cavalry Division swooped into the valley from the northwest, opening up a series of critical landing zones before assaulting the valley floor last week at the old, bomb-cratered French-built airstrip at Aloui. The helicopter units, except for antiaircraft fire, had only sporadic ground contact.

From the northeast, however, units of the 101st Airborne Division began trudging into the valley and came into sharper contact with the enemy.

"It would take too many troops to hold this logistics area permanently, so it's best that we move around trying to find the enemy," General Cushman went on....

New York Times
Allies Control Ashau Valley

DANANG, South Vietnam, May 11 (AP)

Allied forces have taken control of the Ashau Valley and have linked up with United States paratroop units along roads connecting the former enemy stronghold with the old imperial capital of Hue, the United States command said today.

The United States commander in the northern war zone, Lieut. Gen. Robert E. Cushman, Jr., of the Marines, said that enemy resistance in the valley was sporadic in some areas and nonexistent in others.

The enemy bases in the Ashau Valley had been considered a threat to Hue, 30 miles to the east.

New York Times
Ashau Valley Drive Ends

By Douglas Robinson

SAIGON, South Vietnam, May 17

Operation Delaware, the offensive aimed at clearing North Vietnamese troops from the Ashau Valley, has been concluded, the military command said today.

In making the announcement, the spokesman declined for security reasons to say whether United States and South Vietnamese troops had left the valley or were remaining in an effort to block enemy supply routes.

The operation began on April 19 and involved units of the First Cavalry Division (Airmobile) and the 101st Airborne Division, as well as a regiment of South Vietnamese paratroopers.

American and South Vietnamese casualties for the month-long offensive were put as 139 dead and 662 wounded. The North Vietnamese were said to have lost 726 men.

Heavy fighting was reported during the first few days of Operation Delaware, but only light to moderate action has been disclosed since then. One high-ranking officer said a few weeks ago that the fighting had "not been what we expected."

The allies, however, did capture or destroy an enormous amount of enemy equipment and supplies, including heavy weapons, ammunition, trucks, bulldozers, explosives, rice and other foodstuffs....

New York Times
By Douglas Robinson
SAIGON, South Vietnam, May 18

...The vulnerability of the North Vietnamese was also demonstrated in the Ashau Valley, where a large quantity of arms, ammunition and equipment was captured or destroyed by an allied force that spent a month patrolling the thick jungle.

Although the allied generals had expected more opposition than they received, the operation was described as successful because it removed heavy equipment and artillery from the hands of the North Vietnamese.

The initial allied landing in the Ashau was opposed only by enemy engineer and security forces. Despite their limited strength, they shot down a number of helicopters. The main bulk of the North Vietnamese troops were not in the valley, but were closer to Hue and Danang. They stayed there.

Now that the Ashau campaign has ended, the North Vietnamese, according to intelligence estimates, will probably slip back into the valley in an attempt to re-establish it as a vitally needed storehouse.

"If you kill a Vietcong porter and ruin the small amount of ammunition or equipment he's carrying, you haven't hit the enemy very hard," the American intelligence officer said. "If you destroy a batch of North Vietnamese trucks, you're striking a hell of a blow."

New York Times
ENEMY RETURNS TO ASHAU VALLEY
Big North Vietnamese Units Back After Allied Sweep
DANANG, South Vietnam, May 23 (AP)

Highly informed sources said today that there was "quite a bit of evidence" that the North Vietnamese had moved back into the Ashau Valley with large forces.

A major allied operation recently swept the valley east of Danang and 30 miles southwest of Hue. The move ended a week ago.

The sources said the North Vietnamese could be again using truck convoys in the valley to replace the vast amounts of weapons, food and other war material destroyed during the allied operation.

Allied troops never intended to stay in the valley and left just ahead of monsoon rains that would have made their stay highly hazardous because of the difficulties of reinforcing, resupplying and launching air strikes.

For some reason the allies operating on the valley floor did not attempt to destroy major segments of the road there, a direct truck route from North Vietnam through Laos to South Vietnam.

Big Road Building Project

Long called the biggest enemy base camp in South Vietnam, Ashau took on fresh importance with the recent discovery of a major enemy road-construction project from the valley in the direction of Danang, the biggest allied base in the northern war zone.

In one aerial sighting, more than 1,000 construction workers were spotted along one segment of the road. Bulldozers are believed to be in use.

Thick jungle and bad weather make United States operations against the new road almost impossible except by bombing. Finished sections of the road are said to extend from Laos about 7.5 miles inside South Vietnam, with work under way on an additional six miles.

United States planes are spraying the Ashau Valley and likely routes out of it with herbicides in an attempt to kill all foliage that the North Vietnamese are using for cover during road construction.

Still another road spotted farther south could give enemy trucks access to base areas that threaten not only the vital Danang region but Kontum Province as well.

Douglas Coulter
Military Service History

Volunteered for U.S. Army, March 1964
Basic training, Fort Knox, Kentucky
Advanced infantry training, Fort Gordon, Georgia
Tank crew, 69th Armor, Fort Benning, Georgia
Airborne School, Fort Benning, Georgia
Officer Candidate School, Fort Benning, Georgia
Promoted to second lieutenant, August 1965
Deployed to 10th Special Forces, Bad Tölz, West Germany, September 1965
Deployed to 5th Special Forces, Project Delta, Nha Trang, Vietnam, September 1966
Promoted to first lieutenant, September 1966
Project Delta deployed to Kham Duc, II Corps, February 1967
Project Delta deployed to An Lao, II Corps, March 1967
Author conducted 5-man long-range reconnaissance patrols in An Lao until April 1967
Project Delta deployed to Khe Sanh, I Corps, April 1967
Project Delta deployed to A Shau Valley, I Corps, April 1967
Author conducted 5-man long-range reconnaissance patrols in A Shau Valley until June 1967
Project Delta deployed to Nha Trang, II Corps, June 1967
Discharged August 1967

Medals and Awards

Air Medal
Vietnam Service Medal
Republic of Vietnam Gallantry Cross with Palm Device
National Defense Service Medal Campaign Ribbon with Device
Combat Infantryman Badge
Vietnamese Silver Star
Good Conduct Medal

But to go back to the original question about special or unique individuals.

One I remember particularly was Doug Coulter, a Harvard graduate who came to Vietnam when that was not a very popular war and said, "I'm going to do my duty. My number came up and I'm going." He did and was a very professional guy, one of the best officers I saw during my two years over there. Today he teaches Harvard business case studies in China. Before that, he also taught in Russia. He's as professional as they come, and went out on some missions and did some things that would make the hair on the back of your neck stand up. All out of range of U.S. forces and artillery (though we did have air support we could call in). He was truly good.

> —General Henry H. "Hugh" Shelton, Chairman of the Joint Chiefs of Staff, 1997–2001 (answering author Tom Clancy in his book *Special Forces*)

From *Special Forces: A Guided Tour of U.S. Army Special Forces*, by Tom Clancy, with John Gresham (New York: Berkley Books, 2001)

Index